Albert Soboul

NLB

The French Revolution
1787–1799

IN TWO VOLUMES

2: FROM THE JACOBIN DICTATORSHIP TO NAPOLEON

TRANSLATED FROM THE FRENCH
BY ALAN FORREST AND COLIN JONES

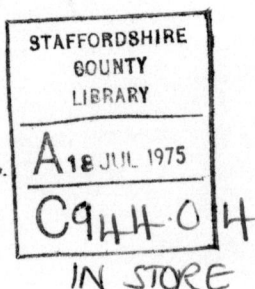

First published as
Précis d'histoire de la Révolution Française
by Editions Sociales, 1962
© Editions Sociales 1962
This edition first published, 1974
© NLB 1974

NLB, 7 Carlisle Street, London W1

Typeset in Monotype Fournier
and printed by
Western Printing Services Ltd, Bristol
Designed by Gerald Cinamon

PART TWO *continued*

Chapter 3

The Montagnard Convention
— the Popular Movement
and the Dictatorship of Public Safety
(June to December 1793)

Scarcely had the Gironde been eliminated when the Convention, now under Montagnard leadership, found itself caught between two threats. For while the forces of counter-revolution were gaining new impetus from the federalist revolt, the popular movement, roused to fury by high prices, was increasing the pressure it exercised on the government. Meanwhile the government was proving incapable of controlling the situation: thus Danton, on the Committee of Public Safety, was negotiating instead of putting up a fight. In July 1793 the nation appeared to be on the point of falling apart.

But whereas the Montagne hesitated, the prisoner of its own contradictions, the popular masses were driven on by their needs and their hatreds to force on the government the great measures of public safety of which the first was the decree ordering conscription for the armies on 23 August 1793. As a result revolutionary government seemed more necessary than ever if the popular upsurge was to be controlled and the alliance with the bourgeoisie maintained, the alliance that alone could provide the trained personnel needed for administration. It was on this twin social platform, of the sans-culotterie and the Montagnard or Jacobin bourgeoisie, that revolutionary government was constructed by a series of steps taken between July and December 1793. The more far-sighted of the revolutionary leaders were determined to defend at any cost the revolutionary unity of the old Third Estate – in other words, the unity of the nation as a whole. But was it in their power to overcome the contradictions inherent in this coalition? For a while the danger that faced the nation sufficed to silence these contradictions. But it was easy to foresee that, once victory was assured, they would once again emerge on the forefront of the political stage.

1. MONTAGNARDS, MODERATES, AND SANS-CULOTTES (JUNE TO JULY 1793)

It was thanks to the sans-culottes of Paris that the Montagne had triumphed over the Gironde, but the Montagnards had no intention of giving in to their pressure. For them the problem in the weeks following the *journée* of 2 June was that of checking the popular movement without at the same time encouraging a reaction favourable to the Girondins. They were most anxious to rally to their side that section of the bourgeoisie which had remained neutral during the conflict with the Gironde and hence they wanted to win over the property owners and the moderates. It was in no sense part of their policy to enact the entire programme of political and social change that had been proposed by the popular militants on the insurrectionary committee on 31 May – a programme that included the arrest of the Girondins but which also demanded the expulsion from the Convention of all those who had voted for the *appel au peuple*, the formation of a paid revolutionary army that would arrest suspects and ensure the provisioning of Paris, the enforcement of the maximum price law on grain and the extension of the principle of price-fixing to all essential consumer goods, and the purging of both armies and administrative bodies, particularly by the dismissal of all nobles. . . . The Montagne attempted to reassure the middle classes by rejecting any idea of terror, by protecting property rights, and by restricting the popular movement to very narrowly-circumscribed limits. It was a very difficult and delicate balance to achieve, a balance that was destroyed in July by the worsening of the crisis.

The conciliatory measures of the Montagnards

During the month of June the Montagne played for time. On 8 June Robespierre persuaded the Convention to reject the plan which Barère and Danton had proposed two days before for the suppression of the committees of surveillance (as Jeanbon Saint-André had declared in the course of the debate, 'We must know whether, on the pretext of creating liberty, we are not killing liberty itself'). But no positive measures were adopted: the revolutionary army was not organized, the discussion on the proposed forced loan was cut short, and Saint-Just's report on those Girondin deputies who were imprisoned or had fled was very moderate in tone. 'Liberty,' he said in this report, read on 8 July, 'will not prove terrible in its treatment of those whom it has disarmed and who have submitted to the laws.' It was a question of rallying the support of the departments by reassuring them and removing their fears of a dictatorship by the sans-culottes of Paris.

In the social field three laws were passed which attempted to give satisfaction to the demands of the peasants. That of 3 June on the manner in which émigré lands should be sold stipulated that they should be divided into small plots which poor peasants would be able to acquire, especially as they were to be given ten years to pay. The law of 10 June on the sharing-out of common lands authorized that this be done on an optional basis, that the shares should be of equal size, divided among all those living in the area, and that the distribution should be decided by the drawing of lots. And the law of 17 June on the feudal system brought about its complete destruction by suppressing all feudal dues without any indemnity, even those that were based on long-established title-deeds; all titles that were lodged with the municipal records were ordered to be burned. For the peasantry the fall of the Gironde meant the final freeing of the soil.

In the political sphere, the Convention rapidly voted a constitution and by this means hoped to clear itself of the charge of dictatorship and calm the anxieties of the departments. The so-called Constitution of 1793, voted on 24 June on the basis of a report from Hérault de Séchelles and following a brief discussion, laid down the essential characteristics of a politically democratic regime.

The Declaration of Rights which precedes the text of the Constitution goes further than that of 1789 and proclaims in its very first clause that 'the aim of society is the happiness of all'. It states the right of people to work, to assistance, and to education:

Public assistance is a sacred debt. Society owes a living to the unfortunate among its citizens, either by finding work for them or by guaranteeing the means of subsistence to those who are not in a fit condition to work (article 21).

Education is a necessity for all. Society must use all its power to advance the development of public education and to bring instruction within the reach of all citizens (article 22).

Finally, the 1793 Declaration recognized not only the right to resist oppression (article 33), as had that of 1789, but also the right to rise in insurrection:

When the government violates the rights of the people, then insurrection, both for the people as a whole and for each group amongst the people, is the most sacred and necessary of duties (article 35).

But there was no thought of altering the definition of property from that which Robespierre had proposed on 24 April:

The right of property is one which belongs to all citizens – the right to enjoy and to dispose at will of one's possessions and income, of the fruits of one's labour and one's industry (article 16).

And economic freedom, a subject on which the 1789 Declaration had remained totally silent, was explicitly affirmed in article 17, which stated that 'no kind of work, cultivation or trade may be forbidden to those citizens who want to work at it'. The Montagnards refused to commit themselves in the direction of a social democracy.

The chief aim of the Constitution was to ensure the preponderant role of the deputies in the Convention, which was seen as being the essential basis for political democracy. The two-tiered voting system proposed in the Girondin plan drawn up by Condorcet was rejected. It was argued that the immediate choice of the people, without electoral colleges, ensures the supremacy of the legislature over the executive, of deputies over administrative bureaucracy. The Legislative Assembly was to be elected by a direct vote cast for a single member; deputies were elected on receiving a simple majority of the votes cast, and the assembly would sit for one year. The executive council of 24 members was chosen by the Legislative Assembly from among the 83 candidates chosen by the departments on the basis of universal suffrage, and in this way ministers were made responsible to the representatives of the nation. The exercise of national sovereignty was widened through the institution of the referendum, already an aspect of Condorcet's plan: the Constitution was to be ratified by the people, as were laws in certain precisely-defined circumstances.

When it was submitted for popular ratification, the 1793 Constitution, the Constitution that was to become the symbol of political democracy for republicans throughout the first half of the nineteenth

century, was adopted by a huge margin of more than 1,800,000 for
to some 17,000 against, while more than 100,000 voters accepted the
Constitution if amendments of only a moderate nature were incor-
porated in it. The results of the plebiscite were made public on
10 August 1793, the anniversary of the fall of the monarchy, at the
Festival held to celebrate the Unity and Indivisibility of the Republic.
But the application of the Constitution, the text of which was
placed in the sacred ark and laid in the debating-chamber of the
Convention, was postponed until peace had been restored.

The onslaught of counter-revolution

The moderate, conciliatory policy of the Montagnard Convention
had proved unable to prevent the spread of the civil war. In those
departments where their strength lay the Girondins rose against the
Convention. The federalist revolt, indeed, became more widespread
at exactly the moment when the war in the Vendée was growing
more intense and when on all sides the frontiers were being pushed
back by the onslaught of the coalition powers.

The federalist revolt was a natural extension of the sectional
movement of the month of May. News of the insurrection in Paris
and the elimination of the Girondin deputies both precipitated the
revolt in Lyons and Bordeaux and widened its appeal. The leaders of
the Gironde whose arrest was ordered but who managed to escape
joined forces with certain of the seventy-five right-wing deputies
who signed a protest against the events of 2 June; together they
roused the departments to revolt. In Brittany and Normandy, in the
South-west and the Midi and the Franche-Comté, the departmental
authorities seceded from the Republic. The leaders of the sectional
movement, transformed into federalists, set up special emergency
committees and tribunals to pass sentence on patriots, closed the
clubs and tried to raise troops. Caen became the capital of the
Girondin West, while Bordeaux, Nîmes, Marseille and Toulon all
fell into the hands of the insurgents who already held Lyons,
where they had executed Chalier on 17 July. Towards the end of
June around sixty departments were openly in revolt against the
Convention. But the royalist Vendée stood between Normandy and
Brittany on the one hand and the South-west on the other. In the
end Toulouse refused to follow the example of Bordeaux, thus
preventing any link-up between Aquitaine and the Bas-Languedoc.

Between Provence and Lyons, the Drôme, politicized by the Jacobin Joseph Payan, proved itself to be a patriotic bastion. And the departments close to the frontier remained loyal to the Convention.

Federalism had a social content that was more striking than its political identity. No doubt it can be explained in part by the survival of regional particularism, but much stronger was the solidarity of the class interests which underpinned it. As early as 15 May 1793 Chasset, the deputy from the Rhône-et-Loire, was writing that 'it is a question first of our lives and then of our property'; after 2 June he reached a Lyons that was already in a state of revolt and placed himself at the head of the movement (later still he was outlawed and did not return from emigration until the Year IV). The rising was essentially the work of the middle classes who dominated the departmental administrative organs and who were anxious about their property, and it received support from all those who supported the Ancien Régime. The municipal councils, on the other hand, bodies which recruited members of more humble origins, were hostile to it. The workers and artisans were unwilling to fight for the rich, and the requisitions of men ordered by the departments which joined the revolt met with indifference or hostility from the popular classes. Besides, the men who were directing the insurrection quickly lost any unity of purpose they may have had. The sincere republicans among them were reluctant to follow the royalists. They became worried by the foreign invasion and by the rising in the Vendée, and they hesitated to play into the hands of reactionaries. On the other hand, in the South-east the royalists very rapidly assumed control of the movement, and nowhere more than in Lyons, where Précy persuaded the King of Sardinia to stage a diversion in the Alps.

Repression was vigorously organized by the Convention, which paid particular attention to punishing the leaders while sparing their minor accomplices. The most serious threat came from Normandy, as no troops were covering Paris. But on 13 July at Pacy-sur-Eure, when faced with several thousand men raised from the Paris sections, the Girondin forces disbanded, and their leaders, Buzot, Pétion and Barbaroux, left Caen and then the whole of Brittany for the safety of Bordeaux. Robert Lindet was sent to Normandy, and he swiftly pacified the country with the very minimum of repression. But if the departments of the Franche-Comté also gave in without fighting, Bordeaux held out for a longer period, not being retaken by the national government until 18 September. In the South-east there was a brief moment when it was feared that the rebels of Marseille and Nîmes might join forces with the people of Lyons. But the Drôme remained loyal to the Montagne and Pont-Saint-Esprit, which had fallen into the hands of the Nîmois, was retaken; equally the Marseillais who had crossed the Durance and seized Avignon were driven back. On 27 July the troops of General Carteaux entered Avignon and on 25 August they were in Marseille. But four days later, on the 29th, the royalists threw open the port of Toulon to the British and handed over the French Mediterranean fleet. Lyons persisted in its revolt. To recapture these towns regular siege tactics had to be resorted to: Lyons fell on 9 October, but Toulon held out until 19 December 1793. Repression in these towns reached terrible proportions. No doubt by the end of August it was clear that the danger had been staved off, but this does not offset the fact that in July the Republic had been on the point of breaking up.

The results of the federalist revolt were the same as those of the rising in the Vendée: it gave added impetus to the movement, already evident, towards the centralization of power, and it increased the degree of control exercised by popular organizations over citizens suspected of hostility or indifference towards the Revolution. Certain of the Girondins had not hesitated to ally themselves with the royalists, who were themselves in league with France's enemies abroad. And since they had depended on the support of the propertied classes, these in turn came to be regarded as suspect. More than ever before, the Montagne and the popular movement identified with the Republic.

In the meantime the revolt in the Vendée was taking a new turn. After taking Saumur on 9 June 1793, the rebels crushed the Republican forces on 18 July at Vihiers in the Maine-et-Loire, and with the capture of Ponts-de-Cé on the 27th they posed a direct threat to Angers.

The threat posed by the foreign invasion was also becoming more distinct. Since becoming a member of the Committee of Public Safety Danton preferred to negotiate rather than fight. But with Belgium and the left bank of the Rhine recaptured by the coalition, France had no longer any counters to bargain with; perhaps it was true that Danton, as was suspected, was intent on serving the interests of the Queen and her children. And yet the Constitution of

1793 made it clear that 'the French people does not make peace with an enemy that is occupying French territory' (article 121).

The British entered the campaign on the northern frontier, where a force of 20,000 Hanoverians under the Duke of York, supported by 15,000 Dutch troops, was preparing to lay siege to Dunkirk. The Austrians under Coburg methodically proceeded to besiege strongholds protecting the northern frontier: Condé fell on 10 July and Valenciennes on the 28th. Le Quesnoy and Maubeuge were then in turn surrounded. And yet Custine, who had been given command of the army in the North, remained where he was without making any move; it was not long before he became suspect in the eyes of patriots.

On the Rhine the Prussians under the command of the Duke of Brunswick captured Mainz. The town had been under siege since April, defended by twenty thousand French soldiers under Kléber and the deputy on mission, Merlin de Thionville, and it held out until 28 July. The armies on the Rhine and the Moselle were forced to pull back to the Lauter and the Saar, and Landau was besieged.

In the Alps the Piedmontese piled great pressure on Kellermann's troops who were already weakened by the loss of detachments which had been diverted to fight against the federalists in the Midi and the Rhône valley and to lay siege to the rebel cities of Lyons and Toulon. It was only with the greatest difficulty that the Maurienne and Tarentaise passes were held, and soon Savoy was invaded. The town of Nice was threatened.

In the Pyrenees the Spaniards forced their way across the frontier and advanced on Perpignan and Bayonne.

On all the frontiers of the Republic, French armies were being forced back. Those troops that were poorly led underwent a very real moral crisis. Command was uncertain and passed from one hand to another. The aristocratic Custine heaped scorn on the sans-culotte Minister of War, Bouchotte, who was a simple lieutenant-colonel. In the Vendée the military situation was one of total confusion. The deputies sent out on mission to supervise the military leadership failed to cooperate with one another, and when they fell out with Biron, a former noble who was the commander at Niort, some of them supported the sans-culotte generals Ronsin and Rossignol, while the others denounced them. They all refused to accept any responsibility for the defeats that were being suffered. The situation appeared to be utterly desperate.

The assassination of Marat on 13 July 1793 drew attention to the sheer size and scale of the danger: in the heart of Revolutionary Paris a young royalist from Normandy, Charlotte Corday, had been able to kill 'l'ami du peuple'. In his person she had wanted to destroy one of the symbols of the Revolution. But her gesture provided the Montagne with new-found strength and gave new life to the revolutionary movement. For Marat was very popular among the sans-culottes for whose welfare he had shown a deep-seated concern and sympathy. His murder caused great anger and bitterness, and to the desire for vegeance was added the demand for measures of public safety. Paris provided Marat with a lavish funeral which the members of the Convention all attended on 15 July; his heart was hung from the vaults of the Cordelier Club. As a 'martyr of liberty' Marat became, along with Lepeletier, who had been murdered on 20 January, and Chalier, beheaded on 17 July, one of the godheads in the Pantheon of the French Revolution.

The revolutionary counter-attack

The economic and social crisis made the task of the Montagnard Convention still more difficult, but at the same time it drove the mass of the people towards revolutionary action.

The crisis in the supply of foodstuffs and essential consumer goods remained the chief cause of popular discontent. The maximum law on grain prices had been passed on 4 May 1793 but it was not enforced; recognizing that it had failed in this respect, the Convention allowed departments and *représentants en mission* to suspend it in July. It is no doubt true that the Paris sans-culottes did not suffer as a result of the high price of bread, since the price in Paris was held at 3 *sous* per pound by the Commune with the help of government subsidies. But the irregularity with which supplies reached the capital gradually reduced reserves, queues once again became a common sight outside bakers' shops, and the people grew anxious. High prices affected other commodities, while the series of departmental revolts on 2 June contributed to the worsening of the meat crisis by cutting down the number of deliveries. In June 1793 a pound of veal was selling at a price 90 per cent above that of June 1790, while the price of beef had risen by 136 per cent. Troubles broke out all over Paris as a result of high prices. On 21 June a man was arrested in the Faubourg Saint-Antoine for shouting: 'In the old days soap cost only 12 *sous*, now it costs 40; long live the Republic! Sugar once 20 *sous*, now 4 *livres*; long live the Republic!'

The food crisis was made even worse by the effects of inflation of the *assignat*. For inflation followed its course unchecked and magnified the increase in prices. Since the death of the King and the formation of the European coalition paper money had not stopped plummeting in value, falling in July to less than 30 per cent of its face value. The discrediting of paper led to the flight of capital abroad, the growth of speculation, the hoarding of goods and the acceleration of price increases.

The Enragés took advantage of this to stir up general discontent, reproaching the Convention for doing nothing in the economic and social sphere. On 8 June 1793, at the general council of the Commune, Varlet read out his *Déclaration solennelle des Droits de l'Homme dans l'Etat social*, arguing that 'the inequality of wealth' should be overturned 'by just means' and that

property that has been acquired at the expense of the public by means of theft, speculation, monopoly or hoarding should become the property of the nation.

On 15 June the Droits-de-l'Homme section asked for a policy of general price-fixing and for a law against hoarders. And on the 25th, at the bar of the Convention, Jacques Roux presented a petition which had a threatening tone:

The Constitution is about to be presented before the sovereign people for their assent. Have you anywhere in that document outlawed speculation? No. Have you imposed the death sentence for hoarders? No. Have you laid down what exactly freedom of trade means? No. Have you forbidden the sale of coin? No. Well, we are making it known to you that you have not done everything in your power to ensure the happiness of the people. Liberty is no more than a vain shadow of its real self when one class of men can with impunity starve another. Equality is no more than a vain shadow of itself when the rich, by dint of the monopoly position they enjoy, can exercise the right of life and death over their fellow men. And the Republic is no more than a vain shadow of itself when counter-revolution is active from one day to the next in the manipulation of food prices, prices which are beyond the reach of three-quarters of the population but for painful sacrifices on their part. So hand down a further judgement. The sans-culottes are ready with their pikes to enforce your decrees.

On the following day soap riots broke out along the quays in Paris and lasted for three days, from 26 to 28 June; the washerwomen unloaded the ships of their cargoes of soap and divided them among themselves at agreed fixed prices. The sans-culottes were taking the initiative and ended by dragging the Montagnards along behind them.

The renewal of the members of the Committee of Public Safety on 10 July 1793 was in response to the seriousness of the crisis. In their eagerness, the popular militants proposed that measures be adopted to defend the nation and the Revolution in proportion to the threat that presented itself. But it was still necessary to avoid extreme measures that might alienate from the Republic the revolutionary bourgeoisie who had so far given it their support. The revolutionary government recognized this need and kept the popular movement in check. The Committee of Public Safety formed in April had proved itself inadequate to the task. It had not been able to repulse the foreign invasion or to prevent the federalist revolt or to solve the problem of inflation and the food crisis. Instead of giving leadership it was following in the wake of events and had allowed the situation to deteriorate. On 10 July the Convention renewed its Committee of Public Safety, and Danton was removed from it.

The new Committee, elected by a roll-call of all the deputies, consisted of nine members. Three of them were swiftly eliminated: Gasparin for remaining a supporter of General Custine right to the end, Hérault de Séchelles for being the lover of a former aristocrat and being highly suspect, and Thuriot as a friend of Danton's. The Montagnard nucleus of the Committee was formed by Couthon, Saint-Just, Jeanbon Saint-André and Prieur de la Marne. Two members of the Plain, Barère and Lindet, rallied to their support. They were convinced that the Revolution could only emerge victorious if it had the strength of the ordinary people, the sans-culottes, at its command. Hence it had to satisfy popular claims, to supply the population of the towns who were vulnerable to both high prices and scarcity, and to turn all the energies of the people against the aristocracy and the coalition.

The murder of Marat on 13 July made the policy of the Montagnards, faced with the worsening of the political crisis, still more intractable and unbending. Hébert and the Enragés fought among themselves over who should succeed Marat as leader of the people. As early as 16 July, Jacques Roux hastened to bring out a supplement to his paper entitled 'The Publicist of the French Revolution, by the shade of Marat, the Friend of the People'. On the 20th there appeared in its turn another *Ami du Peuple* by Leclerc. But on the 21st, at the Jacobins, Hébert declaimed that, 'If a successor is to be found to Marat, if a second victim is needed for the aristocracy, then that victim is ready – me.' An often demagogic auction then ensued among the popular news-sheets as they attempted to outbid one another. One part of the Montagne, that which included men like Hébert and Chaumette, themselves adopted the political programme of the Enragés so as not to be cut off from the Paris sans-culottes. And they all, with growing vigour, took to denouncing the 'merchant aristocracy', the 'bourgeois and mercantile aristocracy'. As shortages became more acute and a large number of bakers were forced to close because of a shortage of flour, the Maison-commune section introduced a system of ration cards on 21 July; meanwhile petitions poured in and the queues at the doors of bakers' shops became noisy and unruly: in issue 263 of his *Père Duchesne* Hébert wrote:

These poor souls, the sans-culottes, have been suffering for far too long till they are nearly at the end of their tether. It was in order to be happy that they brought about the Revolution.

Scarcely had it been installed in office than the new Committee found itself in danger of being outflanked.

It was in these conditions that the law on hoarding was voted on 26 July 1793. It must be seen as a tactical concession by the Convention. Billaud-Varenne, indeed, had put forward the idea as a means of escape, arguing that the cure for shortage lay not in price-fixing but in the punishment of hoarders, that the threat of the death penalty would force them to lower their prices. On the 26th, after hearing a report from Collot d'Herbois, the Convention voted the decree which prescribed the death penalty for hoarders, who were defined as those merchants who refused to declare the stocks of basic consumer goods which they held and who would not post a list of these on the door of their premises. This law might seem to be an important concession to the Enragés' programme since trade now was to be controlled by sectional commissioners appointed to investigate hoarding. But in fact it was only slowly put into practice and soon appeared as a purely symbolical concession to the sans-culottes.

The membership of the Committee of Public Safety was completed on 27 July with the nomination of Robespierre, the man who had defended it so consistently. The authority of the Committee was far from being accepted by the Convention. Thus the law on hoarding had been voted without its being consulted, and its early decisions, especially that concerning the arrest of Custine on the night of 21/22 July, were greeted with hostile mutterings. Robespierre supported the Committee against its enemies, and then, from 27 July, he was one of its members. On 14 August two further members were elected, Carnot and Prieur de la Côte-d'Or, while Billaud-Varenne and Collot d'Herbois were added on 6 September. They were very different men in both their political leanings and their temperament (Carnot and Lindet showing themselves to be socially conservative, while Billaud and Collot leant towards the views of the sans-culotterie), but all were men of probity, diligence and authority, men united in their desire for victory, men who could maintain their solidarity for a year until that victory was won. Such was the Great Committee of the Year II.

Because of his reputation as a revolutionary, Robespierre was able to impose the policies of the Committee on the Convention and on the Jacobin Club. Farsighted and courageous (this he had shown in his solitary struggle against the general movement of opinion that had led to the declaration of war), eloquent and disinterested, he was the only man in French history to merit the description of 'incorruptible' and he enjoyed the confidence of the sans-culottes. Though committed to his principles, he was nevertheless capable of moulding his policies to the needs of the situation and was statesmanlike in his political manœuvres. He placed all revolutionary authority in the Convention, which he saw as the expression of national sovereignty. But if it was to be strong and effective, the government must depend on the support of the people and remain closely united to them. In the course of the insurrection of 31 May–2 June Robespierre had made this note in his diary:

What is needed is one single will. . . . For that will to be republican we must have ministers who are republican and a government that is republican. The dangers within France come from the middle classes, and to defeat them we must rally the people. . . . The people must ally with the Convention and the Convention make use of the people.

Between 13 and 21 July Robespierre read to the Convention the project of Lepeletier de Saint-Fargeau on the subject of national education:

The revolutions which have taken place over the past three years have done everything for the other classes of society but have as yet done next to nothing for what is perhaps most necessary of all, for the citizens of the proletariat whose only property rests in their labour. Feudalism has been destroyed, but that was not for them, since they do not own any land in the country areas that have been freed. Taxes are now more justly divided, but, as a result of their extreme poverty, they were almost outside the range of people paying taxes. Civil equality is established, yet they still lack instruction and education. Now we have come to the revolution for the poor.

If, however, Robespierre and the members of the Committee understood the situation clearly, they were less sure of the means that would have to be used. The great measures that were taken in defence of the nation and the Revolution, the conscription of men for the armies, the Terror, and government direction of the economy, these were all forced on the leadership by outside forces, whether as a result of the crisis of the month of August 1793 or of pressure from the popular movement.

2. THE COMMITTEE OF PUBLIC SAFETY AND THE PRESSURE OF THE POPULAR MOVEMENT (AUGUST TO OCTOBER 1793)

The new Committee was determined to give a vigorous boost to the defence of the nation, which it did not distinguish from the defence of the Revolution. But it intended not to allow itself to be outflanked by the popular movement and in particular by the propaganda of the Enragés. For the popular militants the only means of ensuring adequate defence lay in the introduction of a controlled economy and of universal conscription. But the Committee at first saw conscription as nothing more than a fanciful notion, while it remained hostile to price-fixing and to directing the economy and was horrified by the idea of terror; finally, direct democracy, which the Paris sections practised in a disorganized way, seemed to the Committee to be incompatible with efficient government management. Throughout the month of August it manœuvred from one concession to another until it finally gave in to the popular *journées* of 4 and 5 September 1793.

From the beginning of August, Robespierre did battle with the Enragés in an attempt to rid the government and the Convention of their opposition. On 6 August he denounced them to the Jacobins as the 'new men', the 'one-day patriots' who were seeking to deprive the people of their oldest friends. As Robespierre put it, not without a degree of bad faith: 'Two men paid by the enemies of the people, two men whom Marat denounced, have succeeded or have thought they could succeed that most patriotic of writers.' In particular he reproached Jacques Roux for having attacked merchants. So as to deprive the Enragés of the very basis of their case, the Committee actively concerned itself with foodstuffs, sending into the departments around Paris energetic deputies who requisitioned manpower and saw that the corn was threshed. On 9 August, at Barère's suggestion, the Convention decreed that in each district a public granary should be established. It was pure window-dressing as a response to popular demands, since the purchase of grain by the districts could not solve the problem of high prices. But Paris was supplied, and for a brief moment the Enragés were denied their principal argument in appealing to the sans-culottes.

Against the moderates who were demanding that the Constitution adopted by the people should be put into force and were asking for new elections in the hope that these might lead to the fall of the Montagne, Robespierre reacted with great vigour. It was a demand that was all the more dangerous in that it found unexpected support from Hébert in issue 219 of his *Père Duchesne* some days before 10 August. The Committee of Public Safety intended that the government should remain revolutionary until peace had been signed and that not till then should the Constitution be put into effect. On 11 August Delacroix, the deputy for the Eure-et-Loir and one of the future *Indulgents*, had it decreed that a census be taken of the voters of the country with a view to holding general elections in accordance with the Constitution: Robespierre held that this insidious proposal would merely have the effect of substituting the minions of Pitt and Coburg for the members of the present Convention which had already been purged of counter-revolutionaries. To apply the Constitution before the revolts at home had been crushed and victory won on the frontiers would mean that the whole Revolution would again be put in question. On that same day delegates from the *assemblées primaires* had brought the text of the Constitution to the Convention and it had been solemnly placed in a cedarwood ark. There was no longer any question of bringing it out again, even though the suspension of the Constitution until the return of peace was not to be explicitly stated as a doctrine until 10 October 1793.

Universal conscription (*23 August 1793*)

External war and internal counter-revolution did, however, continue to mobilize the popular movement, which succeeded in imposing the idea of mass conscription on both the Committee of Public Safety and the Convention. This was in accordance with the revolutionary mentality of the sans-culottes, and it was a popular concept in the sections and clubs of Paris. For conscription would give the Revolutionary forces the benefit of numerical advantage and would raise hopes of a speedy victory against enemy armies whose strength was being reduced: Jemappes seemed to provide proof of this. The idea crystallized in the course of the crisis of July 1793 when the Republic, already under attack on the frontiers, was further endangered by the federalist revolt. On 6 July the Luxembourg section proposed that the members of the Paris sections be sent *en masse* against the rebel departments; 'that all citizens without distinction between the ages of sixteen and fifty be permanently requisitioned and formed into the armed forces of the country'. On 28 July the proposal was taken up again by a militant from the Unité section, Sébastien Lacroix, in a speech which already betrays something of the epic spirit of the decree of 23 August:

... stop at once the various jobs done by cartwrights, joiners and wood-workers, so that they can all be used to make rifle-butts, gun-carriages, powder-chests, and waggons; stop the work done by locksmiths, black-smiths, toolmakers and all ironworkers, so that they may be employed solely in the manufacture of guns. ... Let those who love their country take up arms and form large numbers of battalions; let those who have no weapons drive munitions-waggons; let the womenfolk bring provisions or knead bread; and let the signal for battle be given by the singing of the patriotic anthem!

The defeats suffered at the end of July gave irresistible force to the idea of conscription, an idea that was now being championed by the popular press. As Hébert wrote in issue 265 of the *Père Duchesne*:

'Let all men who are in a fit state to march and to bear arms be required to do so at once and let them go without delay to all those places where danger lies.'

The popular demand for mass conscription was first presented to the Jacobins on 29 July 1793; it was subsequently taken up by the Commune on 4 August and three days later by the delegates of the *assemblées primaires* who had come to Paris to accept the Constitution; their spokesman, Royer, proposed to the Convention on the 12th that the people should be conscripted. Yet the Committee of Public Safety held back. What would be done with the disorganized mob that would be created by mass conscription? How could they be armed and provisioned? On 14 August Robespierre told the Jacobins that 'this magnanimous though perhaps over-enthusiastic idea of mass conscription is not practicable'; and he added: 'It is not men that we are short of, but the virtues of patriotism in our generals.' Under pressure, however, from the militants of Paris and the delegates from the primary assemblies, the Convention adopted the principle of a conscript army on 16 August, and finally, on the 23rd, the Committee of Public Safety listened to Barère's report on the subject and decided to put forward ideas on how it could be enacted:

From this moment until such time as our enemies have been expelled from the territories of the Republic, all Frenchmen are in a state of permanent requisition for service in the armies. The young will go to fight; married men will forge weapons and transport foodstuffs; women will make tents and clothes and will serve in the hospitals, while children will shred old linen and old men will be taken to the public squares to rouse the courage of the young soldiers and to preach hatred of kings and the need for Republican unity.

The loophole whereby a man could find a replacement to serve in his stead was abolished. In principle conscription was applied to all, but young men aged between eighteen and twenty-five, those who were unmarried or widowers with no children, were in the first group to be requisitioned and would be the first to march off to the frontiers. They were to be formed into battalions which marched under a banner bearing the words, 'The French people standing up to tyrants'.

Did the decree on conscription correspond exactly to the wishes of the sans-culottes? Their ideal, that of marching to the frontiers, borne along by a spirit of patriotic enthusiasm, was a quite unrealistic dream. It is for this reason that Robespierre appeared so reticent, the Committee so hesitant, and the decree so limited: for if all the resources of the nation were mobilized and extraordinary provisions were made for the manufacture of arms, only those aged between eighteen and twenty-five without family responsibilities were in fact called on to serve. Indeed, the problems involved in arming and provisioning the armies remained vast. The *Père Duchesne*, when establishing its plan of campaign at the beginning of September, asked certain very important questions: 'How can several million men be in action at one and the same time? How are they to be armed and supplied? . . . Above all we must be certain that we have at our disposal all the supplies of food that are held in the Republic. . . . We must requisition all those who are engaged in metalwork, from the blacksmith to the goldsmith, set up forges in all public places, and spend night and day making cannon, guns, swords, and bayonets.'

Hébert was giving explicit expression to the problem of the economic management of a great national war effort: for to arm and feed the huge numbers of men who would fill the conscription lists— and there were seven separate classes of men involved – it was absolutely necessary to impose a controlled economy. The political and economic problems that faced France were indissolubly tied in with the problem of national defence.

The journées of 4 and 5 September 1793

Towards the end of August 1793 no solution had been found to any of the great problems of the moment. The political problem remained in all its enormity: for if the Committee of Public Safety had eluded the attacks of its opponents, revolutionary government was still far from being stabilized and well-organized. Nor had any effective solution been found to the economic and social problem, for the law against hoarding and that establishing public granaries had not provided any real cure to the ills of the country. Up till this point both the Convention and the Committee of Public Safety had refused to sanction price-fixing or economic regulation, despite the fact that the fate of the *assignat*, the only financial resource at the disposal of the Revolution, was dependent on these measures. In the last few days of August the food crisis grew even more serious and pressure on the government from the popular classes became still greater. At the same time the Parisian militants became convinced that what was called for was another day of rioting in order to impose the will of the people on the government authorities.

Though the food crisis was reduced for a short period, it resumed on account of the drought: the work of the mills was slowed down, there were popular disturbances again at the doors of bakeries, and the supplies arriving in Paris amounted to some 400 sacks of flour per day when the consumption needs of the city were of the order of 1,500. For Hébert the shortage proved a powerful lever in political agitation, and he put the food issue at the very centre of his campaign, developing themes which bitterly attacked the rich and the merchant classes and which, he knew, would doubtless please the sans-culottes: as he wrote in issue 279 of his *Père Duchesne*:

Our country, damn it, the merchants don't care about it. As long as they thought that the Revolution might be useful to them they gave it their support; they helped the sans-culottes destroy the nobility and the *parlements*; but they did so in order to put themselves in the aristocrats' place. But there is no longer any such thing as active citizens, since the poor sans-culotte now enjoys the same rights as the rich extortionist; all these scoundrels who don't give a damn about the Revolution have ratted on us, and now they are leaving no stone unturned in their attempts to destroy the Republic; they have hoarded every possible kind of foodstuffs and consumer goods in order to sell them back to us at exorbitant prices or to bring about acute shortages.

In these first days of September 1793 the popular movement reappeared in all its force and with its own particular role to play. It was what Albert Mathiez has termed an 'Hébertist rising'. No doubt the popular news-sheets (though these included the paper edited by Jacques Roux as well as that of Hébert) helped the sans-culottes to realize their true political aims and to identify their social grievances. But they did not cause these aims or grievances. It was a popular and not an Hébertist upsurge: it was under pressure from the sans-culottes that Hébert wrote and organized, resoundingly echoing the ideas that he heard, just as it was their pressure that shook the Jacobins and inspired the Commune and to that pressure that the Convention and the Committee of Public Safety finally gave in.

The popular movement first assumed a political role in the spring of 1789, but its origins would have to be sought in the worsening standard of living of Parisian shopkeepers, artisans, and workers in the years long before the Revolution. This movement, which allowed the bourgeois revolution to sweep it along during periods of crisis, was nevertheless totally different from it (as was shown in the rioting of September 1793); it was characterized by the pre-capitalist mentality of the sans-culottes, a mentality that was essentially the same as that of the peasantry who were bitterly defending their common-land rights against the onslaught of capitalist agricultural methods. The sans-culotte was deeply hostile to the frame of mind of the commerical and industrial bourgeoisie who would not rest till they had, in the name of that liberty that was so necessary to the growth of their businesses, destroyed the economic controls and fixed prices that were so dear to the hearts of shopkeepers and artisans.

Their conception of property throws considerable light on the fundamental opposition that existed between the bourgeois and the sans-culotte. Property, as defined in the Declaration of Rights of 1793 and that of 1789 alike, is an absolute right, a natural human right which nothing should impede. But for the sans-culotte property is conceived of only in terms of a man's personal work and it is limited by the needs of society as a whole. On 2 September 1793, at the culmination of the popular upsurge, the Paris section named Sans-Culottes (previously the Jardin-des-Plantes section) presented an address to the Convention asking the Assembly

to fix at a permanent level the price of essential commodities, the level of wages, the profits of industry and the gains to be made from trade. . . . What's that? The aristocrats, royalists, moderates and intriguers will tell you that that would imply an attack on property rights and that these ought to be sacred and inviolable. . . . No doubt; but do these rascals not know . . ., do they not know that there is no basis to property other than the extent of physical needs?

The sans-culottes went on to ask for maximum prices to be applied to food and to incomes:

2. That the price of all essential goods should be set at a fixed level against the price that was current in past years, starting from 1789 and including 1790, in proportion to the differing qualities of the products; 3. That these matters should be fixed in such a way that the profits of industry, the wages paid for labour and the gains made from trade should all be regulated by law and that the industrious workman, farmer or trader should be able to acquire for himself not only those things which

are essential to the eking out of a bare existence but also those things which may add to his happiness.

In particular the sans-culottes of the Jardin-des-Plantes asked for property rights to be very strictly circumscribed:

8. That a *maximum* be fixed for personal fortunes; 9. That the same individual should not be able to own property above the level of a single *maximum*; 10. That no one should be able to rent more land than the amount that can be tilled with a stipulated number of ploughs; 11. That the same citizen should not be able to own more than one shop or workshop.

This social programme, though it was full of contradictions as a result of its desire both to maintain private property and to limit it in the effects it had on society, was quite basically at variance with that of the bourgeoisie who were running the Revolution. It was as a result of this clash that the revolutionary government was to be destroyed in Thermidor. But in the short term the alliance between the sans-culottes and the middle classes who composed the Montagne was cemented by other factors – their hatred of the common enemy, of the Ancien Régime, of privilege and of the feudal aristocracy, and the sheer size of the danger posed by counter-revolution. The Montagnards could not win through on their own and they had, therefore, to rally to the programme championed by the people. They also had to exercise restraint over them.

The crisis came to a head in the early days of September. While Hébert was denouncing the Convention for inactivity and humbug, feeling in the sections was running high and their initiatives and petitions rapidly increased in number. In the midst of this feverish excitement news came through on 2 September of a quite unheard-of degree of treachery – the news that Toulon had been handed over to the British by the royalists. To the anxieties caused by the food shortage were now added the anguish of offended patriotism and an obsession with the aristocratic plot. And there was nothing that could be more certain to unleash a popular demand for terror. On the evening of the 2nd, to avoid what they regarded as a disaster, the Jacobins decided to take action.

Two days later the popular excitement that had been contained for so long suddenly exploded. From early morning groups of workmen, especially those employed in the building trades and in the manufacture of war materials, made their way to the Place de

Grève to demand bread from the Commune. There is no possible doubt that this was an initiative taken by the workers themselves, a movement that originated from among the most proletarianized members of the sans-culotte ranks, from among those workers who were neither shopkeepers nor artisans, those who had the greatest difficulty in making ends meet with wages paid in *assignats* that were constantly dropping in value. The leaders of the Commune had no success when they tried to calm the demonstrators: 'It's not promises that we need, it's bread – and we need it immediately!' Chaumette climbed on to a table to address the crowd:

I, too, have been poor and as a result I know what poverty means for people. What we have here is open warfare declared by the rich on the poor. They want to crush us. Well, we should warn them; we must crush them ourselves – and we have strength in our hands!

It was decided that a mass demonstration should be held on the following day to impose the wishes of the people on the Convention.

On 5 September 1793 the sections assembled in a long column and marched on the Convention; they had watchwords like 'War on tyrants! War on aristocrats! War on hoarders!' The Convention was peacefully surrounded and invaded; the deputies carried on their discussions under the eyes of the people. After Pache, speaking for the Commune and the sections, had denounced the activities of hoarders and the selfishness of those with property, Chaumette read out a petition asking for the creation of a revolutionary army to ensure that grain requisitions could be made in the country areas and that the convoys reached Paris safely. Billaud-Varenne went further, proposing that suspects should be arrested – a measure which the sans-culottes saw as being quite essential. Without consulting the Committee of Public Safety, the Convention gave way and decreed not only the arrest of suspects but also the purge of the revolutionary committees that were given the job of looking for them. The effect of these steps was to make Terror the order of the day. After listening to a report from Barère, the creation of an *armée révolutionnaire* of 6,000 men and 1,200 artillery was agreed to. Finally the Convention accepted a proposal by Danton, that an indemnity of 40 *sous* per session be paid to those citizens who attended their section meetings, meetings which should in future be reduced to two each week.

The *journées* of 4 and 5 September 1793 were a victory for the popular movement: the sans-culottes forced the government authorities to adopt measures which they had been demanding for some time. But it was not a complete victory, for the decisions taken on the 5th were primarily political ones, while on the 4th the Convention had done no more than to promise to introduce a general maximum law, the measure which contained the very essence of popular claims. The Parisian sans-culottes had to maintain their pressure on the Convention in order to extract from it the national maximum price for grain and fodder (a law passed on 11 September) and the Law of the General Maximum (on the 29th). Such was the repugnance with which the bourgeoisie, even the Montagnard bourgeoisie, interfered with the liberty of trade and commerce.

It was a popular victory, but it was also a success for the government, since they had safeguarded the rule of law and since legal terror had won the day over direct action by the people. The Committee of Public Safety certainly resisted, but it knew to give way in time and on ground which it chose itself. Its authority emerged strengthened, and a further step had been taken towards the reinforcement of Revolutionary Government.

Popular successes and government consolidation (September to October 1793)

After the *journées* of 4 and 5 September popular pressure was maintained, for the Convention and Committee of Public Safety moved only with the greatest reluctance towards a policy of terror and economic controls. The demands of the people also had a second major effect, since they held up the consolidation of Revolutionary government within the Convention itself, where it was already faced with powerful opposition. The militants in the sections and the clubs demanded that the Terror be strengthened by means of a vast operation to purge the numerous administrative bodies, by the elimination of suspects in public life, and by means of increased repression. Besides, the persistence of the food crisis made them stubbornly insistent in their demands for total government direction of the economy and for the general fixing of commodity prices which had been promised but was continually being postponed.

Throughout the entire month of September the Committee of Public Safety was engaged in political manœuvring, playing with the popular movement in order to keep the Convention under control, and with the Convention in a bid to put a brake on the popular upsurge, granting those concessions which were necessary but gradually reinforcing its own position as it was doing so. Billaud-Varenne and Collot d'Herbois, who supported the demands of the people, were nominated to the Committee on 6 September. On the 13th the Committee of General Security was renewed, while in future the Committee of Public Safety would present the Convention with a list of its members. The same decision was taken with regard to the other committees. In this way power became more highly concentrated, and the Committee of Public Safety, now in a position of pre-eminence and given responsibility for controlling the activities of all the other committees which till then had been its equals, now became the real centre of government activity.

The Terror, which had been the order of the day in principle since 5 September, was imposed gradually as a result of popular action. A widespread movement to purge the personnel of the various administrations developed, a movement which was controlled by the sections and which concentrated especially on the offices of the Ministry of War, as a result of the driving force of the secretary-general to the ministry, Vincent. The revolutionary committees were renewed by the general council of the Commune, thus escaping the attentions of the sectional authorities. And the sectional assemblies and committees themselves expelled from their ranks all those who were moderate, indifferent, or lukewarm in their support of the Revolution. The Convention and the government committees tolerated rather than directed this purge. But it was repression, even more than purging, that captured the popular imagination. The demands for Terror were heard all the more strongly as the government refused to order the more generalized use of repression. While the revolutionary committees, spurred on by the Paris Commune, were already proceeding to make arrests of suspects, around mid-September rumours were spread about that massacres had been carried out: on the 8th prisoners who were taken to the Abbaye said that they were afraid of a renewal of the September Massacres of the previous year. The Convention sensed the danger and realized that there was a risk of finding itself outflanked. Hence on 17 September 1793, to avoid any interpretation that might undermine the measures of principle adopted on the 5th, it passed the Law of

Suspects, a law adopted following a report from Merlin de Douai. Under this law the definition of 'suspects' was a very wide one, and the law therefore applied to all those who were enemies of the Revolution. Suspects might be the relatives of émigrés, unless they had given some proof of their love for the Revolution, or all those who had been refused a *certificat de civisme*, or officials who had been suspended or dismissed. Suspect in a more general manner were those who had, whether by their actions or the company they kept, by their words or their writings, shown themselves to be 'supporters of tyranny or of federalism and therefore enemies of liberty', or those again who were unable to justify the means by which they earned their livelihood (by this clause the law sought to include speculators). The revolutionary committees were given the task of drawing up lists of suspects.

Though the principle of a controlled economy was accepted on 4 September, it, too, was finally instituted only under pressure from the popular masses of Paris. The establishment of a national maximum price for flour on the 11th was not enough to satisfy them. Towards the middle of the month rowdy groups of people were again causing disturbances outside bakers' shops and petitions were circulating in ever-greater numbers; on the 22nd the sections, with the full support of the Commune, presented an address to the Convention: 'You have decreed the principle that all essential consumer goods will be subject to price controls. . . . The people await your decision on this question with an impatience occasioned by genuine hardship.' And so the Committee of Public Safety, grappling simultaneously with violent opposition inside the Convention, aimed at holding the support of the Assembly by instilling fear of popular pressure from the streets; for this reason they gave satisfaction to the people by deciding to increase the degree of economic direction. The Law of the General Maximum was passed on 29 September 1793. The law fixed both price and wage levels. Essential consumer goods were pegged in each district at a figure one-third above the average price for 1790, and those who contravened the law were to be added to the list of suspects. It would have been illogical to fix prices for goods without at the same time fixing the rate for a day's labour, and so the law fixed the maximum wage rates in each commune at the level paid in 1790 increased by a half. There were huge difficulties experienced in the application of the law; its enforcement demanded extra severity and stricter centralization, leading to a decisive advance in both terror and political dictatorship.

The strengthening of the powers of the Committee of Public Safety continued apace. It was seen both in the destruction of the Enragés and in the silencing of the opposition in the Convention. The liquidation of the Enragés was possible only on account of the divisions within the popular movement. Jacques Roux, Leclerc and Varlet had taken great risks by providing the vanguard of the movement, in that they provided easy targets for attack by governmental authorities which were anxious not to allow themselves to be outpaced. On 19 September 1793 the official *Journal de la Montagne* could write in these terms:

Popular movements are just and defensible only when they are made necessary by tyranny ...; the rascals who have advocated the formation of ferocious irregular movements, whether to serve our enemies or to satisfy their own special interests, have always incurred shame and obloquy.

Intent on making its policies fully effective, the Committee of Public Safety had no intention of tolerating these irregular movements, that is to say the at times disorganized thrust of the masses of Paris. Jacques Roux was arrested for the second time on 5 September 1793 following a denunciation, and this time he was not released. Varlet encountered the same fate. He was arrested on the 18th, on the orders of the Committee of General Security, for having organized opposition in the Droits-de-l'homme section to the decree which limited the number of sectional meetings to two each week:

Do you want to close the people's eyes, to dilute the intensity of their surveillance? And in what circumstances? At a time when the dangers facing the country oblige them to entrust enormous power to you, the exercise of which must be actively supervised.

Meanwhile Leclerc pursued his campaign against the government in *L'Ami du Peuple*, but, denounced to the Jacobins and threatened with arrest, he suspended publication of his paper on 21 September. There remained the Society of Republican Revolutionary Women under the leadership of the actress Claire Lacombe; this was dissolved on 20 October and women's clubs were banned. In this way the logic of events led the Committee of Public Safety to assume control over popular organizations, a tendency which could only result in the long term in disaffection towards authorities which showed little concern for sovereignty, at least in the sense in which the sans-culottes understood the term.

For a time opposition inside the Convention was also silenced, following one of the most virulent debates ever held on the floor of the Assembly. When Bouchotte announced the dismissal on 24 September of Houchard, the commander in the North who had been defeated at Menin after his earlier victory at Hondschoote, this was taken as the signal for attack. Thuriot, who had resigned from the Committee of Public Safety, made devastating charges against government policy on the 25th, centring his attack on the controlled economy and the purge of personnel and concluding: 'We must bring this impetuous torrent to an end or else it will drag us down to utter barbarism.' This indictment corresponded with the views which the Convention secretly held: the deputies applauded and sent as a new member to the Committee Briez, who was on mission to Valenciennes at the time when the town had capitulated. Robespierre threw the entire weight of his prestige and his eloquence into the debate:

I declare before you that a man who was in Valenciennes when the enemy entered the town is not a fit person to be a member of the Committee of Public Safety. . . . That view will seem harsh, but what is harder still for a patriot to stomach is that over the last two years 100,000 men have been slain as a result of treason and weakness; it is our feeble attitude towards traitors that is our undoing.

The Convention was subdued and maintained the confidence it had had in the Committee of Public Safety.

The strengthening of the powers of the Committee followed from these debates. On 10 October, on the recommendation of Saint-Just, the Convention declared that the government of France would remain revolutionary until peace had been signed. The bases of Revolutionary Government, that is to say the coordination of the various emergency measures under the sole control of the Committee of Public Safety, had been laid down in September. The needs of the economic situation and the enforcement of the general maximum now demanded that it be established definitively. The decree of 10 October 1793 was the first step in this direction. As Saint-Just had said:

The laws are revolutionary, but those who carry them out are not. The Republic will be firmly established only when the sovereign will of the people represses the monarchical minority and rules over them by right of conquest. . . . Those who are not prepared to be governed by justice must be governed by the sword. . . . It is impossible for revolutionary laws to be carried out if the government itself is not constituted on revolutionary principles.

As a result, ministers, generals, and government administration at national and local level were all placed under the overall supervision of the Committee of Public Safety, which communicated directly with the district assemblies, the linchpins of the new organization. The principle of authority was given priority over that of election.

The result of the popular upsurge had been to make terror the order of the day, organized in political matters through the Law of Suspects and in economic affairs by the Law of the General Maximum. The September crisis had given a powerful stimulus to the creation of revolutionary government, and the Committee of Public Safety had in the end emerged from it with its authority increased. The primacy of the Committee was now an established fact. But it was not to become definitively entrenched without being shaken by a number of other incidents.

3. THE ORGANIZATION OF THE JACOBIN DICTATORSHIP OF PUBLIC SAFETY (OCTOBER TO DECEMBER 1793)

Now that it had been declared to be revolutionary until peace was signed, the government gradually got down to the task of organizing itself. All its efforts were concentrated on gaining victory on the frontiers and on crushing the counter-revolutionaries at home. In political matters it was the desire of the Committee of Public Safety to place repression on a regular footing, to keep terror within its legal framework, and to control the activities of the popular movement. But meanwhile the pressure of popular claims did not recede, especially over questions of political and economic repression. For the steps taken in September gave the sans-culottes some degree of satisfaction but certainly did not disarm them; indeed, their influence was at its height during October and November 1793. Already the government was showing itself eager to restrict the activities of the popular movement to certain narrowly-defined limits and to prevent it extending beyond these. But suddenly the dechristianization issue flared up and the popular movement received a new lease of life.

The Committee of Public Safety tried to check it, but this merely accentuated the break that had already appeared between the Committee and the sans-culottes. The decree of 14 Frimaire II (4 December 1793), which stabilized its power and set out the organization of government, gave legal sanction to a trend that had been apparent since 2 June.

The Terror

Though the Terror was organized in September 1793, it was not really introduced until October, and that as a result of pressure from the popular movement. Up until September, of the 260 people who had been brought before the Revolutionary Tribunal, 66 – or around one-quarter – had been condemned to death. The triumph of the sans-culottes opened a new chapter in the history of the Tribunal: on 5 September it was divided into four sections of which two were to be operational at any one time; the Committees of Public Safety and General Security were to propose the names of judges and jurymen; Fouquier-Tinville stayed on as public prosecutor, and Herman was nominated president.

The great political trials began in October. On the 3rd, on the basis of a report from Amar, the Girondins were sent before the Revolutionary Tribunal, as was Marie-Antoinette on the recommendation of Billaud-Varenne. When the Queen was guillotined on 16 October, her execution was hailed as 'the greatest joy of all for the Père Duchesne'. The trial of the twenty-one Girondins started on the 24th. As the discussions seemed likely to be dragged out for ever, the Convention ruled that after three days the jury should be entitled to give its verdict; and hence the Girondins died on the 31st. Hébert's terrorist campaign continued throughout the autumn months and was a factor in the great increase in the sans-culottes' demands for the punishment of their opponents. After the execution of the Duc d'Orléans, Philippe-Egalité, on 6 November, *Le Père Duchesne* gave the Tribunal the benefit of its own opinions, urging it to 'strike while the iron is hot and without delay guillotine the treacherous Bailly, the infamous Barnave . . .'. Issue 312 of the paper sang the praises of the 'holy guillotine' and protested in advance that too much clemency was being shown. Madame Roland was executed on 8 November, Bailly on the 10th, Barnave on the 28th. In the last three months of 1793, out of 395 defendants, 177 received death sentences – 45 per cent of the total. The number of people detained in the prisons of Paris rose from around 1,500 at the end of August to 2,398 on 2 October, and to 4,525 on 21 December.

In the provinces the Terror reflected the gravity of counter-revolution and the temperament of the men sent out on mission from the Convention. Those regions which were not affected by civil war very often did not experience the Terror at all, at any rate before the end of 1793. In Normandy no death sentences were imposed after the collapse of the federalist rising, and Lindet appealed for a general reconciliation. In the departments of the West which had been ravaged by the Vendéan revolt, military commissions of five members were set up in the principal towns, Rennes, Tours, Angers, and Nantes, to condemn to death those rebels taken prisoner with arms on their person; they did so summarily once the identity of the accused had been established. In Nantes, the representative on mission, Carrier, allowed executions to be carried out without trial by drowning the victims in the Loire; in this way some two to three thousand people died in the months of December and January alone, mostly refractory priests, suspects and brigands, as well as those condemned for common-law offences. In Bordeaux repression was directed by Tallien, while in Provence it was carried out by Barras and Fréron, who were responsible for mass executions while trying cases at Toulon. Terror in Lyons was proportionate to the danger which the city's rebellion had posed for the Republic; a siege lasting two months, from 9 August until 9 October, had to be conducted in order to bring the town to its knees. On 12 October the Convention listened to a report from Barère and decreed that Lyons should be razed to the ground:

All that part that was inhabited by the rich shall be demolished; only the houses of the poor and the homes of good patriots, those who have been murdered or outlawed (by the federalists), shall be left standing . . .; and the group of buildings that are left shall in future be known as *Ville Affranchie.*

But if Couthon was content to order the demolition of a few houses on the Place Bellecour, Collot d'Herbois and Fouché arrived on 7 November and organized large-scale repression. The existing court, the Commission de Justice Populaire, was held to be too indulgent and was replaced by a Revolutionary Commission which passed 1,667 death sentences. The guillotine was too slow as a method of dispatch; it was supplemented by the practice of having prisoners shot – the *fusillade* and the *mitraillade*.

Although the Terror was in its essence political, it often quite fortuitously acquired social significance, since the deputies on mission could find support only from the sans-culotte masses and the officers of the Jacobin clubs. Many of these deputies, whose basic task was that of directing conscription, confined their activities to such measures as were necessary for national defence and internal security. Others endowed their revolutionary work with a marked social flavour, imposing levies on the rich, organizing the *armées révolutionnaires*, building public workshops and hospitals, and enforcing the *maximum* with great stringency: such men included Isoré and Chasles in the Nord, Saint-Just and Lebas in Alsace, and Fouché in the Nièvre. On 10 Brumaire II (31 October 1793) Saint-Just and Lebas passed a decree whereby the rich of Strasbourg were to be taxed the sum of 9 million *livres*, of which 2 millions were to be used for the needs of the patriotic poor. When he told the Jacobin Club about Saint-Just's mission, Robespierre declared on 1 Frimaire (21 November): 'You see how the rich have been stripped of their wealth to feed and clothe the poor. That has aroused once more the forces of revolutionary strength and patriotic fervour. The aristocrats have been guillotined.'

The economic aspects of the Terror are no less clear. In Paris the Commune controlled the distribution of goods, especially through the introduction of ration cards for bread; it also authorized the sectional commissioners for investigating hoarding to proceed to make visits to people's homes; and it attempted to see that the fixed prices were adhered to by resorting to acts of repression. Detachments of the *armée révolutionnaire*, which had been created by the decree of 9 September and had been organized in early October, toured the corn-growing areas around Paris, with the result that the farmers released their corn supplies. The authorities did, however, confine themselves to the terms of the existing legislation against hoarding and refused to give in to pressure from the Paris sections: on 23 October 1793 they vainly asked the Convention to introduce special juries chosen from among the poor to hear cases against hoarders. In the provinces even greater severity was required if the *maximum* was to be applied: this the Terror supplied by the simple threat of its existence on the statute book, and no death sentences were passed for purely economic offences. Most of the towns followed the example of Paris in rationing bread, in many cases going so far as to take bakeries into municipal ownership. But bread distribution did presuppose that supplies were coming into the towns in the normal way. In an attempt to coordinate the movement of goods and to stimulate production, the Committee of Public Safety set up a special commission, the Commission des Subsistances, on 22 October, a body which enjoyed the most extensive powers and which had overall control of production, trading conditions, and transportation. The entire economic life of the nation now came within the jurisdiction of the Committee, and the coercive authority enjoyed by its agents and by the deputies on mission allowed it to impose economic direction on producers and merchants who were utterly opposed to it.

But at the very moment when the Terror was being regulated and brought under the ever-tightening control of the Committee of Public Safety, the Committee had to face pressure from the people in a new form which came close to destroying its dominant position and throwing open once again the whole question of how Revolutionary Government should be placed on a stable footing.

Dechristianization and the cult of martyrs of liberty

The origins of dechristianization are to be found both in certain aspects of religious policy in the years after 1790 and in certain characteristics of the popular mentality.

Ever since 1790 refractory priests had risen in revolt at the side of the aristocracy. In 1792, moreover, the constitutional clergy in turn came to appear suspect in the eyes of many of the revolutionaries, for, with the exception of a few curés who, like Jacques Roux, identified with the popular movement, the vast majority of the constitutional priests remained monarchist in outlook, deplored the events of 10 August, and became more forthright in their disapproval after the execution of the King. In 1793 their attitude evolved still further. Moderate by nature, the constitutional clergy naturally tended to favour the Gironde and federalism, which only served to increase the hostility of the people towards them. Many politicians therefore considered that it was no longer very useful to carry on with the Civil Constitution, and as early as November 1792 Cambon proposed that the State should no longer pay priests' salaries. But such men were wrong to imagine that the State could do without a Church and that the people could dispense with religious ceremonies. From 1790 there had gradually come into being a cult of the Revolution itself, a cult which was first and most splendidly shown in the Federation of 14 July. The practices of this new religion were laid down over the years in the shape of civic festivals, memorial ceremonies like that to commemorate the Fall of the Bastille, and funeral services such as that held in honour of Mirabeau. But whereas until 1793 the clergy had always been associated with these ceremonies, the Festival of the Unity and Indivisibility of the Republic on 10 August 1793 was a purely lay affair. At that time, too, a real spirit of popular devotion was building up around the 'martyrs of liberty', Lepeletier, Chalier, and especially Marat.

Several months before the unleashing of full-scale dechristianization there were a number of incidents in Paris which showed that certain of the militants wanted just such a policy: this was clear at the festival of Corpus Christi in June of 1793 and also when the question arose of hunting for precious metals and pulling down the church bells needed for the armament industries. On 12 September 1793 the Panthéon-français section asked that 'schools of liberty' be opened where the horrors of religious fanaticism might be preached to the people on Sundays. So dechristianization was a response to a movement which was becoming clearer and clearer ever since the sans-culottes first took a part in political life. And the movement gained impetus, since to general anti-religious feeling were added the necessities of national defence; the precious metals from the churches would allow the value of the currency to be protected, while the bronze from the bells could be used for making cannon. Thus there was an economic aspect to dechristianization; the hunt for gold was often both one of the causes and one of the consequences of the movement.

What Aulard sees as the most anti-Christian action of the whole Revolution, the adoption of the revolutionary calendar, showed that on this particular matter the feelings of the Convention and the revolutionary bourgeoisie on the one hand and the popular leadership on the other were identical. On 5 October 1793 the Convention adopted Romme's suggestion that the republican era should be deemed to have started on 22 September 1792, the first day of the Republic. The year was divided into twelve months of thirty days each, and each month was further divided into three periods of ten days (known as *décades*); the full number of days in each year was made up by the addition of five or six additional days or *jours complémentaires*, which were in the first instance referred to as *jours sans-culottides*. Thus the new *décadi* replaced Sunday in the calendar and the new holidays every ten days were established in competition with the old religious holidays. On 24 October 1793 another report was produced on the calendar, this time by Fabre d'Eglantine: the poet who had written 'Il pleut, il pleut, bergère' thought up poetic names which might be given to the months (*vendémiaire, brumaire, frimaire; nivôse, pluviôse, ventôse; germinal, floréal, prairial; messidor, thermidor, fructidor*). This attempt to dechristianize everyday life was completed by the decree of 15 Brumaire (5 November) which introduced a list of civic festivals. In the words of Marie-Joseph Chénier in his speech in support of the project:

As men free of prejudices and worthy to represent the French nation, you will understand how to build on the ruins of the superstitions which we have toppled the only universal religion free of secrets and mysteries, whose sole dogma is equality, which is spoken for by our laws and whose bishops are our magistrates; a religion that does not burn holy incense except before the altar of the nation, which is a mother and a divine protector to us all.

But until that moment the Catholic faith remained unscathed, at least within the terms of the law.

Dechristianization in the real sense of the term was first seen in the provinces at the instigation of certain of the deputies on mission. On 21 September 1793, in the Cathedral at Nevers, Fouché attended the unveiling of a bust of Brutus; on the 26th he told the popular club in Moulins that he wanted to replace 'superstitious and hypo-critical religions' with that of the Republic and natural morality; finally, on 10 October, Fouché forbade the holding of any religious service outside church buildings and laicized both funerals and cemeteries, outside which he had placed the inscription 'Death is an eternal sleep'. In Rochefort, Lequinio transformed the Church into a temple dedicated to Truth; in the Somme, Dumont forbade services on Sundays and transferred them to the new *décadis*; in Maubeuge, Drouet ordered the seizure of the precious objects that were used in the course of worship, which he described as 'ornaments of fanaticism and ignorance'; and certain of the deputies encouraged priests to get married.

Dechristianization was imposed on the Convention from outside. Chaumette, who had been travelling in his native area, the Nièvre, at the end of September and had been present at Fouché's side during the ceremony on the 21st, recommended to the Paris Commune that they should take similar steps: and on 14 August the Commune forbade all religious ceremonies from being held outside churches. But the Commune was acting cautiously. Hébert waited until the end of October before launching an attack on the clergy in issue 301 of the *Père Duchesne*. The initiative came from elsewhere. On 9 Brumaire II (30 October 1793) the commune of Ris, near Corbeil, told the Convention that it was adopting Brutus as its patron instead of Saint Blaise; on the 16th (6 November) a delegation from Mennecy in the same district declared that they were renouncing the Catholic faith, asked that their parish be suppressed, and started masquerades against religion at the bar of the Convention. At whose instigation were the sans-culottes of Ris and Mennecy acting in this way? Were these counter-revolutionary intrigues directed against the constitutional curés? Or did the pressure come from commissioners of the Department or of the executive itself who were in charge of grain requisitions in the district of Corbeil, supported by detachments of the *armée révolutionnaire?* ... On that day, 16 Brumaire, the Convention ruled that a commune had the right to renounce the Catholic faith.

From that moment the rate of dechristianization was accelerated. On the evening of the 16th, at the Jacobins, the deputy Léonard Bourdon delivered a violent speech against priests; then the central committee of the sections, at which such extremists as Desfieux, Pereira and Proli were active, read out details of a plan to petition for the suppression of the Church's income. During the night of 16/17 Brumaire the men who had promoted the petition, along with the deputies Anacharsis Cloots and Léonard Bourdon, went to the home of the Bishop of Paris, Gobel, and forced him to resign. The next day, the 17th, he appeared with his vicars-general at the bar of the Convention and solemnly resigned his office. Immediately Chaumette informed the Commune of this 'memorable scene at which the fanaticism and trickery of priests heaved their last sigh', and he persuaded them to celebrate a festival of Liberty in the former metropolitan church of Notre-Dame. This was held on 20 Brumaire (10 November 1793), with a symbolic mountain constructed in the choir and an actress playing the part of Liberty. The

Convention had been present at the celebration of this festival and immediately decreed, at Chaumette's request, that Notre-Dame should be consecrated to Reason. In a matter of days the wave of dechristianizing fervour swept the Paris sections along with it. As early as the evening of the 17th, on the initiative of its president, Thuriot, the Tuileries section renounced the faith, and on the 19th Gravilliers followed suit, encouraged by Léonard Bourdon. Then the revolutionary committees and clubs took up the cry, and on 5 Frimaire all the churches of the capital were consecrated to Reason. On 3 Frimaire (23 November 1793) the Commune sanctioned what had already been done by deciding to close the churches.

The cult of the martyrs of liberty developed alongside the movement towards dechristianization. But while this last was stimulated by men who had nothing to do with the sans-culottes, the cult of the martyrs was born of popular devotion to Marat. During the crisis of the summer months of 1793 the sans-culottes saw in it a confident statement of their republican principles, a means of popular communion, and the extolling of their revolutionary faith. The pomp and ceremony of the new cult did much to replace that of the traditional religion they had always practised, the religion which had become more and more closely supervised, then been restricted to church buildings, and had finally been banned altogether. In the course of autumn 1793 a number of Paris sections and clubs had held funeral ceremonies in honour of Marat or had proceeded to unveil his bust along with that of Lepeletier; in this way the chief characters of the new cult were beginning to emerge. When the sans-culottes won their final victory in September the cult became much more widespread: choirs and soon processions appeared, which gave these republican ceremonies a truly religious ceremonial flavour. In October civic processions became even more numerous. And when to the names of Marat and Lepeletier was added that of Chalier, the Montagnard leader who had been guillotined by the counter-revolutionaries in Lyons, the revolutionary triad was in being. Dechristianization gave a new impetus to the cult of the martyrs, and it became accepted in all the sections of Paris. Once the churches were closed, it seemed to be the one element in the republican faith which the popular militants were eager to establish on the ruins of Catholicism. Devotion to the martyrs of liberty became an integral part of the cult of Reason, a divinity which was much too abstract, even when it borrowed the outward characteristics of a young lady from the Opéra. It was effigies of the martyrs which replaced those of Catholic saints once the churches were converted into temples of Reason. But even in the autumn of 1793 the cult of the martyrs already seemed dangerous to the government authorities, and even more so to certain sections of the Jacobin bourgeoisie, since it exalted in the person of Marat the most extreme variety of revolutionary sentiment. The cult was therefore one of the chief targets of the counter-offensive which was launched by the Committee of Public Safety against dechristianization.

The clamp-down came as early as the beginning of December. When, on 21 Brumaire II (11 November 1793), a deputation from the central committee of the sections asked that the State should not pay out salaries for priests, the Convention refused to make any pronouncement on the question. On the 27th, in his report on the external situation facing the Republic, Robespierre referred to the danger that the dechristianization campaign might alienate neutral nations. And on 1 Frimaire (21 November) he spoke out forcefully at the Jacobin Club in favour of religious freedom. For although he was not in any sense favourably-disposed towards Catholicism, it seemed to him that to abolish religion would be a political blunder: the Republic had quite enough enemies already without stirring up the enmity of a large section of the popular masses who were deeply attached to their traditional religion. Referring to Desfieux, Pereira and Proli as 'agents of foreign powers' and 'these immoral men', Robespierre hinted that those who were overturning altars might easily be counter-revolutionaries in the guise of demagogues:

The man who is determined to prevent religious worship is just as fanatical as the man who says mass. . . . The Convention will not allow persecution of peaceable ministers of religion, but it will punish them severely every time they dare to take advantage of their position to deceive the citizens or to arm bigotry or royalism against the Republic.

The return to Paris of Danton, who had since October been staying in Arcis and who was alarmed by the discovery of the foreign conspiracy, served to strengthen the government's position in this field. On 6 Frimaire Danton spoke out vehemently against religious masquerades, demanding that such demonstrations 'should be stopped'. On the 8th Robespierre returned yet again to the dangers of dechristianization. On the following day, sensing that the wind was changing, Chaumette got the Commune to confirm the freedom of religious worship, but by not continuing to pay priests a salary the Commune was separating Church and State. On 16 Frimaire II (6 December 1793) the Convention in turn passed a solemn decree restating the principle of freedom of worship. But the Assembly limited the consequences of its decree when it went on to make clear on the 18th, taking up a proposal from Barère, that it did not intend to undermine any of the measures already passed and especially the decrees issued by deputies on mission: in other words, those churches which had been closed remained closed. Dechristianization went ahead, but it was masked and unequally applied according to region and the personality of the deputy on mission. In the spring of 1794 the churches that were still open were becoming more and more rare.

Despite the limited nature of its success, victory in this matter lay with the Committee of Public Safety, for it had put a brake on the popular movement and avoided allowing itself to be outflanked in revolutionary zeal by the dechristianizers. And at around the same time its position was still further strengthened by the improvement in the military situation.

The first victories (September to December 1793)

Revolutionary Government had no other reason for its existence and no other goal than victory in the war. The Committee of Public Safety would not have succeeded in imposing its authority or in maintaining itself in power but for the quick victories it had gained against the enemy.

The running of the war effort was coordinated by the Committee, which gave it a powerful stimulus and was vigorously supported by the sans-culotte Minister of War, Bouchotte. The two career officers who became members of the Committee on 14 August 1793, Carnot and Prieur de la Côte d'Or, concerned themselves in particular detail with military matters, the former with the direction of military operations and the latter with the manufacture of war materials. But the plans of campaign and nominations of generals were discussed by the entire Committee. Robespierre, as the notes he made in his diary make clear, played an important role in the direction of the war, as did Saint-Just. In the course of his long missions Jeanbon Saint-André controlled and developed ironworks, gun factories, saltpetre-works and shipbuilding. Lindet at the Commission des

Subsistances busied himself tirelessly with the provisioning of the armies and the war industries. Carnot certainly earned his nickname of 'the organizer of victory', but he shared that honour with all the members of the Committee. The story that Robespierre, Saint-Just and Couthon had no part in the methodical organization of victory is one that was spread in the Thermidorian era by the surviving members of the Committee, men eager to let all the responsibility for the Terror fall on the outlawed Montagnards while claiming for themselves alone the glory of having ensured the salvation of the Republic.

The mobilization of war materials was organized from the summer of 1793 onwards. There was a shortage of everything, corn magazines and arsenals alike were empty, while by July the number of men in uniform was already as high as 650,000. It was necessary to obtain from within the country all the things which had previously been bought abroad. The Committee of Public Safety involved the best minds of the age in its effort, and for the first time scientific research was systematically put at the service of national defence. At their head was Monge, a man of many talents who in Brumaire II edited a *Déscription de l'art de fabriquer les canons*, who organized with Hassenfratz, a mining engineer, the special emergency manufacture of arms in Paris, and who played an essential part in the revolutionary efforts to obtain saltpetre and in the development of factories to make gunpowder. The chemist Berthollet was also concerned with manufacturing powder. Vandermonde wrote a booklet on the *Procédés de la fabrication des armes blanches* ('side arms'). Hassenfratz himself was a commissioner for arms manufacturing. In Paris metal-workers were conscripted for working in an arms factory built to cope with the emergency, while forges were installed in gardens and public places: by the end of the Year II production reached nearly 700 rifles a day. In December 1793 a campaign was launched for the revolutionary production of saltpetre: the citizens were invited to harvest the saltpetre on the earthern floors of their cellars while the municipal councils were urged to set up workshops to wash the saltpetre and extract from it by means of evaporation techniques 'the powder that would kill tyrants'. From that moment saltpetre production became an expression of the patriotic fervour of the sans-culottes. No doubt this vast effort did not really produce results until the spring of 1794; meanwhile the Committee had understood how to ward off the most dangerous attacks and stop the enemy invasion.

Terror in the armies was in part responsible for this. For if the Committee of Public Safety could raise, equip, arm and feed four-teen armies and lead them to victory, it succeeded in doing so because of the introduction of conscription, requisitions, the *maximum*, and the nationalization of arms production, as well as the purging of the military command and the enforced obedience of the generals. All these measures could only be imposed and could only bear fruit because Revolutionary Government enjoyed an authority sanctioned by the Terror. The military command and general staff were purged and a new generation of army officers chosen from among the various groups within the old Third Estate, as well as from the poorer elements among the nobility, for the Committee had always refused to pass any general measure excluding the nobility from the army and public office. Jourdan, born in 1762, was given command of the army in the North; Pichegru, born a year earlier, was appointed to command the army on the Rhine; and Hoche, who was born only in 1768, took over the army on the Moselle. The generals were under the rigid control of the civil authorities and they had to obey. Article 110 of the 1793 constitution stipulated that 'there is no commander-in-chief'. Revolutionary discipline applied to everyone, whether general or common soldier, with equal severity. General Houchard, the victor of Hondschoote, seized Menin on 6–8 September 1793, but suddenly and against the orders he received from the Committee he ordered the retreat which soon changed into a rout. Dismissed from his command, he was brought before the Revolutionary Tribunal, condemned to death and guillotined on 15 November 1793 for having compromised the campaign plans. But it must not be imagined that onerous and inflexible conditions were blindly imposed on the generals: when Hoche, leading the army on the Moselle, failed in his vigorous attack on Kaiserslautern, the Committee of Public Safety understood and knew to console and encourage him. The soldiers regained confidence as the deputies on mission applied themselves to the development in their ranks of patriotic feeling. 'Victory or death' – that was the watchword of the republican armies.

The autumn of 1793 brought victory. The end of the federalist revolt was marked by the capture of Lyons. A long siege had been necessary, since the city, spurred on by the Comte de Précy and the royalists, resisted strongly and was only forced to surrender by a strenuous military effort which weakened the armies in the Alps.

On 29 September 1793 the republicans took control of the hill that dominated Lyons, Fourvière; but it was not until 9 October that they entered the town itself, the town which was now known as Ville Affranchie. Then the Committee of Public Safety could push ahead with the siege of Toulon, where the army was commanded by Dugommier, aided by Bonaparte, a captain of artillery. On 15 December 1793 the assault began and the town fell on the 19th. Toulon was renamed Port-la-Montagne.

The crushing of the Vendéan revolt was the result of the energetic steps taken by the Committee of Public Safety. The garrison of Mainz, which had come out of the war with great honour, struck a decisive blow against the Catholic and royalist army. All the republican forces were grouped together in a single army in the West under the command of Léchelle, with Kléber as second-in-command. Two strong republican columns left Niort and Nantes and, driving the bands of rebels back before them, they joined forces at Cholet, where the Vendéans were routed on 17 October. But La Rochejaquelein and Stofflet succeeded in crossing the Loire with between twenty and thirty thousand men. They advanced as far as Granville in an attempt to seize a seaport and make contact with the British. But Granville was defended by Le Carpentier, a member of the Convention, and the rebels failed to take it when they attacked on 13–14 November; they then fell back towards the south, failed again when they tried to take Angers on 3–4 December, and finally took the road to Le Mans. There, at Le Mans on 13–14 December 1793, Marceau and Kléber crushed them in a street battle of terrible ferocity. The remains of the Vendéan army were scattered or wiped out at Savenay on the Loire estuary on 23 December. That marked the end of the war in the Vendée. Although La Rochejaquelein and Stofflet made their way back across the Loire, and Charette still held on to the Marais, the Vendée had ceased to present an immediate danger.

The war effort of the Committee of Public Safety was reflected in the check administered to the invading forces. All the frontiers had been breached by foreign armies. On the North Sea the Anglo-Dutch force led by the Duke of York was blockading Dunkirk at the end of August, a prize which the government in London was bent on seizing at any price. On the Sambre the Imperial troops led by Coburg first took the fortress of Le Quesnoy and then laid siege to Maubeuge at the end of September. On the Sarre the Prussian army of the Duke of Brunswick seemed fairly inactive, but over by the Rhine the Austrians under Wurmser took the offensive, seized the Wissemburg lines on 13 October, blockaded Landau and invaded Alsace. The Committee issued the order to attack on every front.

The liberation of Dunkirk, which had been courageously defended by Souham and Hoche, followed the victory of Houchard's army over Freytag's force which was covering the siege operations: this battle, at Hondschoote, lasted from 6 to 8 September 1793, and was long, confused, and represented an incomplete triumph. For Houchard allowed Freytag to escape and could not cut off the retreat of the English army besieging Dunkirk. Shortly afterwards Houchard allowed himself to be beaten by the Dutch at Menin, following which he was dismissed and guillotined. Hondschoote, however, was the first victory registered by the republican armies for a considerable period.

The liberation of Maubeuge resulted from the victory at Wattignies on 16 October 1793 of the *armée du Nord*, commanded by Jourdan with Carnot as second-in-command. The deputy on mission led the assault columns at the generals' side. In contrast, the general commanding the fortress had made no move throughout the battle; cashiered, he too was sent to the guillotine. The Austrians fell back to Mons. Victory in this sector was not decisive, but Wattignies, coming soon after Hondschoote, both justified the Committee's policy and gave new confidence to the troops.

It took longer to liberate Landau. While the Austrian general Wurmser invaded Alsace, Brunswick and the Prussian army on the Sarre made no move. Saint-Just and Lebas were sent on mission to Alsace, and Baudot and Lacoste to Lorraine. The Committee of Public Safety regrouped its forces in the East and reinforced the army on the Rhine, under the command of Pichegru. Hoche, appointed to take command of the army on the Moselle, launched an attack on Brunswick at Kaiserslautern between 28 and 30 November; but he failed. Then, promoted to the command of the two armies combined, he resumed the offensive, stormed the Wissemburg lines, raised the blockade of Landau on 29 December, and entered the city of Speier. The Prussians fell back to Mainz, while the Austrians crossed back to the other bank of the Rhine.

By the end of 1793 the invasion was checked on all fronts. On the western side of the Pyrenees the Spaniards were driven back to the

Bidassoa, and on the eastern side to beyond the Tech. As early as October Savoy had been liberated by Kellermann. Around the same time the first results of the mobilization of France's material resources began to make themselves felt: the soldiers conscripted under the *levée en masse* joined the armies, the special war factories were set up, and at the beginning of November the first guns produced by the new workshops were presented to the Convention. The Committee of Public Safety's policy for the defence of the nation was proving to be effective.

The decree of 14 Frimaire II (4 December 1793)

At the beginning of December 1793 the popular movement appeared to be becoming more stable. The government's offensive against dechristianization disconcerted the militants in both the sections and the clubs and shattered the impetus built up by the popular leadership, an impetus which the Committee of Public Safety had been trying since 2 June to moderate and direct. At the same time it became clear that it was necessary to regularize government activity in the departments. There was enormous diversity in the implementation of the Terror. In most cases the deputies sent out on mission depended heavily on the local Jacobins and popular clubs, and left decisions to the sans-culottes on the spot. From this resulted large numbers of power struggles between those of differing leanings and a great diversity in the way in which the Terror and its laws were applied. And if the deputies and the Jacobins did succeed in maintaining national unity, their actions nevertheless lacked both discipline and coordination. In many cases the very fact of having a dual authority in administration – those bodies which were elected and those of revolutionary origin – added to the general disorder. It seemed necessary to define their respective powers, to subordinate them to central government, and to turn the spontaneity of the people once and for all towards goals assigned to them by Revolutionary Government.

This was all the more urgently necessary since the economic situation demanded it quite imperiously. The establishment of the general maximum on a district basis involved a number of inequalities, while it also seemed necessary to define certain points which had not been covered by the decree of 29 September 1793. In this category were such things as the price of transport and the profit margins that should accrue to wholesalers and retailers. Certain areas were suffering shortages – for instance in the Midi – while others were abounding with produce, and this again was the source of disorders and rioting. The Committee of Public Safety judged that it was necessary to step up administrative centralization in order to reorganize the management of the economy, to standardize the rates of the maximum, to nationalize external trade and hence to establish equitable distribution among the departments. It was economic requirements as much as political imperatives which induced the Committee to establish its absolute authority once and for all over the life of the nation in all its aspects.

The decree of 14 Frimaire II (4 December 1793) which established Revolutionary Government was an attempt to achieve this end. The provisional constitution of the Republic for the duration of the war was finally settled and centralization restored:

The National Convention is the sole centre of government initiative (article 1).

But article 2 went on to say that

All constituted bodies and public officials are placed under the immediate supervision of the Committee of Public Safety, in accordance with the decree of 10 October 1793; and for all those officials concerned in the general and domestic police forces, this supervision is the particular responsibility of the Committee of General Security, in accordance with the decree of 17 September 1793.

The *procureur* of the Commune thus became an *agent national*, a simple representative of the revolutionary State and subject to the control of the government committees. The district, whose affairs were directed by an agent of central government who was nominated and not elected, became the most important administrative unit, the department now playing no more than a secondary role. The right to send out *commissaires* was reserved to the government; it was now forbidden for any administrative bodies to communicate with one another through *commissaires* and to form central assemblies, and the same rules applied to popular societies. The central *armée révolutionnaire* was maintained, the departmental armies were suppressed and revolutionary levies prohibited.

The logic of events led to the reintroduction of centralization, the reestablishment of administrative stability, and the reinforcement of governmental authority, conditions necessary if the Committee of Public Safety were to achieve the victory which it had been pursuing so stubbornly. But it spelt the end of liberty of action for the popular movement.

Around the same time this dictatorial centralization was being called into question by the force of circumstances. The Revolution was victorious: Toulon had been retaken on 19 December, the Vendéans were routed at Savenay on the 23rd, and Landau was liberated on the 29th. Could not the Terror be relaxed after that and the degree of dictatorship be reduced? All those who wanted a peaceful life and hoped for the return of economic freedom wished that the Committee of Public Safety would now relax its grip and slacken its control over people's lives. But with the war continuing and the campaign being resumed in the spring, the country faced the same demands and the same exigencies. If the Committee gave way to the rising tide of opinion in favour of an indulgent policy (and with the check it had delivered to dechristianization it had appeared to be doing so), would it succeed in maintaining the confidence of the sans-culottes, which was an essential prerequisite of victory? Scarcely had Revolutionary Government been placed on a solid foundation when it found itself grappling with opposition from two different quarters.

Chapter 4

The Victory and the Collapse of Revolutionary Government (December 1793 to July 1794)

Putting the needs of national defence above all other considerations, the Committee of Public Safety had no intention of giving in to the demands of either the popular movement or the moderates. For the claims of the popular movement would have jeopardized revolutionary unity, while the demands of the moderates would have undermined both the controlled economy, so essential if support were to be guaranteed to the war effort, and the Terror which ensured the obedience of all to its decrees. But how could they obtain a balance between these contradictory demands? The policy of Revolutionary Government was that of maintaining a position half-way between the moderates and the extremists. But at the end of the winter of 1793 the shortage of foodstuffs took a sharp turn for the worse. The combination of a powerful opposition group and popular discontent forced the government to take positive action in Ventôse. It did so by ridding itself of the extremist faction. But once it had condemned, in the persons of the Cordelier leaders, the specific demands of the popular movement, the Revolutionary Government found itself left at the mercy of moderates, the very people whom it had claimed to be struggling against. Harnessing all the energy it had left, it succeeded for some time in resisting their attack. But in the end it was overthrown because it had not been able to win back the confident support of the people; it was the victim of the contradiction which had hung over it since its very formation.

I. FACTIONAL STRUGGLE AND THE
TRIUMPH OF THE COMMITTEE OF PUBLIC SAFETY
(DECEMBER 1793 TO APRIL 1794)

The liquidation of the Enragés, the ending of dechristianization, and the veiled attacks which had been made on popular organizations and especially on the sections, all these developments had shown that in the autumn of 1793 the Committee of Public Safety wanted to hold itself aloof from the popular movement which, until that moment, it had followed rather than directed. But by doing so it placed itself at the mercy of the Convention and opened itself to attacks from its opponents both within the Assembly and amongst the public at large.

Danton had supported Robespierre against those championing dechristianization, but he had done so in part from ulterior motives of both a personal and a political nature: for he hoped by this means to save friends of his who had just been arrested over the question of the so-called foreign plot or who, like Fabre d'Eglantine, were in danger of being charged in connection with the liquidation of the Compagnie des Indes. But Danton was also looking further ahead: he sought to undermine the very base of Revolutionary Government by causing splits within the Committee of Public Safety, where Billaud-Varenne and Collot d'Herbois posed as supporters of the sans-culotte cause. Danton's policy was opposed on every point to the popular programme proposed by Hébert and his friends in the Cordelier Club – a programme based on extreme Terror, a new strengthened *maximum*, and total war. The government's attack on dechristianization prepared the way for reaction and favoured the Dantonist offensive. A factional struggle was unleashed which had the most serious results not only for Revolutionary Government but also for the popular movement and, in the last analysis, for the Revolution itself.

The 'foreign plot' and the affair of the Compagnie des Indes
(October to December 1793)

These two incidents, closely linked with one another both in terms of the men involved and of their consequences, destroyed the unity of the Montagne and led to still deeper dissension within the Convention.

The 'foreign plot' was exposed around 12 October 1793 by Fabre d'Eglantine: breaking with the extremists and denouncing such men as Proli, Desfieux, Pereira and Dubuisson, Danton's friend accused them of complicity in a plot stirred up by foreign agitators in a bid to destroy the Republic by carrying things to excess. Refugees were to be found in large numbers in revolutionary circles. At the start, the Revolution had declared that it was prepared to welcome the victims of foreign despotism, and France had become the home of a considerable number of foreigners. Certain of them even sat in the Convention itself, like Anacharsis Cloots and Tom Paine; others were to be seen at the Cordeliers and in popular clubs and organizations, like Pereira. Soon these foreign refugees came to play a very considerable political role which worried the Committee of Public Safety all the more in that they retained contact with businessmen abroad whose political stand was more than slightly equivocal. Such men were Walter Boyd, a Foreign Office banker who received the protection of Chabot; Perregaux, a banker in Neuchâtel and hence a subject of the King of Prussia; yet another banker, Proli, from Brabant and therefore an Austrian subject, who was friendly with the Jacobin agitator, Desfieux, and with a large number of Jacobin deputies; the two Frey brothers, both businessmen and Austrian nationals, whose younger sister married Chabot (himself a former Capuchin friar) on 6 October 1793; or again Guzman, another businessman, formerly one of the more notable figures in Spanish society who had fallen in the world. ... These foreigners had numerous links with certain of the Montagnard deputies; they urged them to adopt all the most extreme policies, such as territorial annexations and dechristianization (Cloots and Pereira were among those who brought about the abdication of the constitutional bishop of Paris, Gobel); they also made money out of supplying the armies and speculated against the *assignat* on the international money market.

The affair of the Compagnie des Indes broke in the midst of all this and resulted in schisms within the Montagne. A decree of 24 August 1793 had suppressed all joint-stock companies and societies; it had been passed following denunciations by various deputies with business interests, such as Delaunay d'Angers, Julien de Toulouse, Chabot, Basire, and Fabre d'Eglantine, who, at the same time as they were denouncing these companies, were also playing the market as the price of their shares plummeted. The government ordered seals to be placed on the cash-boxes and papers of the Compagnie des Indes. On 8 October 1793 Delaunay very tactfully presented the decree which would regulate the liquidation of the company. Fabre d'Eglantine introduced an amendment (which was then passed) stipulating that that liquidation should be carried out by the State and not by the Company itself. But when the definitive text appeared in the *Bulletin des Lois*, the former version had been restored, and it was to be the Company that would be entrusted with the task of winding up its affairs. The minute dealing with the decree, signed by Fabre d'Eglantine, had been falsified with his complicity; for Fabre, Delaunay and their friends had accepted from the Company a windfall of half a million *livres*. The whole matter was exposed to the Committee of General Security, by Chabot, on 24 Brumaire II (14 November 1793). Under violent attack at the Jacobins for his relationship with the Frey brothers and his marriage to their sister, suspected of currency speculation, and also compromised in the movement for dechristianization, Chabot hoped to protect himself by betraying his accomplices. And Basire confirmed the truth of his accusations.

The Committee of Public Safety believed that there was a 'foreign plot', and their belief was given added force by the fact that the intrigues of foreigners and deputies with business interests became enmeshed in a royalist intrigue led by the Baron de Batz. Chabot's denunciation seemed to confirm that made previously by Fabre. The Committee was more sensitive to the political problem and its implications for the nation than it was to the question of peculation. But at the same time it was under attack in the Convention from the very men who had now been denounced. On 20 Brumaire (10 November) first Basire and then Chabot had again spoken out against the system of Terror and had attacked the tyranny which the government committees exercised over the Assembly: on that same day the Convention decreed that no deputy could be sent before the Revolutionary Tribunal without first being given a hearing by the Convention itself. The debate had demonstrated a degree of collusion between the deputies with business connections and the new faction of *Indulgents*, of men advocating a lenient line, which was in the process of forming. Such men included Chabot and Thuriot, one suspected of speculation, the other of an over-moderate political position, both ardent supporters of dechristianization. The decree was rescinded two days later. But from that moment the Committees, warned by Fabre in his belief that by denunciation he could more successfully protect his own interests, saw foreign complicity and English gold in every plot aimed at dividing patriotic Frenchmen against themselves. When Chabot added his denunciation, their response was to arrest denouncer and denounced alike: Chabot, Basire, Delaunay, and Julien de Toulouse. In his report on 'the political situation in the Republic' on 27 Brumaire II (17 November 1793), Robespierre attacked 'both the cruel moderatism and the systematic exaggeration of false patriots', those 'paid agents of foreign Courts' who 'violently hurl the chariot of the Revolution along dangerous roads in the hope of smashing it into the winning-post'. On 1 Frimaire (21 November), at the Jacobin Club, Robespierre again denounced foreign agents, 'the cowardly emissaries of tyrants' whom he held responsible for dechristianization; and he had Proli, Desfieux, Dubuisson and Pereira excluded from the club.

The 'foreign plot' and the scandal over the Compagnie des Indes gave rise to a huge wave of public anger and came to have considerable political importance because of the prominence of the people who were compromised by them, the degree of corruption which they revealed, and the links which were exposed between business deputies in Paris and the agents of enemy powers. 'Confidence becomes quite worthless,' Saint-Just had written to Robespierre on 15 Brumaire, 'when it is shared with men who are corrupt.' From that moment suspicion lingered for all time and in every quarter, suspicion which poisoned quarrels between the various groups and which made hatreds even more deep-seated. By permanently dividing the Montagnards, the 'foreign plot' and the scandal concerning the Compagnie des Indes gave a new impetus to faction-fighting.

The Indulgents' *offensive (December 1793 to January 1794)*

Danton had left Paris in October 1793; he had remarried the previous summer and was now taking his ease at Arcis-sur-Aube. But on 30 Brumaire, having received warning from Courtois, and suspecting that the affair of the Compagnie des Indes which had already compromised his friends, Basire and Fabre, might now spread to him as well, he hurriedly returned to Paris. Immediately the moderate opposition, which had been searching for an identity, crystallized around Danton. It was a step which was aided in the first instance by the desire of the Committee of Public Safety, and of Robespierre in particular, to end the movement towards dechristian-ization. In its bid to suppress the extremist faction, those who were now referred to as the *Exagérés*, the Revolutionary Government sought Danton's support, without first taking precautions lest the *Indulgents* make use of the situation to ruin the revolutionary organization of government and put an end to the Terror.

The *Indulgents'* offensive, led by Danton, was aimed against all those positions where advanced revolutionaries were in the van-guard. On 2 Frimaire (22 November 1793) Danton spoke out against what he termed anti-religious 'persecution' and demanded that 'human bloodshed should be kept to a minimum'. On 6 Frimaire he protested at anti-religious celebrations, demanded that 'an end be put to such things', and asked the Committees to produce a report on 'what has been called a foreign conspiracy'. On 11 Frimaire (1 December), Danton went still further. When Cambon proposed that people should be compelled to exchange coin for paper money, a measure which was demanded by the sans-culottes and which the Cordeliers had asked for that same day in a petition, Danton opposed this and indicated to the men of the Paris streets that the role of the pike in making the Revolution was now over:

Let us remember that if it is with pikes that things are overthrown, it is with the compass of reason and the human mind that the structure of society can be built up and consolidated.

When on 13 Frimaire he was in his turn attacked in the Jacobin Club, Danton conceded that he had no intention of 'breaking the very sinews of the Revolution'. He was forced to defend himself, and in this he received the support of Robespierre, who was anxious to maintain the unity of the Montagnards: 'The cause of patriots, like that of tyrants, is one single cause: they are all united in its defence.'

The campaign undertaken by the *Vieux Cordelier* gave Danton's offensive very full coverage and posed a threat to the policies of the government. Camille Desmoulins, a great journalist if a poor politician, launched his new paper on 15 Frimaire II (5 December 1793). 'Oh Pitt! I sing the praises of your political genius!' As Des-moulins understood the situation, all the advanced revolutionaries were Pitt's agents. In his second issue, on 20 Frimaire (10 December), Camille delivered a violent attack on Cloots, the man he held responsible for dechristianization; but he associated with his name that of Chaumette, the prosecutor for the Commune of Paris: 'Anacharsis and Anaxagoras may believe that they are pushing the wheel of reason, whereas in fact the cause they are aiding is that of counter-revolution.' On 25 Frimaire (15 December), the third number of the *Vieux Cordelier* appeared, arraigning the whole system of the Terror and of Revolutionary Government itself: cribbing from Tacitus, Camille Desmoulins listed the crimes of the first Caesars and condemned the terrorist practice of repression:

The Committee of Public Safety ... thought that, if it were to establish the Republic, it would need to resort to the legal practice of despots.

This issue of the paper enjoyed enormous success, since it raised hopes of counter-revolution once more and attracted all those who were worried by the Terror into the ranks of the Dantonist faction. The *Indulgents* then became still more bold and outspoken, encouraged by the benevolent neutrality which Robespierre had previously maintained towards them. On 27 Frimaire II (17 December) Fabre d'Eglantine, who had been totally successful in deceiving the Committee, denounced to the Convention two of the most prominent among the advanced revolutionary leadership: Vincent, *secrétaire-général* at the Ministry of War (and through this attack on his secretary the Minister himself, Bouchotte, was also made to seem suspect), and Ronsin, a general in the *armée révolutionnaire*. Both men were arrested. The question was now being posed: was the Terror about to be turned against those who had engineered it? The government Committees had not been consulted over this matter, and the manœuvre had the effect of draining away their authority. On 30 Frimaire (20 December), replying to a delegation from Lyons – asking that 'the reign of Terror give way to one of love' – and to a large delegation of women, the Convention decreed the setting up of a Committee of Justice that would examine the cases of all those held in prison and free any prisoners who had been gaoled without good reason.

The tide turned, however, at the end of Frimaire. On the 29th (19 December), the discovery among the sealed papers of Delaunay of the false decree concerning the liquidation of the Compagnie des Indes, that minute which bore Fabre's signature at the foot of a text stating the very opposite of his amendment, showed up the Dantonists in a very bad light. The ultra patriots now counterattacked with greater ferocity than ever. Collot d'Herbois, warned of what was happening, rushed back from Lyons. On 1 Nivôse (21 December), amidst a great crowd of people escorting him from the Bastille to the Tuileries, and a delegation of sans-culottes from Lyons carrying the head and the ashes of Chalier, Collot appeared before the Convention. He justified the repression in Lyons in terms of the danger which the Republic had faced; and the Assembly approved the action he had taken. In the evening Collot d'Herbois delivered a harangue to the Jacobins, reproaching them for their lack of backbone, praising the energy of Ronsin, and coming out strongly against any false sensibilities that might be felt towards the victims of repression:

What man can have tears left to shed over the bodies of the enemies o liberty, whilst the hearts of patriots are still torn asunder?

The Committee of Public Safety now departed from its attitude of benevolent neutrality towards the *Indulgents'* offensive; and on 3 Nivôse (23 December) Robespierre, in a speech at the Jacobin Club, adopted a position that was above all factional disputes.

The struggle between factions at departmental level posed a real threat to the stability of government. The split between Revolutionary Government and the popular movement which had become evident since the ending of dechristianization led in many places to a change in political orientation. Many of the deputies on mission to the departments broke with the local sans-culottes and turned the full force of repression against the ultras, the most extreme revolutionary elements, while freeing many of those held as suspects. This was what happened at Sedan, at Lille, at Orleans where Taboureau, an Enragé, was imprisoned, at Blois as early as Frimaire, at Lyons where Fouché now busied himself with rooting out the former friends of Chalier, at Bordeaux where Tallien, to conceal his own peculation of public funds, denounced the extreme revolutionary leaders, and in the Gard where Boisset dismissed the patriotic mayor of Nîmes, Courbis. On all sides conflicts raged between moderates and extremists, conflicts in which the *représentants en mission* took sides instead of arbitrating. Aware of the danger which this presented, the Committee of Public Safety intervened in order to re-establish its position as arbitrator.

Robespierre replied to the fourth issue of the *Vieux Cordelier*, distributed on 4 Nivôse (24 December), in his report of the 5th 'on the principles of Revolutionary Government'. In this fourth number Camille Desmoulins demanded the release of 'those two hundred thousand citizens whom you call suspects', declaring that he was 'certain that liberty would be strengthened and Europe conquered if you only had a Committee of Clemency'; this appeal Desmoulins made 'in the name of liberty', and he went on to add that 'this liberty that has come down to us from the heavens, it isn't a nymph in the Opera, nor is it a *bonnet rouge*, a dirty shirt or ragged clothing. Liberty is happiness, reason, equality, justice . . .'. In his reply on the 5th, Robespierre justified the Terror by the fact that France was at war. He outlined to the Convention the theory that whereas the aim of Revolutionary Government is to found the Republic, that of constitutional government is to conserve it:

The Revolution is the war of liberty against its enemies; the constitution is the regime established by liberty, victorious and at peace.

Just because it is at war, Revolutionary Government needs to be able to take 'extraordinary action':

To good citizens it owes all the protection that the nation can give, to the enemies of the people it owes nothing but death.

And Robespierre, assuming the role of arbitrator, condemned both the extremist factions:

Revolutionary Government must sail between two reefs, between timidity and foolhardiness, between moderatism and excess: moderatism which is to moderation what impotence is to chastity; and excess which is in the same relation to energy as dropsy to good health.

The check administered to the advance of the *Indulgents* began to bear fruit on 6 Nivôse (26 December), when Billaud-Varenne had the 'Committee of Justice' which had been established on 30 Frimaire finally suppressed. Yet for some time after this the Committee of Public Safety still tried to hold the balance between the two factions which were dissipating their energies in mutual struggle. On 16 Nivôse (5 January 1794) Camille Desmoulins published the fifth number of his *Vieux Cordelier*, in which he pushed home his attack on Hébert, accusing him of receiving money for his *Père Duchesne* from the Ministry of War under Bouchotte's direction. But two days later the *Vieux Cordelier* itself was denounced at the Jacobin Club, where Robespierre delivered a searing reprimand to Camille and ended by burning his newspapers. 'Burning does not constitute a reply,' retorted Desmoulins. On the 19th (8 January), Robespierre again denounced the two factions which were threatening the future of Revolutionary Government but which had an understanding amongst themselves 'like brigands in a forest'. Meanwhile, on that same day, Fabre d'Eglantine, who had now been finally compromised by the discovery of the proposed decree on the liquidation of the Compagnie des Indes with corrections added in pencil in his handwriting, was denounced by Robespierre at the Jacobin Club, and was arrested on the night of 23–24 Nivôse (12–13 January). When Danton intervened on the following day in support of his friend, Billaud-Varenne shouted back: 'Woe betide the man who has sat by the side of Fabre d'Eglantine and who is still duped by him.' The offensive by the *Indulgents* had now been checked; much more than that, they were already compromised and were soon threatened by their opponents' counterattack.

The Exagérés' *counter-offensive (February 1794)*

Once they were no longer under attack from the *Indulgents*, the extremist faction, the *Exagérés*, began to regain some of their lost influence. For they had first been disconcerted by the government's disavowal of dechristianization, then compromised by the agreements they had made with certain extremist elements abroad, and finally had been the victim of the intrigues of Fabre d'Eglantine. The *Exagérés* induced the Cordelier Club to make common cause with them, for the Cordeliers were tirelessly demanding the release of Vincent and Ronsin. One of their bastions of strength lay in the offices of the Ministry of War, which Vincent had filled with patriots of their persuasion, while through the influence of Hébert they were powerful in the Commune, and through Momoro in the Department. The efforts of the *Exagérés* centred on the freeing of imprisoned patriots, the stepping up of the Terror, and the strengthening of economic controls.

The campaign in favour of Vincent and Ronsin was relentlessly pursued by the Cordeliers; it was also one of the main themes of the agitators in the popular clubs and sections of Paris. On 12 Pluviôse II (31 January 1794), the Cordeliers declared that oppression existed in France and they placed a veil over the board on which was enshrined the Declaration of Rights. This implied threat, the absence of any charge that could be brought against them, and the need for the government Committees to make a few concessions to the ultra patriots to counterbalance the influence of the moderates, all these factors help explain the release of Vincent and Ronsin on 14 Pluviôse (2 February).

This in turn led the Cordeliers to reinforce their campaign for the speedier enforcement of the Terror. Encouraged by their success in this first campaign and spurred on by Vincent who, when he came out of prison, was eager to wreak revenge, they now found added vigour in their denunciations of the 'new moderates'. They demanded the punishment of 'those who oppressed patriots' and, on 18 Pluviôse, 'the destruction of those impure elements of the Plain that are still in the Convention'. They wanted, in other words, another purge of the Assembly. The terrorist campaign was particularly directed against the seventy-five deputies who protested against the measures taken on 2 June, deputies who had been held in custody but against whom Robespierre had decided to level no charges at the Revolutionary Tribunal. They also denounced all those who had signed the moderate petitions of the spring of 1792, the petitions referred to as those of the Eight Thousand and of the Twenty Thousand. On 24 Pluviôse Hébert cried out at the Cordeliers: 'It is necessary that that entire clique be overthrown for all time.' And on 2 Ventôse the Cordeliers decided to resume publication of Marat's newspaper, in which they would unmask 'the traitors who deceive the people and the ambitious and factious politicians who would like to corrupt or seduce them'.

The campaign for the stepping up of economic controls was given an increasingly warm reception in the popular areas of the city; for throughout the winter months the economic situation had grown increasingly worse. The voting of the maximum law had not, despite its intentions, succeeded in solving all the problems. For if bread was now available, it was of very low quality, while shortage and high prices did affect groceries, a sector in which the *maximum* was ignored with complete impunity. From Pluviôse on, a serious crisis in the supply of meat brought popular discontent to a new peak. And popular demands, though they might be less and less persistent on political matters, remained strident when it was a question of foodstuffs. Hostility towards merchants, a hostility so characteristic of the popular mentality, remained as strong as ever, despite the enforcement of various forms of control over the economic life of the nation. Two social groups suffered especially severely as a result of this crisis: those artisans whose skills were not relevant to the needs of the war and who remained almost completely without work, and those dependent on wages. Both these groups believed that violence and increased repression constituted one means of restoring plenty. In his papers Hébert played his part in enflaming the terrorist spirit of the people at such moments as it seemed to have died down; number 345 of his *Père Duchesne* presented

his motion whereby the butchers who treat the sans-culottes like dogs and who give them nothing more than bones to gnaw on should be guillotined like all the enemies of the ordinary people, like the wine merchants who do business under the Pont Neuf.

The idea of another popular *journée* was being formed; the food crisis risked bringing the sans-culottes back as a political force.

The Committee of Public Safety, which had for a brief moment been carried along by the *Indulgents*' offensive, had meanwhile resumed its position midway between the moderates and the extremists. But where, between these contradictory movements, could a point of equilibrium be found? Robespierre could see no possible policy other than that of advocating revolutionary virtue, or even Terror. He explained what he meant on 17 Pluviôse II (5 February 1794) in his report on 'the principles of political morality which should guide the Convention':

If the sphere of popular government in peacetime is virtue, in revolution it is at one and the same time virtue and terror; virtue, without which terror is quite deadly; and terror, without which virtue is powerless. Terror is nothing more than rapid, severe, and inflexible justice; it is therefore something that emanates from virtue. It is not so much a special principle in its own right as a consequence of the general principle of democracy applied to the most pressing needs of the country.

By virtue was meant a lack of concern for one's own personal interests, devotion to the interest of the community as a whole, and, should the need arise, a spirit of sacrifice. Robespierre wanted to buttress this civic virtue with an institutional framework and by legal and judicial guarantees. As for the Terror, the Committee of Public Safety sought to moderate it within the limits of revolutionary legality but to retain it as a means of governing the country.

As winter drew to a close the food crisis grew dramatically worse; the situation in Paris also worsened; and a popular rising appeared likely, a popular rising which could once again call the Revolutionary Government into question.

The crisis of Ventôse and the downfall of the political factions (March to April 1794)

The crisis had gradually come to be more and more clearly formulated as the winter of the Year II progressed. Both social and political life had been evolving perceptibly since the establishment of Revolutionary Government; the character of that evolution was now much more sharply defined. It was this which gave direction to the crisis in Ventôse and which so brutally highlighted the problem of the relations between the popular movement and Revolutionary Government.

First there was the social crisis. Price-fixing, regulation, and the authoritarian direction of the economy all proved incapable of ensuring that provisions got through satisfactorily to the population of Paris. This affected the day-to-day existence of the sans-culottes. Shortage and high prices combined to undermine their standard of living, and wage increases, frequently allowed through the less stringent application of the maximum laws, no longer compensated for the rise in prices. Queues now began to form again outside butchers' shops as they had so recently done outside bakers'. People began to queue as early as three o'clock in the morning; they hustled one another and fought among themselves. There were scuffles in Les Halles, where there was an acute shortage of dairy produce. Wage-earners suffered greatly and responded by making their own demands; thus the building workers demanded wage rises, while in the arms factories disturbances continued throughout Ventôse. The food crisis further aroused the terrorist mentality of the people: 'What need have we of all these aristocrats?' shouted one woman on 8 Ventôse (26 February) at the Droits-de-l'Homme section. 'Should not all these rogues who are starving the people have been sent to the guillotine before now?'

There was also a political crisis. The demands of national defence and its own Jacobin conception of power led the Revolutionary Government both to make sure that it received the passive obedience of the various popular organizations and to reduce, little by little, the practice of democracy by the people until it reached a level acceptable to the bourgeoisie. This affected the sans-culottes in that it interfered with their conduct as revolutionaries. The activities of the Paris sections and the popular societies were diverted far away from the problems of political life in general towards the war effort (the armament of *cavaliers jacobins*, the collecting of saltpetre, the financial support of children and relatives of soldiers on the frontiers). More and more the grass-roots organizations were controlled by the sectional *comités révolutionnaires*, which were now acting directly on government orders, a trend which was not accomplished without numerous incidents and a number of open conflicts. The moderates took advantage of all this to resume their propaganda, which served to increase the general confusion still more. The militants understood only too well what this meant. As an orator declared to the popular society of l'Homme-armé on 4 Nivôse (22 February), 'If you lose control of the revolutionary movement for one single moment, then you can wave goodbye to the patriots! Their end is then imminent.'

The crisis of Ventôse Year II crystallized the antagonism between the patriots of 1789 and those of 1793. This was itself a reflection of the total opposition between sans-culottes on the one hand and Jacobins or Montagnards on the other, between the popular ideas about political life and the organization of society and those of the bourgeoisie, even of the Jacobin bourgeoisie. In these last stages of the crisis the opposition that existed between the two groups, the *nouveaux modérés* and the *patriotes prononcés*, became embittered by personal animosities and grew much more heated. For the supporters of Vincent and Ronsin did not lay down their arms. In vain did Collot d'Herbois, who since his return from Lyons had devoted himself to the task of restoring good and harmonious relations among the sorely-divided patriots, try to reconcile Cordeliers and Jacobins on 8 Ventôse (26 February). On the very next day the Cordeliers again demanded the arrest of the 'traitors who are unworthy to sit in the Convention', and in particular of Camille Desmoulins. The combined impact of the opposition of ultra patriots and of the discontent that raged amongst the people presented a grave threat to the Revolutionary Government which sought to avoid any alliance between them by taking bold measures of social reform.

The decrees of Ventôse Year II were the Committee's answer to these problems. Already, on 13 Pluviôse, the Convention had voted aid totalling 10 million *livres*; on 3 Ventôse (21 February), Barère presented his proposal for a new general maximum law. The decrees of Ventôse went still further. On the 8th (26 February), following his report on the people then held in custody, Saint-Just had a decree passed ordering the sequestration of the property of suspects; then, on the 13th (3 March), a second decree charged the Committee of Public Safety with the job of reporting on 'the means whereby the property of enemies of the Republic could be used to aid the poor'. Saint-Just had made it clear that

circumstances are perhaps pushing us towards results of which we had not the slightest inkling. While wealth remains in the hands of a fairly large number of those opposed to the Revolution, necessity is driving ordinary working people into being dependent on their enemies. Can you imagine an empire being able to exist where profits accrue to the very people who are opposed to the existing form of government?

And he went on to make the point:

The poor are the really powerful ones amongst us; they have every right to speak to governments which neglect them with all the authority of masters.

Saint-Just ended his second report with a scornful and defiant rebuke to the monarchs of the Ancien Régime: 'Happiness,' he said, 'is a new idea in Europe.'

The scope of the Ventôse decrees must not, however, be exaggerated. Albert Mathiez has expressed astonishment that Saint-Just was 'neither understood nor followed by the very people he wanted to please'. But without the slightest shadow of doubt Saint-Just and the Revolutionary Government were understood. That the enemies of the Revolution have no civil rights in the Republic, and that their property should be used to indemnify those patriots who put their lives in danger in order to defend that Republic, these were ideas which had for some time been widely accepted by the sans-culottes and which had first been formulated in the spring of 1793. It was the inclusion of these ideas which removed from the Ventôse decrees any appearance of being purely emergency measures. Nor can we agree with Mathiez when he writes that Saint-Just's conclusions constituted 'a formidable attempt to isolate from amidst the confused aims of the Hébertistes a coherent social programme'. Both sans-culottes and ultra patriotic leaders had for some time been putting forward more radical ideas on the subject. Besides, if the sequestration of the belongings of suspects and the planned indemnification of impoverished patriots provided an answer to the demands of the popular movement and were warmly welcomed as such, they remained measures which could only become effective over a considerable period, measures which did nothing to solve the outstanding problems of the moment; in particular they provided no solution to the food crisis. If we are not to cast doubt on the sincerity of Saint-Just and the Robespierristes, then the Ventôse decrees must be seen as no more than a tactical manœuvre aimed at thwarting the aims of advanced revolutionary propaganda. But it was a manœuvre that failed. Towards the middle of Ventôse, when the Revolutionary Government had taken neither any economic measures to ensure that food supplies got through to the sans-culottes, nor any political steps to fend off the threat from the moderates, the crisis reached its highest and most dangerous point.

The culmination of this crisis in Ventôse was marked in popular circles by a stream of terrorist slogans against merchants and the rich, by seditious handbills, and by rumours of insurrection which, if they served to alert the government Committees, also deceived the Cordeliers and incited them to resort to an action which they thought would be decisive in getting rid of their opponents. They calculated that by increasing their pressure on the government they would be able to win a final and definitive victory. In his *Père Duchesne* Hébert denounced what he termed the new faction of *endormeurs*, the followers of Robespierre. In number 350 of his paper Hébert spoke of 'the sacred guillotine as being like the philo-sopher's stone' and denounced the government's policy of holding the balance between the various factions:

There is no point in trying to look after both the goat and the cabbage; nor in attempting to save the rascals who have been conspiring against liberty. Justice will be done despite the activities of the *endormeurs*. . . .

And Hébert concluded his article by outlining a specific programme of social reforms:

Make sure that all the citizens have a job to do, grant assistance to the aged and the sick, and to crown your achievements organize without delay a programme of public education.

But, forgetful of the lesson of all the popular *journées* of the Revolu-tion, the Cordelier leadership did not take the trouble to organize the movement that they were contemplating, nor to make sure of their alliance with the great mass of the people, who were much more concerned about the food shortage than they were about the danger of moderatism.

The liquidation of the *Exagérés* was an action of considerable dramatic impact which caused consternation among the popular militants and which opened still further the breach between them and the Revolutionary Government. On 12 Ventôse, at the Cordelier Club, Ronsin, the general of the *armée révolutionnaire*, proclaimed that an insurrection was now a clear necessity. On the 14th (4 March 1794), the veil was placed over the board proclaiming the Declaration of the Rights of Man; Vincent, the *secrétaire-général* to the Ministry of War, denounced those 'who appear to have taken the decision to establish a destructive system of moderatism'; and Carrier, referring to the oppression being inflicted on patriots, concluded that they must organize an insurrection, 'a holy insurrection'. Hébert took up the same theme. 'Yes,' he said, 'we must resort to insurrection; and the Cordeliers will not be the last to give the signal that shall bring death to those who oppress us.'

What the Cordeliers envisaged was probably no more than a mass demonstration, but one which would be aimed over the heads of the *modérés* at the Revolutionary Government itself and at its policies. It was in vain that Collot d'Herbois attempted on 17 Ventôse (17 March) to reconcile Jacobins and Cordeliers. Ronsin replied in a violently-worded speech in which he attacked Robespierre and held him responsible for coining the word 'ultra-revolutionary', 'a word which has given these new factions an excuse for oppressing the most ardent of patriots'; and he demanded that steps be taken to ensure that 'moderates, rogues, traitors and self-seeking politicians would soon sink back again into total obscurity'.

Besides the opposition of Cordeliers and Jacobins, and that of the popular movement and the Revolutionary Government, the general picture was one of two opposing policies: that of those who wanted to resist any further change and that of the people who wanted to advance the revolutionary cause. The second was the policy favoured by advanced patriotic opinion, for they saw in it the only policy that would be able to guarantee the wellbeing of the Revolution by attaching to it the definitive loyalty of the sans-culottes. 'One single step backwards and the Republic will be lost,' Hébert wrote in the last number of *Le Père Duchesne*; and he was right if he was talking about that popular republic which the sans-culottes had helped to build. For the moderates, on the other hand, whose ideal was a conservative, bourgeois republic, a step forward was no less fatal.

The Cordelier offensive began in the middle of Ventôse and it put in jeopardy the social balance on which the actions of the government were based. For this reason the Committee of Public Safety lost patience, and in the course of the night of 23-24 Ventôse (13-14 March) the principal Cordelier leaders were arrested and taken before the Revolutionary Tribunal. It was a trial which brought together on the same charge not only the leading Cordeliers (Hébert, Ronsin, Vincent, Momoro), but also a number of patriots with advanced Revolutionary views (like Mazuel, the leader of a squadron of the *cavalerie révolutionnaire*, and the honest Descombes, of the department concerned with food supplies, the Administration des Subsistances), a number of popular militants (such as Ancard of the Cordelier Club and Ducroquet, who played a comparatively humble role as *commissaire* of the Marat section charged with rooting out speculation and hoarding), and various foreign agents (Cloots, the banker Kock, Proli, Desfieux, Pereira, and Dubuisson). All were guillotined on 4 Germinal II (24 March 1794).

The liquidation of the *Indulgents* followed this purge. For a moment Danton and his supporters believed that their hour had come, and from the end of Ventôse they built up their pressure on the government. The seventh issue of the *Vieux Cordelier*, which was seized by the authorities, contained a violently-worded indictment of the policies of the Committee of Public Safety. But the Committee, which had only turned against the *Exagérés* after a great deal of hesitation, had no intention of allowing themselves to run amuck. Already on 28 Ventôse (18 March) the Convention had issued decrees accusing the deputies compromised in the affair of the Compagnie des Indes of various crimes; these charges affected Fabre d'Eglantine, Basire, Chabot, and Delaunay. Anxious at the proscription of Hébert and his friends, and supported by the Committee of General Security, Billaud-Varenne and Collot d'Herbois finally persuaded Robespierre himself that action must be taken, and in the night of 9-10 Germinal (29-30 March) Danton, Camille Desmoulins, Delacroix, and Philippeaux were arrested. This step was ratified by the Convention on the 11th, following an emotional speech by Robespierre:

I, too, have been a friend of Pétion's, but since he has been exposed I have forsaken his company. I also knew Roland well, but he committed treason and it was I who denounced him. Danton now wants to take their place but in my eyes he is nothing more than an enemy of the people.

In addition to Danton and the leaders of his group, the ensuing trial brought together deputies accused of dishonesty, foreign agents (Guzman and the Frey brothers), a speculator, the abbé d'Espagnac, General Westermann – a friend of Danton's – and Hérault de Séchelles. Danton struck out boldly and denounced those who had brought the accusation against him: a decree was thereupon passed which ruled out of order any defendant who insulted the law of the land. On 16 Germinal II (5 April 1794) all the accused were guillotined.

To destroy what remained of the opposition, a third trial was held, on the pretext of a plan for a prison conspiracy that would release those held in custody. Those charged included Chaumette, the *agent national* of the Paris Commune, the widows of Desmoulins and Hébert, and General Dillon. All in all they were an incongruous batch of people; they died on the scaffold on 24 Germinal II (13 April 1794).

The dramatic events of Germinal were decisive. For the adventurous bid by the Cordeliers gave the Revolutionary Government the opportunity to hasten on a development which had been slowly evolving since the very first measures of public safety. Although it had agreed to an alliance with the sans-culottes when faced with the emergency of national peril, and granted a few concessions in order to maintain that alliance, it had never accepted either the social aims or the political methods of sans-culotte democracy. As far as the government Committees were concerned, the struggle which they were waging against both the foreign coalition and the forces of counter-revolution, as well as their own political ideas, fully justified the control of the popular organizations and their integration into the Jacobin ranks, the ranks of the bourgeois revolution. The opposition of the Cordeliers had threatened the delicate balance which the Revolutionary Government maintained, and it had replied by resorting to repression. But when the sans-culottes saw the *Père Duchesne* and the Cordeliers condemned, men whom they were ready to listen to and who gave expression to their aspirations, they began to lose confidence in Revolutionary

Government. It was a vain gesture to add Danton's name to the list of those condemned to die. For the repression which followed these great trials, despite its limited character, nevertheless gave rise to widespread fear among the revolutionary militants which paralysed the political life of the sections. Direct fraternal links between the revolutionary authorities and the sans-culottes of the Paris sections were shattered. 'The Revolution has run cold,' Saint-Just was soon to write. Indeed, the events of Germinal proved to be the prologue to Thermidor.

2. THE JACOBIN DICTATORSHIP OF PUBLIC SAFETY

From the destruction of the factions to the fall of the Robespierristes, from Germinal till Thermidor, no further challenges were offered to the dictatorship of Revolutionary Government. Despite various modifications which were made as the force of circumstances demanded, it enjoyed a certain basic stability. Centralization was reinforced; the Terror gained new impetus; the various authorities, their membership purged, remained obedient to its will; and the Convention voted decrees without any discussion. But the social base on which all this was constructed had become dangerously limited. At the time of the crisis of the summer of 1793 the militants of the Paris sections had imposed emergency institutions which were in keeping with their social and political aspirations: thus in July commissioners were established to investigate hoarding, and in September the *armée révolutionnaire* was introduced. Having gained power with the help of the sans-culottes, the government Committees undertook the vast task of regularizing the numerous institutions and bringing together the scattered revolutionary forces. The crisis in Ventôse and the trials staged in Germinal allowed them to dispense with the autonomy of the popular movement and to sweep aside the institutions which it had either imposed on the government or created independently. Thus the *armée révolutionnaire* was dismissed on 7 Germinal II (27 March 1794), the commissioners investigating food-hoarding were abolished on the 12th (1 April), the Paris Commune was purged, and the sectional popular societies dissolved. The popular movement was brought inside the framework of Jacobin dictatorship; but what the Committees gained in coercive power they lost in trust and spontaneous support.

Between Germinal and Thermidor the relations between Revolutionary Government and the popular movement grew gradually but steadily worse.

Revolutionary Government

The organization and the characteristics of Revolutionary Government, which had been steadily evolving since the previous summer, assumed their final form, at least in broad outline, in April of 1794. Its charter consisted of the decree of 19 Vendémiaire (10 October), and even more markedly that of 14 Frimaire II (4 December 1793). The theory that underpinned Revolutionary Government was frequently made plain, especially by Saint-Just in his report of 10 October 1793 and by Robespierre in two reports, 'On the Principles of Revolutionary Government' (5 Nivôse II – 25 December 1793) and 'On the Principles of Political Morality that should Guide the Convention' (17 Pluviôse II – 5 February 1794).

Revolutionary Government is a wartime government. 'The Revolution is the war of liberty against its enemies', in Robespierre's words, whether its enemies were inside France or outside. Its aim is that of founding the Republic. After the enemy has been defeated, then the country will return to constitutional government, to 'the régime of liberty, victorious and at peace', but not before then. Because it is fighting a war, 'Revolutionary Government needs to have at its disposal extraordinary powers', it must 'act like lightning', destroying everything that stands in its way; for it is not possible to 'place peace and war under the same régime, any more than health and sickness'. For this reason Revolutionary Government must have the right to use coercive power – in other words, Terror. For as Robespierre himself asked, 'Is force to be used only to protect criminals?' ... Revolutionary Government 'owes nothing to enemies of the people except death'. But Terror is used only in order to save the Republic: virtue, 'a fundamental principle of democratic or popular government', provides the guarantee that Revolutionary Government does not turn into despotism. Virtue, defined as 'love for one's country and its laws', as 'that magnanimous devotion which merges all private interests with the general interest of the community', was at the heart of Robespierre's conception of the Revolution:

In the system of the French Revolution what is immoral is impolitic and what is corrupting is counter-revolutionary.

And the aim of the Revolution he describes in these terms:

We want to fulfil the wishes of Nature, to achieve the destiny of the human race, to keep the promises of philosophy, to free providence from the long reign of crime and tyranny. May France, once illustrious among the enslaved countries of the world, eclipse the glory of all the free peoples who have ever existed and become the model for all nations to follow, inspiring terror in oppressors, providing consolation to the oppressed, a veritable jewel for the whole universe to admire. And may we, in sealing the work we have accomplished with our blood, at least glimpse the radiant dawn of universal happiness.

The Convention remains 'the sole centre of impetus in government'. It is there that national sovereignty resides; it retains supreme authority, with the Committees governing under its control and enforcing its decrees. But after Germinal this ceased to be the case: the executive became the dominant element in the system of government, whereas the Assembly was practically subordinated to it.

The Committees of the Convention, twenty-one of them in the Year II, directed or controlled the various sectors of administration and policy-making. In fact, only two of them exercised political power in any effective way – the Committees of Public Safety and of General Security, referred to as the government Committees.

The Committee of Public Safety, reelected from one month to another, was now reduced to eleven members (Robespierre, Saint-Just and Couthon, Billaud-Varenne and Collot d'Herbois, Barère, Carnot, Prieur de la Côte d'Or and Prieur de la Marne, Jeanbon Saint-André and Lindet). 'The very centre of executive decision-making', it had all the administrative bodies and public officials of the Republic 'under its direct supervision'. Through its Bureau Topographique it controlled the country's diplomacy and the war effort, through its Commission des Armes et des Poudres it had overall charge of armaments, through its Commission des Subsistances it supervised the country's economy; in addition, it ordered arrests and thus encroached on the territory of the Committee of General Security through the agency of the Bureau de Police which was set up in Floréal II. Though certain of its members did develop specialist interests, like Lindet (food supplies) and Prieur de la Côte d'Or (munitions), all the members of the Committee were jointly responsible for the direction of overall policy and for the conduct of the war.

Dependent on the Committee of Public Safety were the six

ministers of the Executive Council, and, after 1 April 1794 (12 Germinal II), the twelve *commissions exécutives* which were created to replace them in accordance with a report which Carnot drew up for the Convention. These executive commissions were nominated by the Assembly on the recommendation of the Committee; they were very closely subordinate to the Committee, which thus maintained its preponderant role in government, 'reserving for itself the formulation of overall policy and proposing measures of major importance to the National Convention'.

The Committee of General Security, also reelected on a monthly basis, took rather longer to become established with a fixed membership (Amar, Moyse Bayle, the painter David, Lebas, Louis du Bas-Rhin, Vadier, Voulland ...). In accordance with the law of 17 September 1793, it had 'within its special field of control' 'all those matters concerning individuals and general internal policing'. Entrusted with the task of enforcing the Law of Suspects, it was the Committee of General Security which directed the police and controlled revolutionary justice; it was, in short, the Ministry of the Terror.

In the departments, administrative organization was simplified by the decree of 14 Frimaire II, when the degree of centralization was increased. The departmental administrations, suspected of federalist sympathies, lost the major part of the powers they had previously enjoyed and were henceforth responsible only for taxes, public works, and national lands. The two vital units of government were the districts and the communes, the former entrusted with 'the supervision of the enforcement of revolutionary laws and of all measures of general security and public safety', and the latter with the actual application of these measures. Every ten days the municipal councils had to give a report on their activities to the districts, while the districts in turn reported to the government Committees.

Representatives of the national government, *agents nationaux*, sat on every district administration and every municipal council, where the old *procureurs-syndics* had been abolished. Their allotted task was to 'insist upon and carry through the enforcement of the laws, as well as to denounce any negligence they might detect in that enforcement and such violations as might be perpetrated'. The *agents nationaux* at district level had to return a report on their activities to the two government Committees every ten days.

The *comités révolutionnaires*, the former *comités de surveillance* which had been established on 21 March 1793 and which were now reorganized by the law of 17 September of the same year, were the means by which the Law of Suspects was enforced. Each comprised twelve members, and they were created on the basis of one committee for each commune (though in fact there were many villages where none was ever formed) or one for each section in the case of large towns. The *comités révolutionnaires* had what were essentially police powers; they drew up lists of suspects, visited private homes in search of evidence, and made arrests. Once again, they were called upon to give an account of their activities once every ten days in a report to the Committee of General Security.

Government action was reinforced by the revolutionary vigilance displayed by clubs and popular societies. The Jacobin Club had an extensive network of affiliated societies throughout the departments of France. Recruiting members from the middle ranks of the bourgeoisie, often from among those who had acquired national lands, the Jacobins were men opposed to advanced revolutionary ideas. When faced with the combination of many different dangers, their desire remained that of maintaining the social and political gains they had made in 1789. It was with this aim in mind that they had formed an alliance with the common people of Paris. Themselves supporters of a liberal economic policy, they nevertheless accepted regulation and price-fixing as a war measure and as a concession to the demands of the people. With the development of the Revolution and a succession of purges, their recruitment did become somewhat more widely-based: thus the proportion of members belonging to the middle classes fell from 62 per cent for the years from 1789 to 1792 to 57 per cent for the period from 1793 to 1794, while the percentage of artisans and soldiers rose over the same period from 28 per cent to 32 per cent, and that of peasants from 10 per cent to 11 per cent.

The various *sociétés fraternelles* were more popular in their social composition and gathered together men from sans-culotte backgrounds. These clubs had sprouted in Paris following the foundation by Dansard, a schoolmaster, of the *Société fraternelle des patriotes de l'un et l'autre sexe* on 2 February 1790; it, too, held its meetings at the convent of the Jacobins in the rue Saint-Honoré. These local societies, open to people of humble means who lived in the district, grew in numbers all over Paris following the *journée* of 10 August 1792. And when, on 9 September 1793, the Convention had ended the right of the sectional assemblies to sit *en permanence*, the popular militants replied by turning these old-established popular societies into sectional societies or by creating new ones. These *sociétés sectionnaires* of the new variety formed the grass-roots organization of the popular movement in Paris: it was through them that the militants directed sectional politics, controlled the numerous administrative bodies, and put pressure on municipal and even governmental authorities. From the autumn to the spring of the Year II, the Republic was covered by a whole network of societies, efficient in their operation, and spread throughout the towns and villages of France. It is difficult to estimate how many there must have been throughout the entire country. But in the South-east, which for a time was threatened by counter-revolution, their number seems to have been particularly high: there were 139 popular societies in the 154 communes of the Department of the Vaucluse, 132 in the 382 communes of the Gard, 258 societies for 355 communes in the Drôme, and 117 for 260 in the Basses-Alpes. These organizations, indeed, played an overwhelmingly important role in the defeat of counter-revolution and the enemies of the Republic within France itself.

Meanwhile a certain antagonism was building up between the Jacobins and their affiliated societies, rigid supporters of the policies of the government, and the *sociétés sectionnaires* who gave expression to the autonomy of the popular movement within the general tide of Revolutionary activity. After Germinal the government Committees, with the full support of the Jacobins, made a serious attempt to bring together all the forces working for the Revolution: under this scheme the central Jacobin Club in Paris was to form 'the one and only centre of political opinion'. Under strong government pressure the sectional societies in Paris were forced to dissolve, a move which led to the closure of thirty-nine societies in the Floréal and Prairial of Year II. The government Committees smashed the framework of the popular movement, but in their desire to bring within the ranks of the Jacobins, forcibly if need be, a movement which until that time had enjoyed a large degree of autonomy and which had its own aspirations and its own democratic practice, the Committees drove a further wedge between themselves and the sans-culottes. In this way the unbridgeable antagonism between the sans-culotterie and the Jacobin bourgeoisie once more found expression.

Centralization of government was strengthened still more in the spring of the Year II by the decision to recall the *représentants en mission* from the departments. These deputies, invested in the first instance with very considerable powers, had already seen their competence limited by the decree of 14 Frimaire II. And if a large-scale mission, the last they would be asked to undertake, intervened in December of 1793 when they were ordered to see that that decree was enforced, the *représentants* were on that occasion closely supervised by the Committee of Public Safety, to which they were obliged to report every ten days. No longer were they able to delegate their powers to others, nor yet to raise armies or impose revolutionary price controls. On 30 Germinal (19 April 1794), twenty-one *représentants* were summoned back to Paris. For the Committee of Public Safety preferred to use its own agents, men like Julien de Paris, the son of the deputy for the Drôme, who denounced the excesses committed by Carrier at Nantes and Tallien at Bordeaux and who secured their recall. Sometimes the Committee would delegate authority to one of its own members – as in the case of Saint-Just, despatched to the northern frontier in Messidor.

Centralization could not, however, be pushed to its logical limit. The Committee of Public Safety had always to take account of the Convention and the other Committees. It never succeeded in gaining control of finance, which remained the preserve of Cambon. The Committee of General Security was very jealous of its prerogatives and was unwilling to tolerate the activities of the Bureau de Police which the Committee of Public Safety established. It was, indeed, conflict between the two Committees which sparked off the collapse of Revolutionary Government. In the departments, in spite of all the efforts of the Committee of Public Safety, local factors still counted for a great deal in the manner in which government decrees were implemented.

'Coercion' and Terror

Ever since 1789 the desire to mete out punishment had always been one of the essential characteristics of the revolutionary mentality: when they were faced with the aristocratic plot, as Georges Lefebvre has shown, the popular movement and the clearheaded revolutionary leaders alike reacted with a defensive mentality and a desire to punish those who threatened them. From this desire stemmed the outbursts of popular feeling and massacres of the revolutionary years, but also, even in 1789, a whole succession of *comités permanents, comités de recherches*, and finally *comités de sûreté générale*. The decree of 11 October 1789 had granted the right of supreme justice in cases of sedition to the Châtelet in Paris. On 17 August 1792 a special tribunal was set up, which was granted the right of summary procedure two days later and against which there could be no appeal. The September Massacres marked the culmination of popular Terror. And since the Girondins found the use of repression utterly repugnant, even where that repression was carried out through legal channels, the tribunal of 17 August was annulled as early as 29 November 1792.

As the crisis grew worse, the Terror became more deeply engrained. As Revolutionary Government became established and grew stronger, the Terror was institutionalized and legalized. On 10 March 1793, in a bid to prevent further massacres by the people, the Revolutionary Tribunal was set up to deal with 'all cases of counter-revolution'. It was finally organized on 5 September. Its members were nominated by the Convention, and it passed judgement in accordance with a simplified criminal procedure, the Grand Jury having been dispensed with and the defendants having no right of appeal or retrial. The *comités de surveillance*, set up on 21 March 1793 to investigate suspects, were themselves brought under the Law of Suspects on 17 September of that year and supervised by the Committee of General Security. To an increasing extent the Convention set up Military Commissions which again enjoyed special simplified legal procedures: on 19 March 1793, for instance, one was set up to deal with the rebels in the Vendée, and another on the 28th to hear cases against émigrés. For rebels, émigrés and refractory priests who returned to French soil, all of them considered as outlaws, trial was reduced to the simple establishment of the defendant's identity and the formality of pronouncing the death sentence.

In the course of this second period of Terror, its intensity varied according to the department, the personality of the deputy on mission in the area, and the influence exercised by local terrorists. The scope of repression might widen or narrow according to the scale of danger threatening the locality and also in accordance with the mood of the local leaders and the interpretation which they chose to give to the laws they had to enforce. Certain of them launched an attack on former members of the Feuillants, on men who had previously been noted for their moderate views, and on those who had protested against the *journées* of 10 August or 31 May–2 June. The worsening of the economic crisis and the introduction of economic controls increased the number of possible suspects to include the rich who hoarded money, as well as those producers and traders who defied the law of the *maximum*. Then again, dechristianization extended the Terror still further, and repression was also aimed at constitutional priests who were too slow in renouncing their ministry and at those of the faithful who stubbornly continued to practise their religion.

The Terror was centralized even more following the destruction of the various political factions and the trials in Germinal. Hitherto it had been directed against the enemies of the Revolution, but now it was extended to include those who opposed the government Committees: in this way the Committees used the Terror to tighten their grip on political life. Gradually the most notorious of the terrorists were recalled to Paris – Fouché, Barras and Fréron, Tallien, Carrier. The decree of 27 Germinal II, voted following a report from Saint-Just on 'policing and the crimes of the factions', established the principle that 'those accused of conspiracy will be brought from all corners of the Republic and tried before the Revolutionary Tribunal in Paris'. On 19 Floréal (8 May), the revolutionary tribunals and commissions instituted in the departments by individual deputies on mission were in turn closed down. Yet the revolutionary tribunal in Arras, set up by Lebon, was kept in being until 22 Messidor (10 July), while on 21 Floréal (10 May), the *commission populaire* of Orange was actually inaugurated. These were exceptions made necessary by particular local circumstances.

The Great Terror emanated from the Law of 22 Prairial II (10 June 1794). Again it can be explained by the special circumstances prevalent at that moment. On 1 Prairial (20 May), a man called Admirat had made an attempt on the life of Collot d'Herbois; and on the 4th (23 May), Cécile Renault was arrested when it appeared that she intended to attack Robespierre; what is more, she made no secret of her counter-revolutionary convictions. Hence it seemed that the old aristocratic plot was still extant, and counter-revolution was shown to be a permanent force in political life. All this happened, moreover, as Republican troops were about to fight another campaign. A wave of terrorism aroused the Paris sections and the desire for punishment and vengeance was again enflamed. But the time for spontaneous reactions of that kind was now past. The Terror was simplified and strengthened. As Couthon made clear when he presented his plan for the Law of 22 Prairial: 'It is not a question of making an example of a few men, but rather of exterminating the implacable lackeys of tyranny.'

The defence and preliminary cross-questioning of the accused were abolished, juries could convict on nothing more than moral proof, and the tribunal's choice was limited to that between acquittal and the death sentence. The definition of 'enemies of the Revolution' was extended considerably: 'It is not so much a question of punishing them as of wiping them out.' Article 6 enumerated the different categories of individuals who were regarded as enemies of the people:

Those who have aided and abetted the plans of the enemies of France by persecuting and slandering patriotism, those who have sought to spread a spirit of discouragement, to deprave the morality of the people, to undermine the purity and energy of revolutionary principles, all those who, by whatever means and under whatever pretext, have attacked the liberty, the unity and the security of the Republic or have worked to prevent these from being established on a firm, lasting basis.

In the course of this last period the practice of holding communal trials for a large number of suspects became common: the widespread notion of an aristocratic plot allowed charges to be brought in the same trial against defendants who had nothing in common, but who were held to be united inasmuch as they had all intrigued against the nation. The accumulation of suspects in Paris prisons – there were more than eight thousand of them at one stage – gave rise to the fear that the prisoners might rise in revolt. The so-called prison conspiracies which a number of signs seemed to point to but which were very considerably exaggerated, served as justification for three *fournées*, or mass trials, in June and a further seven in July 1794. The victims were drawn from the principal gaols in the city, the Bicêtre, the Luxembourg, the Carmes, and Saint-Lazare. Between March 1793 and 22 Prairial II a total of 1,251 people were executed in Paris; but between the passing of the Law of 22 Prairial, the establishment of the Great Terror, and the *journée* of 9 Thermidor there were as many as 1,376 executions. In the words of Fouquier-Tinville, the public prosecutor at the Revolutionary Tribunal, 'heads were falling like tiles'.

The balance-sheet of the Terror must, however, take account of its diversity. The number of suspects detained has been estimated by some to be around 100,000, while the figure of 300,000 seems quite probable to others. The number of deaths is estimated by Donald Greer in *The Incidence of the Terror* to be around 35,000–40,000 if account is taken of all the executions carried out without any semblance of a trial in such places as Nantes and Toulon. The number of capital sentences passed by the Revolutionary Tribunal and the other special courts totalled, according to Greer's calculations, 16,594: between March and September 1793 there were 518 death sentences; from October 1793 to May 1794, 10,812; in June and July there were 2,554; and in August 1794 a mere 86. If the regional distribution of these sentences is examined, we find that whereas 16 per cent of death penalties were imposed in Paris, 71 per cent were passed in the main areas of civil war – 19 per cent in the South-east and 52 per cent in the West. The charges, too, are related to this regional distribution, for in 78 per cent of the cases, the sentences were passed for rebellion or treason. Crimes arising from political opinions (agitation by or in favour of refractories, federalism, and various instances of conspiracy) accounted for 19 per cent of the cases, while offences of an economic nature (the forgery of *assignats*, or misappropriation of funds) added up to no more than 1 per cent. As for the social composition of those sentenced, 84 per cent belonged to the old Third Estate (25 per cent bourgeois, 28 per cent peasants, 31 per cent sans-culottes), whereas only 8·5 per cent were nobles and 6·5 per cent clergy. But in such a struggle, as Georges Lefebvre has pointed out, 'those who run counter to their own class interests are treated with much less circumspection than the original adversaries'.

The Terror, therefore, was in essence an instrument of national and revolutionary defence against rebels and traitors. Like the civil war of which it was no more than one aspect, the Terror had the effect of cutting off from the rest of the nation elements incapable of being assimilated into society, either because they were aristocratic or because they had attached themselves to the aristocracy. It conferred upon the government Committees that coercive power which allowed them to restore the authority of the State and to impose on all citizens the rules demanded in the interests of public safety. It contributed to the development of a feeling of national solidarity by silencing for a brief moment the selfish interests of particular social classes. Above all it allowed the government to impose the controlled economy which was necessary for the war effort and for the safety of the nation. In this sense it was an important factor if victory were to be won.

Economic regulation

The introduction of a controlled economy was caused by the demands of national defence: it was a question of feeding, clothing, equipping and arming the men who had been recruited under the general conscription law, the *levée en masse*, and of provisioning the urban population, at a time when external trade had dried up on account of the blockade and when France was in virtually siege conditions. It was for these reasons that, from the summer of 1793, the Revolutionary Government was gradually induced to take over the overall direction of the economy.

All the material resources of the country were included in the requisition that was decreed. The Law of 26 July 1793, which imposed the death penalty for hoarding, also compelled both producers and merchants to make a declaration of the stocks they held, and appointed commissioners, *commissaires aux accaparements*, to make sure that these returns were truthful and to seek out hoarders. The peasant surrendered his grain, his fodder, his wool, and his hemp; the artisan the products of his craft. In certain exceptional circumstances civilians handed over arms, shoes, blankets or sheets; in Strasbourg, for instance, Saint-Just requisitioned 5,000 pairs of shoes and 1,500 shirts on 10 Brumaire II (31 October 1793), following this up on the 24th (14 November) with a further requisition of 2,000 beds, all taken from the rich citizens of the town in order to look after the wounded. Primary materials were hunted down and collected – metals, ropes, parchment for making cartridge-cases, saltpetre. . . . Church bells were hauled down and sent away to the foundries for the bronze they contained. All companies worked for the nation, under the control of the State, in order to bring production levels up to the maximum possible and to apply the new techniques developed by the scientists employed by the Committee of Public Safety. The requisition greatly limited free enterprise.

The necessary complement to the requisition was the use of price controls. The decree of 4 May 1793 had introduced maximum prices for grain and flour, but in practice it was not enforced. That of

11 September established fixed prices once again. And the decree oₓ 29 September imposed the general maximum on all essential consumer goods, at a rate one-third above 1790 prices, and on wages fixed at a level half as much again as that current in 1790. The *maximum* on prices was to be enforced by the districts, whereas that on wages was left to the municipal councils to implement. To draw up the new legislation and supervise its application in practice, the Convention created a Commission des Subsistances on 6 Brumaire II (27 October 1793), a commission that was to be answerable to the Committee of Public Safety. This commission undertook the enormous task of rationalizing price levels. On 2 Ventôse (20 February 1794) it published a tariff sheet listing the nationally-permitted maximum prices of goods at their point of production. Each district was to add on the costs of transport (laid down in the case of grain and flour as 4 *sous* 6 *deniers* per league travelled), the profit margin of the wholesaler (5 per cent), and that of the retailer (10 per cent). In this way the *maximum* determined margins of profit and thus reduced the spirit of speculation and placed a limit on the freedom of the individual to make profits.

The national control of the economy affected production and foreign trade in differing degrees, but it was used especially to serve the needs of the armies. Indeed, the Committee of Public Safety did not extend national control over civilian provisioning. Clearly this system of production and exchange which placed limits on economic freedom assumed great social value in the eyes of the sans-culottes. Yet the Committee of Public Safety had not undertaken to pursue a policy of economic controls except where such measures were demanded by sheer necessity. For the Committee it was no more than an expedient in the interests of the defence of the nation and of the Revolution, since the bourgeoisie remained strongly hostile to any nationalization which limited its economic freedom.

Production was nationalized in part, either directly through the creation of state factories or indirectly by such means as the supply of raw materials to manufacturers, regulation and control of production, and requisitions and price-fixing. The munitions industry received a powerful boost when national factories for making arms and ammunition were set up: these included the great factory for rifles and side-arms that was built in Paris, those opened by Lakanal in Bergerac and Noël Pointe in Moulins, and the powder-works established at Grenelle in Paris. But the Committee of Public

Safety refused to build large numbers of state factories – a policy to which Carnot in particular was opposed – and avoided nationalizing the mines.

For a few months state control was extended to cover foreign trade. From November 1793 the Commission des Subsistances took charge of this, sending agents to foreign countries, requisitioning cargo vessels, and setting up national warehouses in the ports. In order to finance this trade with neutral countries and to ensure that goods bought in Hamburg, in Switzerland, in Genoa and in the United States were actually paid for, the Commission requisitioned goods for export, notably wines and spirits, silks and cloth. On 6 Nivôse II (26 December 1793), Cambon requisitioned foreign currency, paying for it at par. After the execution of Hébert, controls on external trade were eased. From 23 Ventôse (13 March 1794), commercial facilities were made available to merchants: from this point on the government sought to cooperate with the great merchant firms in order to ensure that provisioning and production could continue without interruption. The merchants in the various ports were grouped together in *agences commerciales* and the agents who had been sent abroad by the Commission were recalled to France. This change, which suited the interests of the commercial and industrial middle class, could not but provoke opposition from the sans-culottes.

The provisioning of civilians was never brought under state control. The Commission des Subsistances, which as from 12 Germinal II became the Commission du Commerce et des Approvisionnements, made use of its right of requisition primarily for the benefit of the armies and paid little attention to the needs of civilian consumers. Indeed, because capitalist development was still at such an early stage, the general statistical information which would have allowed the Commission to determine the exact needs of the population and to draw a map showing the pattern of food supply throughout the nation, was unobtainable. Hence the task of ordering requisitions to keep markets supplied fell to the districts, while the municipal councils were left with responsibility for supervising millers, imposing restrictions on the activities of bakers, and establishing food rationing. In many towns, as in Troyes, bakeries were taken completely under municipal control, a measure that was more rarely applied to butchers (in Clermont-Ferrand, for instance). As for other products, the Commission took little interest in them, with the sole exceptions of sugar and soap; it did nothing more than publish lists of maximum prices, while the Committee of Public Safety went so far as to forbid local authorities to undertake any requisitioning. In vain did the sans-culottes try to compel traders to respect the fixed prices laid down for their goods by means of revolutionary surveillance of their premises: for especially in the case of farm products a black market developed on a considerable scale. On 12 Germinal II (1 April 1794), the *commissaires* who had been employed to track down cases of hoarding were abolished. As it was now treating producers, whether peasants or artisans, with the same leniency as it showed towards merchants, the Committee of Public Safety had no option but to relax, little by little, the control it exercised over civilian provisioning, in spite of the recriminations hurled at it by the sans-culottes. In the end the Committee came to tolerate all violations of the maximum on food prices, with the sole exception of the maximum on bread.

A new economic policy was therefore being formulated in the spring of 1794 at the same time as the schism between the Revolutionary Government and the popular movement was growing deeper. Sensitive to the demands of the middle classes, the Committee of Public Safety was now moving back from its earlier position, was reassuring the business interests and softening the impact of economic controls and mandatory legislation. Economic controls essentially benefited the armies and the State. It could not escape the notice of the Committee of Public Safety that the application of the maximum had the effect of loosening the bonds between the members of the old Third Estate: for whereas the bourgeoisie and such of the peasantry as owned land tolerated economic direction only with considerable repugnance, the artisans and shopkeepers demanded that the *maximum* be applied to foodstuffs but grew angry when they found that it was also being imposed on themselves.

Meanwhile the maximum on wages was a considerable source of irritation to the workers. As the *levée en masse* and the war effort had both had the effect of making labour scarce, the workers had taken advantage of market conditions to gain wage rises, and a large number of communes, including Paris in particular, had never published the official tables listing fixed wage rates. The State, however, applied these rigorously in its own factories, refusing to waive it for the benefit of their workers. Following the events of

Germinal the new Commune in Paris repressed any attempts made to form unions, and the Committee of Public Safety adopted an attitude of resistance to the claims of wage-earners, estimating that the entire economic and financial structure rested on the double maximum and that abandoning it would lead to the collapse of the system and the undoing of the paper currency. Strikes were repressed: as harvest approached, agricultural workers were requisitioned and fixed wage rates were laid down. On 5 Thermidor (23 July 1794), the Paris Commune at last published the list of maximum wage rates, a move which meant for many categories of artisans a mandatory reduction in their wage for a day's work. Hence the discontent of the workers grew stronger, a discontent that was to be added to that of a peasantry overwhelmed by the demands of requisitions, that of businessmen annoyed by price-fixing, and that of property owners ruined by the devaluation of the *assignat*.

And yet our final judgement on the controlled economy cannot be purely negative. It allowed the armies of the Republic to be fed and equipped; without these measures victory was out of the question. Thanks to economic controls, too, the popular elements in the towns did have an assured ration of bread every day: the return to free economic conditions in the Year III made them fall back into quite appalling poverty and misery.

Social democracy

The ideal of social democracy was shared, with some slight differences of interpretation, by both the popular classes and the middling bourgeoisie who formed the revolutionary leadership. It was a commonplace of eighteenth-century social philosophy that inequality of wealth reduces political rights to the point where they are almost meaningless and that the basis of inequality among men lies not only in nature but also in the possession of private property. Few people, however, went on from there to the idea of overthrowing the social order by abolishing private property. 'Equality of possessions is a quite impracticable dream,' declared Robespierre in the Convention on 24 April 1793. Like all the revolutionary leaders, he condemned the *loi agraire*, the more equal division of land holdings. On the previous 18 March, indeed, the Convention had unanimously decreed that those advocating the *loi agraire* should suffer the death penalty. And yet, in that same speech, Robespierre still pointed out that 'the extreme disparity between rich and poor lies at the heart of many of the troubles and crimes of our society'. Sansculottes and Montagnards alike spoke out against 'opulence', against men of vast property or excessive wealth. Their common ideal was a society of small independent producers, peasants and artisans, each owning his own field, shop or workshop and capable of providing for his family without having to fall back on working for a wage. It was an ideal that reflected the condition of people's lives in France at the end of the eighteenth century, conforming to the aspirations of the small peasant and agricultural labourer, the artisan and the journeyman, or, indeed, of the shopkeeper. It was an ideal in keeping with the economic condition of the majority of those involved in the productive process at the time, but one which conflicted with the freedom of production demanded by others, a freedom which was leading to capitalism and the concentration of industry in fewer hands.

This social ideal was given more detailed expression both by the militants in the sections and by the supporters of Robespierre.

On 2 September 1793 the section previously known as the Jardin-des-Plantes but now calling itself the Sans-Culottes section, in the course of making a demand for a maximum law for food prices and a rise in wage levels, declared that 'there is no basis for property other than the extent of physical needs'. It asked the Convention to decree 'that a *maximum* should be passed for personal fortunes, that any one individual should not be allowed to hold more than one *maximum*, that no one should be able to rent more land than was needed for a given number of ploughs, and that no one should be allowed to own more than one shop or workshop'.

In the meantime Robespierre had, as early as 2 December 1792, claimed that the right to own property should be considered of less importance than the right to exist. 'The first human right,' he said, 'is the right to exist; it therefore follows that the first law in any society is that which guarantees all its members the means by which they may stay alive; all other laws are secondary to that one.' On 24 April 1793, in his speech on a new Declaration of Rights, he went still further and stated that property was not a natural human right but a right defined by law:

Property is the right of each citizen to enjoy and dispose of that portion of the possessions of a society which is guaranteed to him by law.

Saint-Just gave vigorous expression to this social aspect of property: 'We must have neither rich nor poor; opulence is a disgrace.' In his *Fragments d'Institutions républicaines*, he argues for the strict limitation of property by the abolition of the right to bequeath it freely and for its equal distribution among direct descendants only, the State appropriating the possessions of those citizens without such heirs. The purpose of this social legislation was to

give to all Frenchmen the means whereby they could obtain the essential goods they need without having to depend on anything other than the laws and without being forced to depend on their relatives.

Or again he proclaimed that 'Man must live an independent existence'. In this way the ideal of social rights was restored to republican thinking: the idea that the community that is the nation, invested with the right to regulate the organization of private property, may intervene to maintain relative equality by reestablishing small property-holdings as fast as these were being destroyed by the evolution of the economy. This was deemed desirable in order to prevent the development once again of high concentrations of wealth in the hands of a few men, accompanied as that would be by the formation of a proletariat dependent upon them.

Montagnard legislation proceeded from these basic principles. The laws of 5 Brumaire II (26 October 1793) and 17 Nivôse (6 January 1794) ensured that inheritances must be equally divided among all heirs, including illegitimate children; these measures were to be applied retrospectively to all legacies since 14 July 1789. But it was not enough to ensure that inheritances were equally divided; it was also necessary to make property available to those who did not own any. This was the idea behind the insistence on 3 June 1793 that émigré lands should be sold off in small lots, with payment staggered over ten years – stipulations which were extended to cover all national lands on 2 Frimaire II. The law of 10 June 1793 authorized the free sharing out of common lands to every citizen in the commune. And yet, if the parcelling out of land in this way allowed a certain number of peasants to round off their holdings or to own land for the first time, most of them derived no benefit whatever from this legislation. The pure and simple abolition of feudal rights on 17 July 1793 led to the disappearance of peasant solidarity, and the crumbling of rural society quickened in tempo. For the landowning peasants and large-scale farmers, desperately in need of manpower on their holdings, could not fail to be hostile to any move that would give land to agricultural labourers and thus transform a rural proletariat into independent producers. The decrees of 8 and 13 Ventôse II (26 February and 3 March 1794) indicated that the Robespierristes were prepared to go still further by giving some satisfaction to the poor sans-culottes: indigent *patriotes* were to receive indemnities through the distribution of property confiscated from suspects. But whereas Saint-Just had talked in his report in terms of granting that property freely to the poor, there was no longer any question of that when the decree was issued. The procedures to be adopted were never precisely laid down. Indeed, the Ventôse Decrees were incapable of solving the agrarian problem. For like the Montagnards, Robespierre and his friends were at heart believers in economic freedom and were unwilling to intervene in agrarian questions. Both groups were equally deaf to the claims of the poor peasants; they never thought in terms of reforming *métayage* or dividing up the big farms into small holdings. In short they were incapable of conceiving of an agrarian programme that would accord with the aspirations of the poor in the countryside.

Social legislation in the real sense of the term remained in the same tradition as the reforms attempted by the Constituent Assembly, reforms which the Convention managed to take somewhat further. The decrees of 19 March and 28 June 1793 introduced aid for the indigent, for children, and for the old. The Declaration of Rights of 24 June 1793 recognized in article 21 that 'public assistance is a sacred debt'. The right to assistance was granted by the law of 22 Floréal II (11 May 1794), which laid down the principle of social security and opened in each department a register of those receiving aid, the *Livre national de la bienfaisance nationale*, in which were inscribed the names of the aged and infirm in the country areas, and those of mothers and widows with children to support. They would all now receive an annual pension and assistance and would benefit from free medical care at home. Saint-Just, on 13 Ventôse II (3 March 1794), exclaimed:

May the whole of Europe understand that you no longer want to see a single unhappy creature or a single oppressor on the soil of France. May this example sow riches in the soil, spreading the love of virtue and human happiness. Happiness is a new idea in Europe!

Republican morality

Virtue, Robespierre explained on 17 Pluviôse II (5 February 1794), is both the principle and the source of popular government:

I am talking of that magic virtue which was responsible for so many marvels in Greece and Rome . . .; of that virtue which is nothing other than the love of one's country and its laws.

Virtue was the corrective for Terror. The Committee of Public Safety dealt severely with those revolutionaries who were dishonest and recalled those terrorists who showed themselves to be lusting after blood. And if it did not resume the dechristianization campaign, it did intend to purify and perfect the civic religion which had become entrenched almost everywhere and also to give it some sense of unity. The belief was that the civic spirit of the great mass of the people had to be fortified by public programmes of education and by the republican religious creed.

Education was recognized as one of the rights of man by clause 22 of the Declaration of 24 June 1793. This was conceived of essentially as a national system of education, an *institution civique* which would teach the citizens, in the words of the Paris Droits-de-l'Homme section on 14 July 1793, 'the duties they are expected to perform and the practice of civic virtues'. Above all it was seen to be necessary to develop public spirit and to strengthen national unity. On 21 October 1793 the Convention passed a decree setting up state primary schools, whose curriculum was to include the training of the mind and the body, morality and gymnastics, teaching and experiment. Immediately brought into question, this decree was replaced by that of 29 Frimaire II (19 December 1793), which ordered the establishment of compulsory primary schools, free and under lay control, following an education system controlled by the State but decentralized in accordance with the wishes of the popular movement. But because it was so busy with the conduct of the war effort, the Revolutionary Government omitted to enforce this law, despite the force of popular demand. Time and money alike were in short supply. As a result the organization of a civic religion became all the more necessary.

Revolutionary religions had developed from the very beginning of the Revolution: the Federation of 14 July 1790 had been one of the first and most splendid symptoms of this. Civic festivals became more and more numerous, a new art form to which David was to lend all the resources of his genius. On 10 August 1793 the Festival of Unity and Indivisibility, organized by David, was celebrated in Paris. When the dechristianization movement was at its peak, in the autumn of 1793, the worship of Reason replaced the Catholic religion in the churches, and soon this, too, changed into a *culte décadaire* based on the qualities of Republican citizenship and morality.

The worship of the Supreme Being, promoted by Robespierre, claimed to be placing the republican doctrine on metaphysical foundations. From his education at a Catholic *collège* Robespierre had received a spiritualistic training. And as a disciple of Rousseau he had a horror of the sensualism of Condillac and even more strongly of the atheistic materialism of *philosophes* like Helvétius, whose bust he smashed in the Jacobin Club. Robespierre, the Incorruptible, believed in the existence of God, in the soul and in after-life: his declaration to the Jacobins on 26 March 1792 can leave us in no doubt on that score. Given the task of presenting a report on the new *fêtes décadaires*, he read a paper on 18 Floréal II (7 May 1794) which gave as their principal purpose the development of civic consciousness and republican morality:

The sole foundation of secular society is morality.... Immorality is the basis for despotism just as surely as virtue is the very essence of the Republic.... Revive public morality. Lead the people on to victory, but take special care to cast vice into total oblivion.

But, acting at one and the same time out of personal conviction and as a politician anxious to give the people a religion that would mould their habits and consolidate public morality, he went on:

In the eyes of the legislator truth consists of all that is useful in the world and good in practice.... The idea of the Supreme Being is a constant reminder of justice; it is therefore something that is both socially valuable and republican.

The first clause of the decree of 18 Floréal proclaimed that 'the French people recognizes the existence of the Supreme Being and the immortality of the soul'. Four great republican festivals were instituted as days of homage to the glorious Revolutionary *journées* (14 July 1789, 10 August 1792, 21 January and 31 May 1793); and every rest day or *décadi* was consecrated to a civic or social virtue.

The Festival of the Supreme Being and of Nature served to in-augurate the new religion on 20 Prairial II (8 June 1794). Robes-pierre, who had been elected president of the Convention a few days earlier, presided over the occasion with a bouquet of flowers and corn in his hand. Surrounded by a huge crowd, the civic procession moved slowly from the Tuileries to the Champ-de-Mars, a magnificent display created on the instructions of David and inspired by the majestic music of Gossec and Méhul. The festival of 20 Prairial made a deep impression both on those who were there and on foreigners. Girbal, a wage-earner from the Guillaume-Tell section, noted in his diary for that day:

I do not think that there has ever been such a day in the whole of human history. It was sublime, both in a physical and in a moral sense. . . . Men with sensitive minds will cherish its memory for the rest of their lives.

And the counter-revolutionary Mallet du Pan wrote: 'We really thought that Robespierre was going to close the abyss of the Revolution.'

Robespierre's political aim in instituting the cult of the Supreme Being was, however, doomed to failure. In the circumstances of the spring of the Year II and following on the events of Germinal, the decree of 18 Floréal was intended to bring together within the same faith and moral outlook the diverse groups which had until then supported the Revolutionary Government but which were now turning against one another as a result of class antagonisms. Unable to analyse economic and social conditions, Robespierre believed in the omnipotence of ideas and appeals to virtue. In fact the cult of the Supreme Being gave rise to a new conflict, one that smouldered inside the Revolutionary Government itself. Neither those who supported an extreme policy of dechristianization nor those who believed that the State should be completely secularized could for-give Robespierre for introducing the decree of 18 Floréal II.

The national army

It was one of the side-effects of the war that the Revolutionary Government was organized and its authority sanctioned by terror; it was in order to feed and equip the armies of the Republic that the controlled economy was instituted; and it was so that the people might devote themselves wholeheartedly to the struggle that social democracy was encouraged to improve their lot and that Republican morality was fostered to strengthen their sense of civic responsibility. Robespierre had declared that 'the revolution is the war of liberty against its enemies'. The Revolutionary Government devoted all its energies to providing for the army of the Year II.

The total strength of French forces in the spring of 1794 was in excess of a million men distributed among twelve armies. They came from widely-differing backgrounds: regular regiments, battalions of volunteers, and the conscripts raised by the *levée* of 300,000 men in the spring of 1793 and the subsequent *levée en masse*. All these men had been brought together into one force as a result of the decree of 21 February 1793 and had been regrouped in *demi-brigades* in the course of the winter of 1793–94. In this way the army was moulded into a truly national force.

The officers were purged and replaced. The Convention laid down the principle that the troops should elect their own leaders, the principle already operative in the National Guard, but qualifying it by giving some consideration to the claims of seniority. The law of 21 February 1793 gave the soldiers the right to elect their corporals. For two-thirds of higher ranks they were to nominate from among the officers of lower rank three candidates for the vacant post, and those officers of the same rank would then select the man to be promoted; the other third were to be decided on the basis of long service. Generals were appointed by the executive, with, once again, one-third chosen on the grounds of seniority and the other two-thirds selected quite freely. Saint-Just explained why on 12 February 1793: 'The election of the leaders of particular bodies of men is the civic right of the soldier,' he said, 'but the right of electing the generals belongs to the entire community.' In practice, the Committee of Public Safety assumed very wide-ranging powers in this field, often delegating its authority to *représentants-en-mission* who themselves intervened in the choice of officers. The principle of election was always, however, respected in the case of officers of subaltern's rank. What gradually emerged through the sieve of this selection process was a military command unequalled in quality: Marceau, Hoche, Kléber, Masséna, Jourdan, and a host of others, backed by officers who were sound both in their abilities as soldiers and in their sense of civic responsibility. To train young officers the Ecole de Mars was established by the decree of 13 Prairial II (1 June 1794): six young men from each district were sent there 'to receive, through revolutionary training, all the knowledge and principles of a soldier of the Republic'.

Discipline was restored. In his proclamation to the army on the Rhine in Brumaire Year II Saint-Just told them to 'have respect for the discipline which leads to victory'. On 27 July 1793 the Convention had imposed the death penalty for looting and desertion; but in fact, though the military tribunals showed no mercy to émigrés and rebels, they did show considerable clemency when dealing with their own soldiers. Above all, the Revolutionary Government knew how to retain the army's democratic spirit. 'It is not only the numbers and discipline of the troops that can lead to victory,' said Saint-Just on 12 February 1793; 'you will only have victory as the spirit of republicanism spreads through the ranks of the army.' The political education of the soldier was provided at the same time as his military training. The soldiers of the Year II went to club meetings and read the patriotic newspapers. An account drawn up on 26 Ventôse II (16 March 1794) gives a list of the newspapers sent to the various armies of the Republic by Bouchotte, the sans-culotte Minister of War: at the head of the list was the *Père Duchesne*, then Charles Duval's *Journal des Hommes Libres*, *Le Journal de la Montagne* (the mouthpiece of the Jacobin Club), and the *Antifédéraliste* published by Jullien de la Drôme. The army of the Year II was a revolutionary army which fought to end privilege, to abolish feudalism, to destroy despotism. Their enemy was the counter-revolutionary, the refractory priest, the émigré noble, every bit as much as the English, Prussian or Austrian soldier. By identifying the Republic with liberty and equality, the Committee of Public Safety succeeded in persuading the citizen-soldiers who composed the fighting strength of the armies that, as soldiers, they must obey orders.

The military command was kept tightly controlled by the power of the civil authority: since the army was no more than the instrument for carrying out their policy, it followed that, as far as the Revolutionary Government was concerned, the conduct of the war was an essential prerogative of the political leadership. Article 110 of the Constitution of 24 June 1793 made it clear that 'there is no commander-in-chief'. After the treason of La Fayette and Dumouriez, the Committee of Public Safety used the Terror to make sure that it was obeyed by the generals. Custine, Houchard and others were sent to the guillotine, their negligence or incapacity appearing to provide proof of their lack of civic consciousness, of *civisme*. The speeches of Saint-Just, who followed military questions very closely, abound in maxims like 'Praise shall not be showered on the generals until the war is over', or 'The rank of general still belongs by its very nature to the system of monarchy'. In a famous circular the Committee of Public Safety made, for the benefit of the generals, this comment on the decree of 14 Frimaire II, the decree which established Revolutionary Government:

In a free State the power of the military is that which must be most firmly controlled, for it is a passive lever for manipulating the will of the people. ... Generals, the time for disobedience is over.

Even in the field, on questions of military operations, the overall control of the civil authority was exercised through *représentants-en-mission*, whose powers, if in practice unlimited, were finally fixed in law on 30 March 1793. On the eve of the 1794 campaign, on 1 Floréal II (20 April 1794), Billaud-Varenne again issued this warning to the Convention:

When you have twelve armies in the field, it is not only defections that have to be feared and guarded against; the influence of the military and the ambition of a leader of some enterprise who suddenly steps out of line, these also are things that should cause us alarm. For history teaches us that that is how all republics have perished. ... Government by the military is the next worst thing after theocracy.

Tactics and strategy were transformed into an aspect of the new political and social situation. Fed, equipped, and armed thanks to the mobilization of material goods which was at last bearing fruit, the Republican troops in their new brigades and divisions now enjoyed the benefits of numerical superiority. No doubt their arms remained the arms of the Ancien Régime: their rifles dated from 1777 and had an accurate range of around a hundred yards, and they were still using the artillery of Gribeauval which consisted primarily of cannon with the capacity to fire four-pound balls over a distance of some 400 yards. But, in the words of Saint-Just on 10 October 1793, 'the methods of warfare favoured by the monarchy do not suit us any more; the system employed by French armies must be that based on shock tactics'.

These new tactics were forced on the army by its lack of military training. The soldiers of the Year II generally fought as riflemen, making use of the lie of the land and then charging in a solid mass with their bayonets drawn. Columns became in the last analysis the tactical formation most typical of the revolutionary armies, a formation that was easier to keep in order and to handle than the traditional linear formation. The new tactical unit for the army was defined in 1794 – that of the division, consisting of two brigades of infantry, two regiments of cavalry, and one battery of artillery, some eight or nine thousand men in all.

The strategy was also revised because of the need to make use of the great masses of recruits that were available. Yet the former practice of siege warfare did persist, with the strongholds serving as the base for military operations. Carnot prescribed repeated attacks by waves of men in tightly-packed lines on vital points in the enemy's defence, a method in which energy and tenacity played a greater part than the science of war. On 14 Pluviôse II (2 February 1794), the Committee of Public Safety outlined its ideas on the subject:

The general rules are these: always to go into action *en masse* and to take the offensive, to maintain strict discipline in the armies without indulging in pedantic detail, to keep the troops constantly in training without over-straining them, to leave behind in barracks only a small number of men who are absolutely indispensable for guarding the premises ... to engage in combat with bayonets in all possible circumstances and to harass the enemy constantly until such time as it is completely destroyed.

Again on 8 Prairial came the reminder to 'attack, be on the attack all the time'. And finally, on 4 Fructidor (21 August 1794): 'Surprise them like a flash of lightning and smash them like a thunderbolt.' Speed of movement, energy in attack, and enthusiasm on the battle-field were seen as being more important than skill in military manœuvres in achieving success.

Victory was gained in June 1794 as a result of the tremendous efforts made by the Revolutionary Government. But at the same time there was a renewal of the political crisis within France and divisions appeared amongst the revolutionary leadership.

3. THE NINTH OF THERMIDOR YEAR II (27 JULY 1794)

Towards the end of the spring of 1794 the difficulties encountered by the Committee of Public Safety in the Convention and in the politi-cal circles of Paris grew much more serious. On the one hand the split between the popular movement and the Revolutionary Government became evident, while on the other the opposition was reforming in the National Assembly. Moreover, this occurred at a time when the worsening of the economic situation made the continued use of Terror necessary if the régime were to be maintained, and when success in obtaining a military victory was making that policy more difficult to accept or to defend in law.

The victory of the Revolution (*May–July 1794*)

The foreign policy of the Committee of Public Safety was essentially a policy of war. The policy of negotiation which Danton had undertaken was now abandoned, since it would have favoured the *Indulgents* at home and would have contributed to a slackening off in national commitment. The Committee did nothing to exploit the divisions among the members of the coalition or to support the Poles who had risen under Kosciuszko. But the Committee of Public Safety did exert pressure on the neutral nations. After hearing Robespierre's report 'on the political situation in the Republic' (27 Brumaire II – 18 November 1793), the Convention proclaimed its willingness to respect the interests of neutral powers and demonstrated its 'feelings of equity, goodwill and esteem' towards the Swiss cantons and the United States of America. The war of propaganda was now finished.

On the northern frontier the military strength of the Republic on on the eve of the 1794 campaign amounted to three armies, which faced Coburg's troops deployed between the sea and Namur. The Armée du Nord of 150,000 men under the command of Pichegru was to attack the enemy in Flanders and push towards Ypres; the Armée des Ardennes, 25,000 strong, was to advance towards Charleroi; and the Armée de la Moselle, the 40,000 troops under Jourdan, was to advance on Liège. Pichegru manœuvred badly and was unable to prevent Coburg from taking Landrecies; but he went on to defeat him at Tourcoing on 29 Floréal II (18 May 1794), thus relieving the frontier from the Scheldt to the sea. Regrouping the armies of the Ardennes and the Moselle and reinforcing them with 90,000 men under the command of Jourdan and supported by Saint-Just (this was soon to be the Armée de Sambre-et-Meuse), the Committee of Public Safety unleashed them against Charleroi, which surrendered on 7 Messidor (25 June 1794). At the same time Coburg, following his defeat at Ypres by Pichegru, retired. To protect his rearguard he attacked Jourdan near Charleroi, at Fleurus, on 8 Messidor (26 June 1794), but after a hard day's fighting he was defeated. Saint-Just had played a highly important part in the victory, bringing up column after column to join the attack; but he refused to make any report on this to the Convention:

I like it very much when victories are announced, but I do not wish them to become pretexts for personal vanity. The victory of Fleurus has been announced, and others who have said nothing about it were there; there has been much talk of sieges, and others who have said nothing about them were there in the trenches.

The liberation of Belgium followed Fleurus. Jourdan and Pichegru joined forces in Brussels. Then Pichegru drove back the British and Dutch to the north, while Jourdan pushed the Austrians back eastwards. On 9 Thermidor (27 July 1794) Pichegru entered Antwerp and Jourdan Liège.

On the Pyrenean front Dugommier stormed the camp of Boulou (12 Floréal – 1 May 1794) and invaded Catalonia, while in the west Moncey crossed the Spanish frontier and occupied San Sebastian (7 Thermidor – 25 July 1794). On the Alpine front the invasion of Italy seemed imminent.

At sea, while the British fleets dominated the Mediterranean and seized Corsica with aid from Paoli, the Republican squadrons in the Atlantic were still succeeding in holding their position. On 9, 10 and 13 Prairial (28–29 May, 1 June) the fleet under Villaret-Joyeuse left Brest and attacked the British off Ouessant in order to protect a convoy of corn from America. The French losses were heavy – one ship, the *Vengeur*, was sunk – but the English, under Howe, were forced to withdraw and the convoy got through.

The Revolutionary Government appeared to be able, by a supreme effort, to avert the internal crisis, achieve victory in the war, and force the coalition powers to make peace. Speaking in the name of the Committee of Public Safety, Billaud-Varenne declared to the Convention on 1 Floréal (20 April 1794):

We are advancing not to conquer territory but to inflict defeat, not to allow ourselves to be swept along by the blind joy of triumph but to stop fighting as soon as the moment arrives when the death of another enemy soldier will not serve the cause of liberty.

But at the very moment when it was about to achieve that objective, the Revolutionary Government fell apart.

The political crisis: the impossibility of conciliation (*July 1794*)

There were many different aspects to the political crisis of July 1794. While Jacobin dictatorship was becoming more centralized and stronger within the framework of Revolutionary Government, its social base never stopped narrowing both in the Convention and in Paris. The division between the two government Committees and disunity within the Committee of Public Safety itself served to bring the crisis to a head.

In Paris and throughout the country public opinion was becoming tired of the Terror at the same time as the popular movement was moving away from Revolutionary Government.

People felt even more weary of the Terror in that victory was now achieved and hence there seemed no further need for repression. The business interests among the bourgeoisie were unwilling to tolerate government control of the economy; they wanted as quickly as possible to return to the total liberty of production and exchange which they had gained from the Revolution of 1789. They also feared possible attacks on their property rights. For though the enforcement of the Ventôse Decrees had been held up for a long period, it now seemed that they would be issued once more; popular commissions were set up to sort out various categories of suspects. The Committee of Public Safety tried to place the Terror on a regular footing by recalling the most notable terrorists from their missions and by reestablishing the centralized working of both justice and repression through the law of 22 Prairial. But the Committee proved unable to apply the law: the Committee of General Security distorted it in the manner in which it carried it out, bringing together under one head the most diverse cases in order to condemn suspects in batches and using the pretext of prison conspiracies to accelerate the rate of repression. Thus the Revolutionary Government found that it had to face not only great economic difficulties but also a large section of public opinion alienated from it by a feeling of revulsion at the scale of the slaughter, by *la nausée de l'échafaud*.

The popular movement had gradually drifted away from the Revolutionary Government in the months following the events of

Germinal. During the spring of 1794, despite the pretence of demonstrations of loyalty to the Convention and the government Committees, there was an irreparable degeneration in the political life of the sections, accompanied by an insuperable sense of alienation from the régime among the Paris sans-culottes. Saint-Just noted that revolutionary fervour had cooled. There were both social and political reasons why that had happened.

In the political sphere, the general assemblies of the sections had been reduced to comparative inactivity, and the elections of municipal and sectional magistrates, which the sans-culottes looked on as an essential aspect of their political rights, were called off. Repression, masked by the political situation, was then unleashed against militants accused of *hébertisme*. This proved a convenient term which allowed the government to strike at those active in the ranks of the sections who were hostile to Jacobin centralization and who remained attached to the system of popular democracy. Some incidents of sectional agitation were reported which, though quickly put down, still demonstrated the persistence of popular opposition. In Floréal the Marat section revived the cult of the 'ami du peuple'; but on 3 Prairial (22 May 1794) the government Committees forbade all 'partial' festivals not celebrated throughout the Republic. At the end of Messidor most of the sections staged a campaign of 'fraternal banquets', but these, too, were immediately denounced and condemned.

In the social field the new direction that economic policy seemed to be following caused widespread discontent among consumers in popular quarters. For the Commune, now purged and controlled by the Robespierriste Payan, was taking steps to revive the fortunes of trade. 'What has been achieved by the continual stream of railing at the leeches sucking the life-blood of the people . . ., against grocers?' he asked on 9 Messidor (27 June 1794). Essential consumer goods were subject to fixed-price laws; but the government did not requisition these goods, contenting itself with providing bread for the people, the distribution of which caused great inconvenience for the municipal authorities. By letting it be known that there was now no restriction on individuals bringing goods into Paris from outside and by ordering the arrest of those who tried to hamper trade, the Paris Commune favoured the black market and ruined any scheme to enforce fixed prices. By these measures it dealt with the demands of the producers and the artisans, but it did so at the expense of the lowest social groups among the sans-culottes, workers and wage-earners who were forbidden by other laws from taking any action to support their demands. From Floréal 1794 onwards, the rise in food prices which followed the publication of the new *maximum* lists and the relaxation of government control gave rise to agitation among the workers for increases in their wages, agitation which spread through the various trades in the city. This was brutally put down by the Commune, which enforced the Loi Le Chapelier. The publication of the lists of maximum wage rates for Paris on 5 Thermidor (23 July 1794) was the culmination of this policy of repression. This table, the strict application of the law of 29 September 1793, imposed on the workers a cut in pay which in many cases was considerable: a stone-mason on the building-sites at the Pantheon who in Ventôse was earning 5 *livres* now received no more than 3 *livres* 8 *sous*. Discontent amongst the working population erupted at the very moment when the Robespierriste authorities of the Paris Commune most desperately needed the confident support of the great mass of the people.

In the Convention the opposition had meanwhile regrouped around the deputies who had been recalled from their missions in the provinces, prominent among whom were certain bloodthirsty terrorists who now felt themselves threatened: Carrier, Fouché, and especially unprincipled men like Barras, Fréron, and Tallien. Once again the faction of corrupt politicians had reformed. They were supported by the new *Indulgents*, who took advantage of the military victory to press for the end of the Terror, and the Plain, which had accepted Revolutionary Government only as a temporary expedient. Now that they had no longer any need to fear a revolutionary *journée*, since the popular movement had been brought to heel, what possible reason could the Convention have for continuing to tolerate the overlordship of the Committees? The Revolutionary Government found itself caught, as if suspended in mid-air, between the Convention which was impatient to throw off its yoke and the popular movement of Paris now irrevocably hostile to it.

But it was as a result of their internal divisions that the government Committees finally fell.

The Committee of General Security, which was in charge of police activities, did not take kindly to encroachment on its territory by the Committee of Public Safety, in particular the work done by its Bureau de Police. The Committee of General Security was composed of determined men, like Amar, Vadier, and Voulland, whose attitude came close to one of arrant extremism, and it wanted to prolong the Terror on which its own authority was dependent. As atheists, they found new sources of grievance in the ending of dechristianization and the cult of the Supreme Being. With the exception of David and Lebas, they were men noted for their hostility to Robespierre, both for personal reasons and because of their principles.

The Committee of Public Safety could quite easily have neutralized this opposition if it had remained united. But divisions crept into the great Committee. As a result of his outstanding services to the Revolution, Robespierre had become the real leader of the government in the eyes of the country. But he made no concessions to the susceptibilities of his colleagues. He was as severe in his standards for others as he was for himself, making few friendships and retaining for the most part an aloofness which could be taken for scheming or ambition. This accusation, one that had already been thrown at Robespierre first by the Girondins and then again by the Cordeliers, was brought up yet again in the Committee by Carnot and by Billaud-Varenne, who declared in the Convention on 1 Floréal II (20 April 1794):

Any people that is jealous of its liberty must guard itself against the very virtues of the men who occupy the highest positions.

To violent differences of temperament and conflicts over the allocation of responsibility (Carnot had violent quarrels with Saint-Just and was roused to anger by criticisms of his military plans by both Saint-Just and Robespierre) was added another factor, that of differences in outlook on social matters. Carnot and Lindet, men who had crossed to the Montagne from the ranks of the Plain, were bourgeois and conservative: they were unwilling to accept economic control and were repelled by the idea of social democracy. Billaud-Varenne and Collot d'Herbois leant towards the other extreme. Robespierre himself, irritated and embittered by the oblique political manœuvring of the Committee of General Security where Vadier was setting out to pour ridicule on the cult of the Supreme Being over the case of Catherine Théot, an old woman who claimed to be 'the mother of God', stopped attending the Committee towards the middle of Messidor. His withdrawal proved helpful to his opponents.

The attempt at reconciliation between the two government Committees, which met in a joint session on 4 and 5 Thermidor II (22–23 July 1794), failed. The members of the Committees had calculated that if agreement could not be reached, Revolutionary Government would not be able to last or to resist the offensive of the *corrompus* and the new *Indulgents*. But if Saint-Just and Couthon were prepared to be conciliatory, Robespierre was not; he was utterly determined to smash the alliance forming between his opponents in the Montagne and the Plain, which until that moment had given him its support.

The dénouement: the insurrection that could not succeed

Robespierre decided to take the conflict to the floor of the Convention. In doing so he was making it the judge of whether or not Revolutionary Government was to continue and he was quite openly taking a huge risk, for the popular movement was then in the course of being demobilized, while the Paris sans-culottes remained indifferent or even hostile to him.

On 8 Thermidor (26 July 1794) Robespierre attacked his opponents before the Convention, hurling back at them the charge that they, terrorists hungry for blood now appearing in the guise of *Indulgents*, had been responsible for the excesses of the Terror. But by refusing to name the deputies whom he was accusing of these crimes, he lost his case, for all those who had some reason to reproach themselves felt that it was they who were being threatened. In the evening, while Robespierre was receiving the plaudits of the Jacobin Club and the Committees were flailing around helplessly, his opponents took firm action. Around midnight the plot was sealed between the deputies who had for a long time been planning Robespierre's downfall, and the Plain, to whom they gave the assurance that they would bring the Terror to an end. It was a coalition formed as a result of political circumstance and cemented by fear.

The meeting of the Convention on 9 Thermidor (27 July 1794) opened at eleven o'clock. At midday Saint-Just got up to speak, and from that moment things happened very quickly. The tactics of obstructionism decided on by the conspirators succeeded in silencing first Saint-Just and then Robespierre. The arrests of Hanriot, the commander of the Paris National Guard, and Dumas, the president of the Revolutionary Tribunal, were decreed. Amidst frightful uproar an unknown deputy called Louchet proposed that a warrant be issued against Robespierre, and this was accepted unanimously. His brother asked to be allowed to share his fate, and the names of Saint-Just and Couthon were added to the list. Lebas claimed the honour of appearing on the list of those proscribed. 'The Republic is a lost cause,' shouted Robespierre, 'the brigands are now triumphant!' The spectators in the galleries of the Convention left to go and take the alarming news to the sections. It was not yet two o'clock.

The attempt at insurrection made by the Paris Commune was badly organized and badly directed. Before three o'clock the mayor, Fleuriot-Lescot, and the *agent national*, Payan, were warned of what had happened; they asked the members of the General Council to disperse to their sections, sound the tocsin and call the men to arms. By six in the afternoon all the sectional militants were alerted and the sections themselves were in session. But only sixteen sections out of forty-eight sent detachments of National Guardsmen to the Commune at the Place de Grève: such were the overt consequences of the government's repression, in the months since Germinal, of the sectional office-holders. The companies of artillery, however, the vanguard of the Parisian sans-culottes, showed greater revolutionary initiative than the infantry battalions, and by ten at night the leaders of the insurrection had at their disposal seventeen of the thirty or so companies of artillerymen then stationed in the capital, together with thirty-two cannon, while the Convention had on its side no more than the one company on guard duty. For several hours the Commune enjoyed an overwhelming superiority in artillery power – a decisive asset if only there had been a leader who could have directed the force. Rescued from the Convention, the deputies whose arrest had been decreed succeeded in reaching the Commune, where they discussed what should be done. But in the meantime the Convention pulled itself together and proclaimed that the rebel deputies were henceforth outlaws; Barras was given the task of mustering an armed force, and the moderate sections gave this their support. The National Guardsmen and artillerymen assembled outside the Hôtel de Ville were left without either instructions or provisions. Soon the rumour of the outlawry decree began to spread through their ranks, and little by little they dispersed and left the square deserted. Around two o'clock in the morning Barras marched on the Hôtel de Ville and took it at a moment when the Commune was quite unprepared. They were defeated before they had even begun to fight.

On the evening of 10 Thermidor (28 July 1794), Robespierre, Saint-Just, Couthon and nineteen of their political allies were executed without trial. On the following day it was the turn of a large batch of seventy-one men, the largest mass execution in the entire course of the Revolution.

If we consider only the attempted insurrection itself, the responsibility for defeat lies with the leaders of the Paris Commune and the Robespierristes who did not know what action to take. Despite the strengthening of the government machine and the defection of a large number of sectional authorities (especially following the reduction of the powers of the *comités révolutionnaires*), the sans-culottes had still rushed in their thousands to the Hôtel de Ville. If their efforts proved futile, the responsibility lies with Robespierre and his friends, who waited for the final blow to fall instead of coming down into the Place de Grève and placing themselves at the head of the popular movement, the men of the revolutionary *journées*. But if we look for more fundamental reasons, it is the contradictions inherent in the revolutionary movement and in the sans-culottes themselves which alone can explain the historical necessity of the Ninth of Thermidor.

As we have seen, Robespierre, a disciple of Rousseau and yet a man almost totally devoid of scientific and economic understanding, regarded with utter horror the materialism of *philosophes* like Helvétius. His spiritual conception of society and of the world left him defenceless when faced with the contradictions that became clear in the spring of 1794. For if he was well able to give a theoretical justification for Revolutionary Government and the Terror, he was incapable of making an accurate analysis of the economic and social realities of his time. There is no doubt that he could not underestimate the strength of the balance of social forces or neglect the preponderant role played by the bourgeoisie in the struggle against the aristocracy and the Ancien Régime. But Robespierre, like Saint-Just, remained the prisoner of his own contradictions: they were both too conscious of the interests of the bourgeoisie to give their total support to the sans-culottes, and yet too attentive to the needs of the sans-culottes to find favour with the middle classes.

Revolutionary Government was based on a social foundation which comprised diverse and contradictory elements, elements which were therefore deprived of class-consciousness. The Jacobins, on whose support Robespierre and his friends were dependent, could not provide it with the strong framework it needed, for they, too, were not united by class interest, and still less were they a class party, strictly disciplined, which could have been an effective instrument for political action. The régime of the Year II rested on a spiritual conception of social relationships and democracy, a fact which proved fatal to its chances of success.

On the political front, much more important than an opposition thrown together by momentary circumstance was the fundamental contradiction that existed between the Montagnard bourgeoisie and the sans-culottes of Paris, between the militants in the sections and the Revolutionary Government. The war situation demanded an authoritarian government, a fact which the sans-culottes accepted since they contributed to its formation. Thus, the war and its demands entered into contradiction with the democratic system which both Montagnards and sans-culottes alike called for but of which they had totally different conceptions. Democracy as the sans-culottes practised it led spontaneously towards direct government; the Revolutionary Government thought that this practice was incompatible with the conduct of the war. Control by the people over the men they elected, the right of the people to withdraw their mandate, voting aloud or by acclamation – such were the claims of the sectional militants which indicated that they would not be content with a formal democratic process. But this style of conducting political affairs was radically opposed to the sort of liberal democracy which the bourgeoisie had in mind. The sans-culottes had demanded a strong government in order to crush the forces of aristocracy; they did not forgive the Revolutionary Government for having reduced their authority and compelled them to obey.

The problem of the relationship between the popular movement and the Revolutionary Government was also seen in another sphere. As a result of their very success in the spring and summer of 1793, the sans-culottes had seen their own officers and leaders dissolve before their eyes. Many of the militants in the Paris sections, without being driven on by personal ambition, nevertheless considered that to obtain a government post was merely a just reward for their devotion. The efficacy of the Revolutionary Government could thus be guaranteed by buying their services. In the autumn of 1793 the various administrations were purged and staffed with good sans-culottes. It was in this way that a new conformism grew among these militants, a conformism well illustrated by the behaviour of the revolutionary *commissaires* sent out by the Paris sections. These men, who came from among the most popular elements and the most fervent revolutionaries in the sections, were originally the most aggressive group amongst the revolutionary personnel. Their economic means and their success in carrying out their allotted tasks alike demanded that they should receive a salary, and as the Year II progressed these militants gradually changed into officials who were all the more prepared to do the government's bidding in that they were afraid they might lose the benefits they had acquired. This development was the inevitable consequence of the worsening of the class struggles both in France itself and on the frontiers: those elements in the popular movement which were most politically aware joined the state apparatus and reinforced the power of Revolutionary Government. But there resulted from this a weaken-ing of the popular movement and a change in its relations with the government. The political activity of the sectional organizations was now thwarted, especially in view of the increased demands of national defence. At the same time democracy was growing weaker inside the sections themselves, as the growth of bureaucracy gradu-ally paralysed the critical spirit and political militancy which had previously characterized the Parisian masses. In the end popular control yielded to the various organs of government, which were in turn strengthened in their authoritarian policies. In this way a new contradiction developed between the Revolutionary Government and the popular movement which had carried it to power. The Robespierristes looked on, powerless. Saint-Just was right to think that 'the Revolution had run cold'. But he was unable to explain why.

In economic and social matters the contradiction was no less insurmountable The men on the Committee of Public Safety, and Robespierre above all, were believers in the liberal ideal of economic freedom and accepted economic direction only because they could not do without price-fixing and requisitioning if they were to bear the burden of a great national war; the sans-culottes, on the other hand, were thinking much more about their own subsistence when they imposed the *maximum* on the government. However democratic the Revolution might have become, it nonetheless remained firmly in the hands of the bourgeoisie, and hence the Revolutionary Government could not peg the prices of foodstuffs without also fixing wage levels, a measure necessary if the balance were to be maintained between businessmen and wage-earners. This policy could work only on the basis of the alliance between the Montagnards and the sans-culottes. It was a policy which ran counter to the interests of the middle classes, even the Jacobin middle classes, for it abolished the free economy and restrained profits; and except for the war materials paid for by the State and the requisitions of grain and fodder imposed on the peasantry, the *maximum* was flouted by producers and traders. The sans-culottes, on the other hand, arguing essentially from the relationship of prices to wages, tended to take advantage of the situation to force their employers to agree to pay rises. It goes without saying, in a society that was essentially bourgeois in structure, that when the Committee of Public Safety intervened to try to solve the crisis, its arbitration should benefit the property owners and producers rather than the wage-earners: it was this that brought about the wage *maximum* for Paris on 5 Thermidor. As it did not rest on a solid class base, the experiment in economic control of the Year II was left hanging in mid-air.

Revolutionary Government, undermined by these contradictions, was unable to recover from the attack on Robespierre and his followers; with them the democratic and egalitarian republic which they had hoped to found was also lost. As for the popular movement, over a period of ten more months it was to mount a bitter and desperate rearguard action against the Thermidorian bourgeoisie, who found themselves more and more seriously hampered by the reaction which they had unleashed. It was a dramatic struggle which finally shattered the vigour and buoyancy of the revolutionary movement.

Chapter 5

The Thermidorian Convention, the Bourgeois Reaction, and the End of the Popular Movement (July 1794 to May 1795)

The Revolutionary Government did not long outlast Robespierre, and the reaction quickly set in after his fall. Behind the relentlessness and confusion of the political struggles in the ensuing Thermidorian period, it is the social character of the reaction which is especially intriguing. The régime of Year II had possessed a popular social content that measures such as the Ventôse decrees and the plan for a wide-ranging programme of public assistance had underlined; on the political level it had allowed the people to participate in the management of affairs. This system had severely impaired the privilege accorded wealth and the political monopoly which the Constituent Assembly had established to benefit the bourgeoisie.

The popular movement and the Paris sans-culottes, who had been the driving force behind the formation of the Revolutionary Government, had given ground as far back as Germinal Year II. Thereafter, the orientation of the social and economic policies of the Committee of Public Safety had become progressively less popular. From this standpoint, the *journée* of 9 Thermidor marks less of a break with the past than an acceleration of existing trends. From Thermidor Year II to the following spring, the reaction advanced, though without gaining any firm footholds. In this key period, bourgeois revolution and popular movement, *honnêtes gens* and sans-culottes, came face to face in a struggle in which were clearly apparent the fear of the one, and the hopes of the other, for a great popular *journée* which would seal the destiny of the Revolution once and for all.

The people of Paris had remained unconquered since 1789. The defeat of Prairial Year III, however, was to mark the end of the

Paris sans-culottes and the definitive liquidation of the popular movement. The Revolution resumed its bourgeois course.

I. THE PROGRESS OF THE THERMIDORIAN REACTION

Among the distinguishing features of the Thermidorian period are the political struggles, whose tangled complexity cannot conceal what was really at stake: the *honnêtes gens* – soon to be called the 'notables' – were wanting to eliminate the sans-culottes from public life. The latter were essentially a petty bourgeois force composed of artisans and shopkeepers and also of *compagnons*. For a short time during Year II they had had the temerity to dictate their law to the *honnêtes gens*. In much the same way as in 1793, when the popular movement was making great strides, the parliamentary struggles which brought the Montagnard minority up against an increasingly large reactionary majority was duplicated at base-level and in all quarters by an even more epic conflict between the reactionaries and the men of Year II. However, the popular movement, which in 1793 had helped to quicken the pace of the Revolution, had now lost its bearings and was disorganized and leaderless. Henceforth it was to prove nothing more than an ordinary resistance force, only capable of fighting as it retreated.

The dismemberment of the Revolutionary Government and the end of the Terror (Summer, 1794)

The intention of the Committee of Public Safety, though now rid of its Robespierrist members, was still to maintain the existing system of government. Barère, speaking before the Convention on the Committee's behalf on 10 Thermidor (28 July 1794), declared that the *journée* of the previous day had been merely 'a slight disturbance which left the government untouched', and went on to state that 'the might of the Revolutionary Government will be increased a hundredfold now that power has returned to its source and produced a more energetic moving spirit and Committees better refined by the purge'. In the same speech, Barère attacked a 'few disguised aristocrats who were speaking of indulgence. . . . Indulgence! There can be no indulgence save for involuntary errors; but the intrigues of the aristocrats are heinous offences and their errors crimes.'

As it turned out, the loss of the basic characteristics of the governmental system of Year II – its stability, the centralization of power within it and, once the Terror had been dropped, its 'coercive force' – caused its disintegration within a few weeks.

Stability of government was destroyed on 11 Thermidor Year II (29 July 1794) when the Convention voted Tallien's motion that a quarter of the members of the Committees of government should be renewed monthly, and that retiring members should only be re-eligible after an interval of a month. Prieur of the Côte-d'Or and Jeanbon Saint-André were immediately excluded from the Committee of Public Safety and replaced by Tallien and the Dantonist Thuriot. This clearly revealed the trend of opinion in the Convention. Soon only Carnot remained from the Great Committee of Year II. David, Jagot and Lavicomterie, all reputed Robespierrists, were removed from the Committee of General Security and replaced by men like Legendre and Merlin de Thionville. Although some deputies gained influence in the government, any stability in governing personnel had gone for good.

The centralization of power within the government did not last beyond the decree of 7 Fructidor Year II (24 August 1794). The predominance of the Committee of Public Safety which had till then ensured the government's unity was attacked as early as 11 Thermidor. Leading the assault was Cambon, who headed the Committee of Finances and under whose orders lay the Treasury, which in Year II had been the only government department to escape the authority of the great Committee. Barère riposted on 13 Thermidor, criticizing the 'moral federalism' which certain persons seemed intent on. The Convention wavered, but ultimately, on 7 Fructidor, voted a decree which was based on Cambon's proposals. There were to be sixteen committees; the twelve main ones each had control over one executive commission. The Committee of Public Safety saw its powers restricted to questions of war and diplomacy. The Committee of General Security retained police affairs and general supervision. The Committee of Legislation acquired a new importance, receiving power over internal administration and the judicial system. With power now split between these 'Three Committees' of government, all centralization was at an end.

The Revolutionary Government's 'coercive force' disappeared in much the same way as the two other mainsprings of its action, with the abandonment of the terror. The law of 22 Prairial was repealed on 14 Thermidor (1 August 1794). Fouquier-Tinville was gaoled, and the Revolutionary Tribunal ceased to function. Following a report by Merlin de Douai, the Tribunal was reorganized on 23 Thermidor (10 August 1794). The most notable change was that the *question intentionnelle* – the question of whether the act had been committed with intent – now allowed the acquittal of any accused person, even if found guilty, who pleaded that he had not been motivated by any counter-revolutionary purpose. The *comités révolutionnaires*, which had been the target for a violent campaign unleashed after 9 Thermidor, were suppressed and, on 7 Fructidor (24 August), replaced by *comités de surveillance*. These were established at arrondissement level in big towns, and at district level in the departments. The 48 Paris sections were grouped into 12 arrondissements, whose new *comités de surveillance*, like their *comités civils*, were as good as government organs. In particular, they were to be independent of the sectional general assemblies, which had in any case been restricted to one meeting per ten days since 4 Fructidor (21 August 1794). The prisons were opened and suspects freed: nearly 500 in Paris alone, from 18 until 23 Thermidor (5–10 August 1794). The Terror was now at an end.

Moderates, Jacobins and Sans-culottes (August to October 1794)

In spite of the exertions of the former terrorists, who had been denounced on 9 Fructidor (26 August 1794) by Méhée de la Touche in his violent pamphlet, 'La Queue de Robespierre' ('Robespierre's Tail'), the political reaction quickly grew stronger. Barère, Billaud-Varenne and Collot d'Herbois were attacked by Lecointre on 12 Fructidor (29 August 1794), and resigned from the Committee of Public Safety. In the space of a month, all the personnel of government from Year II had been eliminated.

The Montagne had lost all its influence in the Convention, where it had been reduced to what was ironically called the 'Crest'; even this was gradually being whittled away by large numbers of defections. The dominant force in the Convention was now the Plain – the centrist majority, reinforced by repentant terrorists and dissenting Montagnards – among whom Cambacérès and Merlin de Douai were especially prominent. The men of the Plain made it quite clear what their social orientation was: they were equally as opposed to social democracy as to the directed economy, and wished to restore the dominance of the bourgeoisie, of which they were members, to reestablish the social hierarchy and to return the people to its subordinate position. When, therefore, on 27 Fructidor (13 September 1794), one of the members of the Crest, Fayau, proposed new terms and conditions for the sale of national lands which would have favoured 'republicans who own little or no property', Lozeau, the deputy for the Charente-Inférieure, retorted:

In a republic composed of 24 million men, it is impossible for all to be farmers; it is equally impossible for the majority of the nation to be landowners, since, according to this hypothesis, if each man were obliged to cultivate his own plot or his own vineyard in order to live, then commerce, industry and the arts would soon be annihilated.

The Thermidorians thus set aside the popular ideal of a nation of independent small producers. However, the men of the Plain were steadfastly attached to the Revolution and were set upon defending the Republic. Thus on 25 Brumaire Year III (15 November 1794), they maintained and codified the punishments for émigrés. Their policy was to unite all the 'Patriots of '89' so as to bar the way to counter-revolution and to stabilize the régime. As in 1793, however, the last word did not rest with the Convention, and was imposed on it from outside.

In Paris from Thermidor to Brumaire Year II (August to October 1794), moderates, Neo-Hébertists and Jacobins met in three-cornered conflict in a series of confused political struggles. The moderates were wanting to reestablish the predominance of the *honnêtes gens*, that is to say, the well-to-do bourgeoisie, along the lines of 1791. The Neo-Hébertists, who were grouped together in the Electoral Club, and who also held the Museum section, represented the popular trends of opinion hostile to the Revolutionary Government: they demanded the restitution of Paris's elected municipality and the enforcement of the democratic Constitution of 1793. Finally, the Jacobins were still supporting the maintenance of the centralization of the government's power and the continuation of repressive methods until a peace was concluded.

By splitting the popular forces and by isolating the Jacobins, the Electoral Club's campaign promoted the progress of the reaction. United with the moderates solely by the vehemence of their hostility towards the terrorists and the Robespierrists, the Neo-Hébertists helped to set in motion a course of events whose results they consequently deplored. Their Electoral Club had been organized after 9 Thermidor, and its moving spirits were men like the former Hébertist Legray and the ex-Enragé, Varlet. It launched a campaign against the system of Year II, in which it was supported by Babeuf's *Journal de la liberté de la presse*. Babeuf wrote on 19 Fructidor (5 September 1794):

10 Thermidor was the end of our confinement; since then we have been in labour to be reborn into liberty.

It is clearly apparent from such passages that the social conflict which underlay the political struggles went unperceived by Babeuf. In the copy of his newspaper for 1 Vendémiaire Year III (22 September 1794), he distinguished only two parties in France:

One in favour of the maintenance of Robespierre's government, the other for the reestablishment of a government backed exclusively by the eternal rights of man.

If there was no collusion between Babeuf, the Electoral Club and the moderate reactionaries, it is nevertheless certain, as Georges Lefebvre noted, that their campaign helped towards the latter's success — as indeed Babeuf later acknowledged in his *Tribun du peuple* of 28 Frimaire (18 December 1794).

The resistance of the Jacobins was channelled through the Jacobin Society, which was reopened by Legendre as early as 11 Thermidor (29 July 1794), and from which, at Carrier's request, the turncoat terrorists, Fréron, Lecointre and Tallien, were excluded on 17 Fructidor (3 September). Supported by Audouin's *Journal universel* and by Chasles and Lebois's *L'Ami du peuple*, the Jacobins demanded a return to the system of the Terror 'in order to annihilate the aristocrats who dare to show themselves'. On 19 Fructidor (5 September), the Club provided itself with a programme by adopting the Petition from the Dijon Jacobins which called for the enforcement of the Law of Suspects, for a new decision on the decree relative to the *question intentionnelle*, for the exclusion of nobles and priests from all public offices and finally for the restriction of press freedom. Eight Paris sections adhered to this petition. The month of Fructidor was marked by a real Jacobin upsurge, culminating on the fifth *jour sans-culottide* with the removal of Marat's remains to the Pantheon. Then, on 10 Vendémiaire Year III (1 October 1794), the Jacobin majority in a dozen Paris sections keenly criticized Lindet's report to the Convention on the fourth *jour sans-culottide*, which had encapsulated a compromise programme, on the one hand promising protection to former terrorists, but on the other hand strongly opposing any extension of revolutionary repression, condemning those who were contemplating a 'transfer of wealth' and proposing to restore to commerce its freedom of activity. The Jacobin-inspired sectional agitation alarmed the majority in the Convention, which let itself be swayed by the reaction. Thus the two movements – the Neo-Hébertists and the Jacobins – which were out to attract popular support, destroyed each other by thwarting each other's plans: victory rested with the moderates.

The moderates' offensive led to an odd coalition between all the right-wing opponents of the system of Year II and of the Jacobins in particular: conservative bourgeois, absolutist and constitutionalist monarchists – in fact all the more or less open supporters of the Ancien Régime. Their purely negative programme encompassed taking revenge on the terrorists, forcing the sans-culottes into obedience and preventing a return to social and political democracy. The two weapons in their armoury were the press and, still more important, the gangs of the *jeunesse dorée*.

The reactionary press, which was able to rely on ample funds from private sources just at the time the Jacobin newspapers were deprived of government subsidies, now held the upper hand. According to a reactionary journalist, the younger Lacretelle of the *Républicain français*, the journalists of the right formed a committee to prepare a common counter-revolutionary strategy, whose aim was to 'drive the Convention back on its tracks after two solid years of anarchist divagations'. The committee included Dussault of the *Correspondance politique*, the Bertin brothers of the *Débats* and Langlois from the *Messager du soir*. On 25 Fructidor (11 September 1794), Fréron started up his *Orateur du peuple* again, while on 1 Brumaire Year III (22 October), Tallien launched his *L'Ami du citoyen*. A stream of pamphlets assailed the Jacobins: *Les Jacobins démasqués* in late Fructidor, and *Les Jacobins hors la loi* in Vendémiaire, for example. The usual weapons employed were abuse and denunciation, calumny and blackmail against the so-called *buveurs de sang*, *anarchistes* and *exclusifs*. The social component of these press campaigns is emphasized by attacks against Cambon, for example, as 'property's Robespierre', or 'the rentier's hangman', and against Lindet who had been set up in Year II in charge of the economy. The *honnêtes gens*, that is, the moneyed notables, were unable to pardon such men for their former actions.

Gangs of youths – *jeunes gens* – constituted from late Fructidor onwards the foremost weapon in the reaction's arsenal. The gangs were organized by the turncoat terrorists, Fréron – indeed, they were often referred to as Fréron's *jeunesse dorée* – Tallien and Merlin de Thionville, and were drawn from the sons of bourgeois, from members of the legal profession, bank-clerks and shop-assistants, and were reinforced by shirkers from active service, deserters and *insoumis*.

We were all, or nearly all, absentee conscripts [wrote one of them, Duval, in his *Souvenirs thermidoriens*]. They considered that we would serve the public interest more usefully in the streets of Paris than in the Sambre-et-Meuse army.

The youths were recognizable by their ringlets and the square collars on their coats; armed with cudgels, they rallied to the slogans 'Down with the Jacobins! Long live the Convention!' or else to their song, the 'Reveil du peuple', whose refrain was 'They shall not escape us'. The *muscadins*, as their opponents called them, had their headquarters in the Café de Chartres in the Palais-Egalité. Here, in late Fructidor, they provoked the first brawls, attacking Jacobins or those with a reputation for Jacobinism. Soon, aided by the complicity of the Committee of General Security and the purged *comités de surveillance*, the *jeunesse dorée* were masters of the streets. The pressure of bourgeois reaction which they brought to bear on the Convention was all the more insidious in that they posed as the defenders of the representatives of the nation. It was not long before they forced the hand of the hesitant majority in the Convention and led it into more extreme positions than it would have wished.

The proscription of the Jacobins and the sans-culottes
(October 1794 to March 1795)

Brumaire Year III was a turning-point of fundamental importance in the political evolution of the Thermidorian period: the Jacobin Society was broken up; the Electoral Club stopped meeting; and the Paris sections fell before the power of the reaction.

The end of the Jacobins was largely consequent on lack of popular support in the last weeks of their existence. Since the people had 'handed in their resignation', as Levasseur put it in his *Mémoires*, the Club was nothing more than 'a powerless lever'. On 25 Vendémiaire Year III (16 October 1794), the Convention crippled Jacobin organization by prohibiting collective petitions and the reciprocal affiliation of the clubs. In Brumaire, defections multiplied, as the attacks of the *jeunes gens* became more forceful. On 19 Brumaire (9 November), they organized their first sortie against the Jacobin Club. Two days later, the Carrier affair gave them a decisive opportunity. The Revolutionary Tribunal had acquitted the 132 inhabitants of Nantes whom Carrier had dispatched to Paris the previous winter, and had put Carrier himself in the dock. On 21 Brumaire (11 November 1794), Romme made a rather reserved speech in the Convention summing up for the prosecution. In order to bring pressure to bear on the Convention, Fréron, the same evening, took his gangs to the rue du Faubourg Saint-Honoré, to the Jacobin Club, urging them 'to surprise the beast in its lair'. The two sides came to blows, and the police had to reestablish order. At once, the government Committees decreed the Club's closure, and the Convention ratified this decision the following day.

The end of the Electoral Club followed soon after. The advance of bourgeois reaction silenced the Left Opposition's virulent anti-Jacobinism, and for a short while following the closure of the Jacobin Club, the Electoral Club became a rallying ground for all the popular opposition. However, ousted from its meeting-place in the Museum section, the Electoral Club disappeared in early Frimaire Year III (late November 1794).

The disappearance of these two centres of popular resistance – the Electoral and Jacobin Clubs – facilitated the conquest of the Paris sections by the moderates. The *jeunesse dorée* had begun participating in sectional assemblies from late Vendémiaire on: one of their chiefs, Jullian, became one of the leaders of the Tuileries section. The Jacobin sections were gradually won over: Piques, Robespierre's old section, seems to have held out until 10 Frimaire (30 November 1794). With the sectional militants out of the way, no popular force remained which could offer resistance to the moderate bourgeoisie and stand out against the reaction, which now trained its fire away from institutions to individuals: the White Terror was in sight.

Anti-terrorism and the extirpation of militant sans-culottes from the sections – which together comprised an embryonic version of the White Terror – progressed throughout the winter of 1794–95, from Frimaire to Ventôse Year III. No longer a question of purges in the true sense of the term, like that which had followed directly after 9 Thermidor – for the terrorist cadres had already been eradicated – the element of personal vengeance now predominated. After having first turned against the main terrorists, the repression widened its scope to include the whole of the former sectional personnel. As it did so, it acquired a social complexion, attacking in the former militants a whole system of republican values. Babeuf, in the *Tribun du peuple* of 28 Frimaire Year III (18 December), complained that the proscription of Jacobinism was being followed up by the proscription of everything sans-culottism stood for.

Anti-terrorism continued its course with the trial of Carrier, who was brought before the Revolutionary Tribunal on 3 Frimaire (23 November 1794) and executed on the 26 (16 December). In his trial, Carrier had denied any responsibility in the Nantes drownings, but had accepted responsibility for the executions by firing squad, basing his defence on the decree against rebels captured in arms. On 18 Frimaire (8 December 1794), following a report by Merlin de Douai, the seventy-five Girondin deputies who had protested against the revolutionary *journées* of 31 May to 2 June, and whom Robespierre had saved from the scaffold, were recalled to the Convention, along with several other deputies who had resigned or been expelled. Seventy-eight deputies in all, some of them moderates like Daunou, others reactionary like Lanjuinais, or even tending towards royalism like Saladin, strengthened the right. Moreover, on 7 Nivôse (27 December), the Convention gave way to the ever-increasing attacks on the former members of the Committees, instituting a commission to examine the case of Barère, Billaud-Varenne, Collot d'Herbois and Vadier. Cambacérès's proposal for an amnesty was in vain. With the business still under consideration, the *jeunesse dorée* gangs intensified their pressure, so as to break the resistance of moderate deputies.

The accompaniment to this anti-terrorism was the systematic rooting out of former sans-culotte militants from the Paris sections. Commissions were set up in at least 37 of the 48 sections to scrutinize the conduct of the former sectional personnel. Two hundred ex-militants, including 152 ex-members of *comités révolutionnaires* were put on trial in eleven sections. Those on trial, deprived of their political rights and condemned to 'public contempt', were as good as social lepers. When the government did not actually encourage the movement of reaction – as it did, for example, by the law of 13 Frimaire (3 December 1794), which insisted on the auditing of the administration of the exceptional revenues of Year II (that is, forced loans and voluntary subscriptions) – it left well alone. The social aspect of this anti-sans-culotte movement was clearly evident in the basic grounds for complaint stressed by sectional reactionaries – that the social and economic system of Year II had wounded the bourgeoisie to the quick. The former hoarding commissioners were one of the main targets: their requisitioning, their forced loans, their confiscations of hoarded goods were nothing less than crimes against property. Not only *hommes de sang*, they were also termed Levellers, for, after all, they had preached 'the redistribution of property'. This movement to root out former sans-culotte militants from the sections was the reaction of a bourgeoisie whose political security, economic interests and social prerogatives had been adversely affected in Year II.

The anti-terrorist fever rose throughout the winter. On 11 Pluviôse (30 January 1795), the Temple section denounced its former *comité révolutionnaire* to the Convention, urging the deputies to 'strike down these tigers!' On 11 Ventôse (1 March), the Montreuil section demanded of the Convention:

What are you waiting for, in order to cleanse the land of these cannibals? Do not their ghastly hue and sunken eyes proclaim enough their foster-parents? Have them arrested. . . . The trenchant blade of the law will deprive them of the air they have too long infected.

The Muscadins were by now harrying their opponents in the streets, in what the *Messager du soir* called 'civic outings'. They looted cafés with a reputation for Jacobinism. They unleashed a war of theatres in Pluviôse, constraining Jacobin actors to make honourable amends, proscribing the singing of the 'Marseillaise', and calling for their own distinctive tune the 'Réveil du peuple contre les terroristes'. Then there was the hunting down of busts of Marat. With the sans-culottes putting up some resistance and with street brawls proliferating, the Committees of government gave way. First, on 21 Pluviôse (9 February), the busts of the martyrs of liberty, Lepeletier and Marat, and David's paintings depicting their deaths, were removed from the hall of the Convention, to the applause of the *jeunesse dorée* packing the public galleries. The remains of Marat and of the young heroes, Bara and Viala, who had died for their country, were then removed from the Pantheon. Exhortations to murder proliferated: 'If you do not punish these men,' proclaimed Rovère in reference to the former terrorists, on 4 Ventôse (22 February), 'then there is no Frenchman alive without the right to slay them.' The next day, Merlin de Douai had the Convention decree that all officials discharged from their office since 10 Thermidor should return to the communes where they had been resident before that date, to remain under the supervision of the local municipality. In some areas, this was tantamount to sending them to their deaths. On 12 Ventôse (2 March), the Convention, giving way at last, decreed the immediate arrest of Barère, Billaud-Varenne, Collot d'Herbois and Vadier. From this time on, the Convention was the prisoner of the *jeunesse dorée* gangs, who were drawing for reinforcements on the increasing numbers of deserters and *insoumis* and also on émigrés who had returned eager to demand the restitution of their sequestrated lands.

In the departments, the White Terror had begun. At Lyons, on 14 Pluviôse Year III (2 February 1795), there occurred the first massacre of imprisoned ex-terrorists. Individual murders had got under way all over the South-east as early as Nivôse. Later, the murder gangs had been organized: the Companies of Jesus, of Jehu and of the Sun, all of which hunted down terrorists, Jacobins and eventually the 'Patriots of '89', especially those who had purchased national lands. The *représentants en mission* either encouraged the formation of these gangs – as Chambon did at Marseille, and the Girondin Isnard in the Var – or else left them well alone. Massacres proliferated. In Lyons, Jacobins, nicknamed 'Mathevons', were murdered daily. In Nîmes there was a prison massacre on 5 Ventôse (23 February 1795). Attacked by the government and denounced by the *représentants*, the Jacobins were unable to offer any resistance.

Impotent in the face of events from now on, the Convention did not intervene. Indeed, with inflation, famine and the freezing cold increasing the people's sufferings and thereby stirring their spirit of revolt, the Convention was too afraid of an aggressive come-back on the part of the Paris sans-culottes not to tolerate the excesses of the ultra-right reaction and the murders of the White Terror.

Old and new rich, Merveilleuses *and* Incroyables

A moral reaction accompanied the social and political reaction. In Year II, the people had been regarded and extolled as the natural custodian of the republican virtues. Now, they were held in contempt. According to Jullian, in his *Souvenirs*, the lower classes were 'doubtless very praiseworthy when they honour their estate by private virtues'; they ought not, however, he maintained, concern themselves with public affairs. Their erstwhile 'simplicity' came to be viewed as coarseness. By Prairial 1794, *sans-culottisme* was considered a sufficient motive for arrest. A new lenience was extended to the sort of extravagance which in Year II had been the object of searing criticism. Republican austerity gave way to a frenzy of hedonism as the propertied classes shook off the shackles they had endured for a short while.

The graces and laughter which the Terror had put to flight have returned to Paris [wrote the *Messager du soir*, the newspaper of the pleasure-seeking bourgeoisie on 2 Frimaire (22 November 1794)]. Our pretty ladies in their blonde wigs are ravishing; the public concerts and the high-society concerts are equally delightful. . . . The *hommes de sang*, the Billauds, the Collots and the enragé gang call this sudden veering of opinion 'the counter-revolution'.

Fashion now proscribed the clothing of the sans-culotte: trousers, overalls and above all, straight hair and the *bonnet rouge*. Now, bourgeois youths distinguished themselves by their sartorial extravagances, which Cambon condemned on 8 Nivôse (28 December 1794): 'Men formerly covered with rags in order that they might seem to be sans-culottes now affect an attire and a language both as ridiculous as one another.'

Dancing became all the rage, public dance-halls opening everywhere, even in the Carmes, which had witnessed the September massacres, and in the old cemetery of Saint-Sulpice. Only those who had lost a relative on the scaffold were admitted to 'Victims' Balls': guests came with Titus haircuts, the nape of their necks bared as if by the executioner, and with a thread of red silk around their necks. *Tutoiement* was proscribed: 'monsieur' and 'madame' reappeared, replacing 'citoyen'.

Fashionable life blossomed anew in the salons. La Cabarrus, Tallien's wife since 6 Nivôse (26 December), whom her admirers dubbed 'Our Lady of Thermidor', had been installed at Cours-la-Reine in a house called her *chaumière*, from which she set the tone for the *Merveilleuses* by launching the fashion of short, semi-transparent Greek dresses. Madame Hamelin and Madame Récamier were soon famous. Financiers, bankers, contractors for the armies and speculators resumed their primacy of place, and nobles, great bourgeois and – soon – returned émigrés revived the urbane traditions of the Ancien Régime. In this way the new bourgeoisie began to be formed from the fusion of the old dominant classes with men made wealthy by speculation on the *assignat*, by national lands and by war-contracting. Theirs was a highly mixed society, in which actresses in vogue such as La Contat played an important part. Many deputies in the Convention, bored with virtue, allowed themselves to be won over, or else bought.

The republican party suffered many defections [wrote Thibaudeau in his *Mémoires*]. Some made concessions, while others sold themselves completely to the royalist cause.

Brazenly displayed luxury, the extravagances of the *Merveilleuses* and the *Incroyables* – that is, a rich and idle minority – antagonized the population as a whole which clung to traditional mores, as well as scandalizing the political minority who had remained faithful to the republican ideal. The contrast between the dreadful distress of the masses and the scandalous wealth of a minority further emphasized the social aspect of the reaction. This was accentuated, and indignation increased as, with winter coming on, famine grew worse.

The religious reaction and the amnesty to the Vendéan

The religious reaction contributed its share to the advance oɪ counter-revolution. The separation of Church and State had actually been established by the decree of the second *jour sans-culottide* Year II (18 September 1794) when, for reasons of economy, Cambon had ended the salaries of sworn priests: thus the Civil Constitution of the Clergy was implicitly repealed and the State completely secularized. The measures against non-sworn priests remained in force, however, and the churches stayed closed. Increasingly as the reaction became stronger, a great many Frenchmen regretted the passing of the old religious ceremonies and the faithful came round to demanding the opening of the churches. The civic religion was too intellectual – as well as now being completely shorn of its formerly democratic and patriotic character – to be able to arouse enthusiasm among the sans-culottes any longer.

The constitutional priests gradually revived their church. Grégoire, for example, insisted on complete freedom of worship in the Loir-et-Cher on 1 Nivôse (21 December). The non-juring priests, who in the department of the Nord were called 'suitcase curés', continued to celebrate 'out-of-sight masses' in secrecy.

Once freedom of worship had been granted to the Vendée rebels – by the Peace of La Jaunaye, 29 Pluviôse Year III (17 February 1795) – then the way was open to an increased measure of liberalization in religious policy. Hence on 3 Ventôse (21 February), after the presentation of a report by Boissy d'Anglas, the Convention authorized worship in buildings which the priests and laity could obtain for themselves. The separation of Church and State was ratified, and the churches preserved for decadal worship. Though worship remained private, all priests could practise their religion provided that they had sworn the 14 August 1792 oath, called the 'small oath', to liberty and equality. Bell-ringing, the wearing of ecclesiastical dress and subsidies to churches from public funds were still strictly forbidden. The constitutional church was immediately reorganized under the leadership of Grégoire, who issued his *Annales de la religion* while the Roman Catholic priests who had sworn the 'small oath' brought out the *Annales religieuses, politiques et littéraires*. The non-jurors expanded clandestine worship more than ever, which brought them into a whole series of conflicts with the constitutional priests.

By re-creating Catholics [wrote Mallet du Pan on 17 March 1795], the Convention is re-creating royalists. . . . There is not a single priest who does not represent to his flock his attachment to this régime as a question of conscience.

The discontent of the Catholics thus persisted. To silence it, the Convention was prepared to envisage the most extreme concessions, not least because the deputies were at the same time at grips with a popular opposition whose size was being increased by the economic crisis.

Concessions to the rebels in Western France were a further component of the political strategy of the Thermidorians. On 9 Thermidor, Charette was still holding the Marais, Sapin the Bocage and

Stofflet the Mauges, though their bands were being harassed by flying columns and their numbers decimated. Brittany and its wooded borders, where the Chouans held sway, had turned into a second Vendée. Having abandoned the Terror and its repressive methods, the Thermidorians were looking to pacify the West by a policy of conciliation. As he took up his command here on 29 Fructidor (15 September 1794), Hoche recalled that the Terror had come to an end. Prisoners were therefore released, and an amnesty proclaimed for *insoumis*. On 12 Frimaire Year III (2 December 1794), this amnesty was extended to rebels who laid down their arms within a month. In January 1795, negotiations were begun with the Royalist leaders. Encouraged by the drift of events, and while still continuing their murders and banditry – 'we are fighting like sheep against tigers', wrote Boursault, the *représentant en mission*, on 4 Pluviôse (23 January 1795) – the rebels compelled the government to accept their terms.

The Peace of La Jaunaye, near Nantes, which was negotiated in particular with Charette, was signed on 29 Pluviôse (17 February 1795). It granted an amnesty to the rebels, restored their property, conceding an indemnity if their property had been sold, even if they had emigrated. The treaty also dispensed the rebels from military service, while allowing them to keep their arms. Finally, freedom of worship was conceded, even to the non-sworn clergy. The Peace of La Prévalaye, near Rennes, on 1 Floréal (20 April 1795), contained the same terms for the Chouans.

The surrender of the Thermidorian to the rebels in the West was ineffective, peace an illusion. The Vendéans and Chouans were able to make preparations at their leisure to resume the struggle. Chouannerie soon spread to neighbouring departments. The Thermidorians were powerless to fight back, since the revival of the popular movement, provoked by the economic crisis, was diverting their attention and their energies, and necessitating the alliance of all branches of the reaction.

2. THE ECONOMIC CRISIS AND THE MONETARY CATASTROPHE

The abandonment of the directed economy was fully commensurate with the strategy adopted by the Thermidorian reaction. The

Convention had only accepted the *maximum* when constrained to do so by popular pressure, and all sectors of the bourgeoisie gauged it to be contrary to their interests. The dismemberment of the Revolutionary Government and the end of the Terror prevented the former's 'coercive force' from imposing its economic policies on producers and traders, who supported free profit and the liberal economy. This inevitably led to first the slackening and then the abolition of the directed economy. Relinquishing the economic constraints, however, could only bring about the collapse of the *assignat* and the rise of inflation, which in turn helped to produce popular distress. Thus the social character of the Thermidorian reaction was emphasized yet again.

The return to economic freedom (*August to December 1794*)

The general *maximum* on essential foodstuffs which had been proclaimed on 29 September 1793 had only functioned properly – in regard to non-military provisioning at least – for grain. The Committee of Public Safety had connived at the non-enforcement of the *maximum* on other foodstuffs, though it did not allow it to be flouted publicly. Clandestine trading had started up, but while the Terror lasted prices rose only slightly. 9 Thermidor changed all this. On 21 Fructidor Year II (7 September 1794), the Convention prolonged the *maximum* on grain and flour of 11 September 1793 and the general *maximum* of 29 September for the whole of Year III. Yet once repression had been abandoned, the rise in prices became more pronounced and the clandestine market made great progress. Transactions gradually became unregulated. 'No one observes the *maximum* in the markets,' observed a police report as early as 20 Vendémiaire Year III (11 October 1794). 'Everything is up for sale by free bargaining.'

The system whereby markets were supplied with grain by means of requisitioning carried out at district level, established by the decree of 11 September 1793, fell into disorder. Because the fear of being treated as suspects no longer acted as a restraining influence on farmers, they only handed over their grain with ill will and were beginning to make secret sales. The peasants found supporters in the Convention, who obtained a few concessions for them in the decree of 19 Brumaire (9 November 1794), which in particular stipulated that requisitions which were not supplied should no longer entail the confiscation of the required quota. This gave a great boost to the resistance of the peasants, and the supplying of the towns became proportionately more difficult. Thus, once the Revolutionary Government had been dismembered and the Terror abandoned, it proved impossible to insist on the enforcement of requisitioning and the observance of price-fixing.

The nationalization of several important sectors of the economy – war manufactures, internal transport and external trade – provoked just as many difficulties. Basically, it could only work within the framework provided by the general *maximum*. The system continued to function after Thermidor, still under the general supervision of Lindet who, though he retired from the Committee of Public Safety on 15 Vendémiaire (6 October 1794), was appointed President of the Committee of Commerce, Agriculture and the Arts.

The nationalization of the war industries had provoked numerous powerful oppositional movements. Artisans and industrialists, who only grudgingly endured state control and the schedule of prices laid down by the *maximum*, were even more embittered by seeing national industries deprive them of work. The Committee of Public Safety made an initial concession to these groups by returning a certain number of factories to private enterprise: the Toulouse foundry, for example, in Fructidor, and the Maubeuge one in Frimaire. Furthermore, the Committee gradually dismantled the great arms factory in Paris, first reducing it to repair work, then dispersing the workers into departmental workshops because they feared political opposition from them. By Pluviôse, there remained only a thousand workers in Paris, on piece-work rates.

The nationalization of foreign trade was prejudicial to the interests of the shipping magnates, the businessmen and the financiers, for whom large-scale maritime trade and speculation in foreign exchange comprised an essential source of profit. In his report on the state of the Republic on the fourth *jour sans-culottide* Year II (20 September 1794), Lindet admitted that it was necessary to revive foreign trade. The harvest was bad, dearth was forecast for the spring. The Committee of Public Safety therefore busied itself with procuring grain by authorizing businessmen and neutrals to import supplies freely. The Convention entered on a policy of concessions. On 26 Vendémiaire (17 October), a decree authorized manufacturers to import freely the products required by their workshops. On 6 Frimaire (26 November), imports of non-prohibited merchan-

dise became free. Freedom to import could not, however, be reconciled with the functioning of the *maximum*, especially after 25
Brumaire (15 November), when the deputies permitted free trade
with neutrals in French ports.

The offensive against the directed economy and the *maximum*
became more general towards the end of the autumn. On 14
Brumaire Year III (4 November 1794), the Convention demanded
a report on the 'disadvantages of the *maximum*'. The attack was
now aimed especially against the administration of the bureaucracy
dealing with the national economy which, in the absence of any
statistical organization, was not managing to get an exact idea of
needs and resources. The fact that this department was staffed by
supporters of the régime of Year II added an extra pungency to the
criticisms. Beyond this department, it was the very principle of the
directed economy which was the target, and in particular the supplying of the armies. For this latter task, the financiers were wanting to
return to former practices, and to compel the State to rely on the
services of suppliers and finance companies, which would thus be
given supplementary trading and huge fortunes. The campaign of
the supporters of economic freedom was ultimately successful: on
19 Frimaire (9 December), a report submitted to the Committee
of Commerce, from which Lindet was soon ousted, concluded in
favour of the abolition of the *maximum*.

The decree of 4 Nivôse (24 December 1794) suppressed the
maximum and all trade controls; it allowed the traffic in grain to
operate completely freely within the Republic; and it empowered
the Commission of Commerce and Provisions to retain a pre-
emptive right to channel scanty grain supplies towards the armies,
though only at current market prices. A terrible crisis ensued.

The collapse of the assignat *and its consequences*

The collapse of the *assignat* was the immediate consequence of the
abandonment of the *maximum*. Prices soared, and speculation on
essential foodstuffs progressed by leaps and bounds. Paper money
lost all its value, exchange collapsed. The *assignat*, which had
climbed back to 50 per cent of its nominal value in December 1792,
had fallen to 31 per cent in Thermidor Year II (July 1794), and the
retreat from the *maximum* made it drop to 20 per cent in Frimaire
Year III (December 1794); by Germinal (April 1795) it was 8 per

cent, and by Thermidor (July) only 3 per cent. The rise in prices doomed the State to inflation, the scale of which was amplified by the fact that taxes were not coming in in their full proportions, or else in devalued *assignats*. Continuous issues augmented the volume of *assignats*, which in December 1794 had reached the figure of 10 billion *livres*, 8 billions of which were in circulation. From Pluviôse to Prairial (January to May 1795), 7 billion *livres* were issued, and the amount in circulation rose to 11 billions. Peasants and tradesmen refused *assignats*, accepting only metal currency. This in turn increased depreciation: thus while from November 1794 to May 1795 the volume of *assignats* in circulation increased by 42·5 per cent, the value of the *assignat* fell by 68 per cent, 100 *livres* in paper money falling from a metal currency equivalent of 24 *livres* to an equivalent of 7·5 *livres*.

The rise in the prices of essential foodstuffs varied from one department to the next. In general terms, however, it was steeper than we might suppose from the depreciation of paper money in relation to metal currency. In March to April 1795, the index of the *assignat* – working on 1790 levels – stood at 581, while the general price index had reached 758, and the price index for foodstuffs alone 819.

Food scarcity further increased the disastrous consequences of the rise in prices. Although requisitioning had been prolonged until 1 Messidor (19 June 1795), the peasants were no longer bringing their stocks to the markets, since they feared being paid in *assignats*. They had a profitable alternative, also, for they were authorized to sell directly either to the agents of the commission which ensured army supplies, or else to the businessmen who were provisioning the propertied classes. Coercive measures were resorted to: district administrations installed National Guard detachments in the villages until the grain required had been delivered. As spring advanced, however, the deficiency of the previous year's harvest rendered these measures futile. The government's desire to initiate purchases abroad was to no avail, since the penury of the treasury obliged it – apart from the exceptional cases of Paris and the armies – to rely on private individuals' capital. This helped to make the predominance of the big commercial bourgeoisie even more pronounced. Consignments from abroad only started to get through in May 1795. Yet in the Midi, which was always dependent on imports of grain, the situation had been calamitous since the beginning of the winter, while even Orléans, which opened on to the grain-producing Beauce region, was in the same position from early spring. Bread rations diminished as prices rose: in Verdun, for example, the worker's ration of one pound of bread, as compared with three-quarters of a pound for the remainder of the population, was reduced by half at the beginning of spring 1795, while the price of bread rose to 20 *sous* per pound. A great many municipalities returned to trade controls, mixing grains together, rationing bread hand-outs and fixing the price of bread below cost-price. They failed, however, to relieve the sufferings of the popular classes, which were made even more difficult to endure by the contrast they provided with the flaunted extravagance of the new rich.

The social consequences of the collapse of the *assignat* did in fact vary from one social group to the next. Thus whereas the popular classes were swamped by despair, the extremely harsh winter of Year III adding still more to their misfortune, and whereas the Ancien Régime bourgeoisie which lived off its income from government bonds, and creditors, who were reimbursed in *assignats*, were ruined, debtors and speculators grew wealthy with great rapidity. Their trafficking in national lands and their war-contracting had raised these men to among the highest ranks in society. True adventurers of the new bourgeois stamp, they infused fresh blood into the old bourgeoisie, and from their number were drawn many of the businessmen who initiated capitalist production in the Directorial and Napoleonic periods.

Inflation completed the social revolution. Prices of foodstuffs and fuel in Paris experienced a staggering rise, under the twofold impetus provided by the shortage of commodities and the distrust of the *assignat*. A pound of beef, assessed in the Halles at 34 *sous* on 6 Nivôse (26 December 1794), had reached 7 *livres* 10 *sous* by 12 Germinal (1 April 1795). The Parisian cost of living index, on the base of 100 for 1790, rose from 580 in January 1795 to 720 in March and to 900 in April. Fluctuations in salaries and revenues diversified the social consequences of the rise in prices. The big business and industrial bourgeoisie – the inflation's new rich – obtained their supplies on the open market, and were hardly affected. The mass of the Paris population, however – wage-earners and lower-grade clerks, artisans and shopkeepers, small rentiers – saw their purchasing power diminish with each advance prices made. Unemployment made great strides because of the shortage of raw materials and the closure of the armament workshops, the number of workers in which was reduced from 5,400 to 1,146. Despair weighed crushingly on the popular classes, whom death was decimating. The cold increased the blighting consequences of malnutrition. The winter of Year III experienced temperatures among the lowest in the entire eighteenth century: minus ten degrees at the start of 1795, and minus fifteen on 23 January. The death rate shot up. At the end of the winter, the bread and meat rations distributed by the *agence des subsistances* which formed the basis of the diet of the popular classes in Paris, were drastically cut. Grain reserves to keep Paris fed had gradually dwindled to next to nothing, as a result of insufficient requisitioning and lack of available transport. On 25 Ventôse (15 March), the bread ration – 'the poor man's sole standby' – was cut back to one pound, except for manual workers, who received one and a half pounds. Furthermore, in a great many sections, such as Jardin-des-Plantes, the bakers were unable to provide enough bread for all the ration cards. In the Gravilliers section, on 7 Germinal (27 March), the ration stood at half a pound, while in the Fidélité section on 10 Germinal (30 March), it was a mere quarter pound.

In these first days of Germinal Year III, popular despair changed to anger, and then to revolt. On 29 Ventôse (10 March), the Committee of Public Safety wrote: 'We may well go without bread one day, but we shall have no control over the consequences.' The Committee promulgated a series of measures appropriate to the emergency, but they had little effect. On 7 Germinal (27 March), for example, when it prescribed the distribution of six ounces of rice to every half pound of bread, it completely overlooked the fact that a large proportion of housewives could not cook it, because they lacked fuel. Gnawed by hunger, the sans-culottes started to get under way again. Back on 8 Nivôse (28 December 1794), a police report had noted the slow rise of popular anger: 'The indigent class is causing alarm in those honest folk who fear the consequences of this excessive dearness.' From the end of Ventôse, conflict seemed inevitable. The Committees themselves prepared for it by increasing the numbers of arrests of Jacobins and sans-culottes, by arming *bons citoyens* and by allowing a completely free hand to the *jeunesse dorée*. Now that they were confronted with the popular movement, which dearth had relaunched into activity, all the forces of bourgeois reaction were closing their ranks.

3. THE LAST POPULAR INSURRECTIONS (GERMINAL AND PRAIRIAL YEAR III)

During the winter of Year III, with the *assignat* in a state of collapse and with the economic crisis forcing the masses towards despair, two trends of opinion clashed in a frontal encounter: first, there was the advance of the reaction and the establishment of the régime of *honnêtes gens*; then there were the first attempts to give political direction and aims to the hunger riot which was looming.

The rise of the popular opposition in Paris (winter 1794 to 1795)

The popular opposition took its bearings from the grass-root organizations which had been able to escape the Thermidorian repression. The 'Société des Défenseurs des droits de l'homme', reinforced by the Jacobins who had obtained admission following the closure of their club, formed the core of an enthusiastic sans-culotte opposition in the Faubourg Saint-Antoine, in particular in the Montreuil and Quinze-Vingts sections. In the Gravilliers sections, the 'Société des Amis de la liberté et de l'humanité', which comprised, according to an opponent, 'almost entirely workmen and men with little education', ensured the patriot party the majority in the sectional general assembly. The sans-culottes still held power besides this in the Bondy, Lombards and Museum sections.

Slowly, all the opponents of the Thermidorian reaction came together. On 28 Frimaire (18 December 1794), Babeuf started up a second campaign. He now regretted having been one of the first to inveigh against the 'Robespierre system', and maintained that only two parties were now confronting each other, the *peuple doré* and the *peuple sans-culotte*. He called the latter to insurrection in the 9 Pluviôse (28 January 1795) edition of his *Tribun du peuple*, which led to his arrest. Lebois too in *L'Ami du peuple* preached social war against the *million doré*. The former Jacobins, for their part, were now reconciled with Babeuf since he had renounced his anti-terrorism, and were in agreement with him over the demand for the enforcement of the democratic Constitution of 1793, which was threatened by a projected revision.

The popular militants had recourse to clandestine activity after the alarmed government Committees had resorted to repression in Pluviôse. The 'Société des Défenseurs des droits de l'homme' was dissolved on 20 Pluviôse (8 February 1795). A number of the government's opponents, including Babeuf, were arrested, and the *honnêtes gens* seized control of those sections which till then had reputedly been in favour of the popular movement, most notably the Museum section. The former sectional militants regrouped in secrecy, and throughout Ventôse denunciations of secret plots proliferated. At the end of this month, a secret system of subscriptions enabled the patriots to launch a campaign of posters and anonymous tracts of an insurrectionary nature. On 22 Ventôse (12 March), the appeal *Peuple, réveille-toi, il est temps* was posted in huge numbers in the faubourgs. On 3 Germinal (23 March), it was the turn of the *Tocsin national*, and then on 5 Germinal, of the *Adresse à la Convention et au peuple*. The worsening of the shortage brought the popular agitation to its highest pitch. A further complicating factor superimposed over the popular agitation was the political crisis which broke out in the Convention.

The journées of Germinal Year III (April 1795)

The political crisis at the beginning of Germinal saw the Thermidorian majority of the Convention at loggerheads with the 'Crest', the Montagnard minority, whom the progress of the reaction had temporarily strengthened. The unyielding antagonism between the two sides crystallized around two points. Firstly, the Constitution of 1793, which Fréron represented as the 'work of a few scoundrels', and which the Thermidorian majority was intending to deck out with organic laws, was considered by the 'Crest' as the very safeguard of the French people. The second focal point of opposition was the proposed arraignment of the 'Four' – Barère, Billaud-Varenne, Collot d'Herbois and Vadier – which the Convention began to debate on 2 Germinal (22 March). The acrimonious debate inflamed popular opinion, but exasperated bourgeois opinion. The Convention settled matters by two decrees: on 9 Germinal (29 March), it set aside all ideas of an amnesty, and determined to proceed to the indictment of the 'Four'; then, on 12 Germinal (1 April), it appointed a committee with instructions to prepare the organic laws.

By this date, the mobilization of the popular forces had already been accomplished. Gatherings at the doors of bakers' shops had been leading to riots since the end of Ventôse. On 27 Ventôse (17 March), a crowd from the Faubourgs Saint-Marceau and Saint-Jacques came before the Convention, and told the deputies: 'We have no bread and are on the verge of regretting all the sacrifices we have made for the Revolution.' On 21 Germinal, the three sections from the Faubourg Saint-Antoine appeared in turn, demanding the implementation of the Constitution of 1793, measures against the shortage, going on to attack the enemies of the people as 'slaves of wealth'. Street brawls proliferated between exasperated sans-culottes and groups of *jeunesse dorée*. The government went ahead with the preparations which would enable it to stand an insurrection. On 1 Germinal (21 March), Sieyès had obtained the passing of a police law decreeing the death penalty for all those who moved against the Convention in a concerted manner and uttering seditious slogans. On 2 Germinal (22 March), the Committees had one hundred rifles per section distributed to citizens on whom they could count. The disturbances worsened on 7 Germinal (27 March) in the Gravilliers section, and lasted two days. On 10 Germinal (30 March), the sectional assemblies were in a ferment, the sans-culottes emerging victorious in ten of them. The following day, the Quinze-Vingts section appeared at the bar of the Convention again, and set out a truly popular programme. The militants were particularly critical of what had happened since 9 Thermidor and of the abolition of the maximum, and demanded an elected Paris municipality, the reopening of the clubs, and the implementation of the Constitution: 'We are on our feet to support the Republic and Liberty!' they concluded. This was the signal for the popular uprising.

The *journée* of 12 Germinal Year III (1 April 1795) highlighted the degree of disorganization to which the popular movement had been reduced by the loss of its cadres in the repression. It was less an insurrection than a demonstration, the disorderly gathering of an unarmed crowd which, after invading the Convention, was satisfied with merely declaring its demands for the enforcement of the Constitution of 1793 and the enactment of measures against the shortage. The National Guard from the rich neighbourhoods dispersed the demonstrators without undue trouble. The *journée* failed because it had neither leaders nor a clear plan of action. The hours during which the sans-culottes were masters of the Convention were wasted in noisy and empty speechifying. Although the agitation continued the following day – notably in the Quinze-Vingts section in the Faubourg Saint-Antoine – the Convention decreed a state of siege and order was swiftly reestablished.

It was not long before the political consequences of the popular failure were clear. The Right had triumphed: 'This day,' declared André Dumont, one of its leaders, 'must be completed.' On the night of 12–13 Germinal, the Convention decreed the deportation of the 'Four' to Guiana without trial. The Left was again decimated by the arrest of eight Montagnards, including Amar and Duhem, who were sent forthwith to the fortress of Ham, and by the arrest some days later of eight other deputies including Cambon. On 17 Floréal (6 May), Fouquier-Tinville was condemned to death along with fourteen jurymen from the old Revolutionary Tribunal. The problem of the Constitution now came under consideration. Till that time, the Constitution of 1793 had not been compromised by the Left's support for it, and the political debates had merely focused on how it was to be hedged round by organic laws. The Constitution itself came under fire, however, from the République section which on 25 Floréal (14 May) criticized it as 'a Constitution of decemvirs, dictated by fear, and accepted in an atmosphere of fear'. The course of the reaction, combining at this time with the transformation of the shortage into famine, relaunched the popular movement.

Prairial Year III (May 1795)

The repression of the Germinal uprising and the persecution of the sectional militants had not been able to crush the Parisian popular movement, and had on the contrary helped to arouse the spirit of revolt of the sans-culotterie. On 21 Germinal (10 April), in a law which was tantamount to a law of suspects against all those who had participated in the system of Year II, the Convention had decreed the disarming of 'men known in their sections to have participated in the horrors perpetrated under the tyranny'. In the Midi, the disarmament of the former terrorists encouraged the murderers of the White Terror, which reached its apogee in Floréal and Prairial. Although the number of those disarmed in Paris seems to have been fairly limited – about 1,600 from all the sections – the disarming struck against the best of the militants of Year II, who felt it, as one of them put it, 'like a political branding, a kind of physical wound'. Since bearing arms was one of the most deeply ingrained values in the popular ideology of equality, disarmament implied exclusion from the community of free men and the loss of civil rights. It exacerbated the spirit of revolt among the popular militants.

The famine of Floréal was driving the masses, however, towards despair. As spring advanced, the system of supplies grew worse. In Paris, stocks were exhausted, and the authorities were utterly dependent on the daily arrivals of grain. The daily ration of a quarter pound, which was the lowest level before Germinal, became standard measure. Furthermore, the distribution was badly organized, and housewives often waited in vain outside bakers' doors. Disturbances swept through France: in Normandy and along the Seine valley, famished rioters attacked grain convoys destined for the capital. Price-rises continued. At the same time, the breakdown in the haulage system – particularly acute for fuel consignments – led to increased unemployment. The famine of Floréal and Prairial Year III had catastrophic effects on a population which had already been long under-nourished and which inflation had rendered completely penniless. This was a truly social famine, which hit the popular classes above all, since the government refused to establish a general system of rationing, and since the workings of the open market meant that the rich could rely on their wealth to prevent them suffering any real hardship. Men and women starved to death in the streets, the death rate soared, suicides proliferated.

One only meets in the streets [wrote the reactionary *Messager du soir* on 8 Floréal (27 April)] pallid and emaciated countenances, on which are depicted pain, weariness, hunger and distress.

The propertied classes' feelings of compassion were given an added twist by their fear of a famine which would prove a threat to property by provoking looting.

Popular anger was gradually being diluted with despair. Famine led to a widespread reappraisal of the régime of Year II:

When Robespierre was in power, blood flowed and no one went without bread [ran a terrorist remark often reported by the police]. Today, blood no longer flows and there is a shortage; therefore, blood must flow if we are to have bread.

The Constitution of 1793 seemed more than ever a promised land:

For the people [wrote Levasseur of the Sarthe in his *Mémoires*], all hopes were tied up with this promise of democracy.

Sectional agitation restarted in Floréal. On the 10th (29 April), the Montreuil section declared itself *en permanence*, and invited other sections to follow its lead, in order to debate the problem of food supplies. On 11 Floréal (30 April), a riot broke out in the Bonnet-de-la-Liberté section. Incendiary pamphlets and placards soon appeared. The government became alarmed and concentrated heavy forces around Paris, though to prevent the popular agitation from spreading it took especial care not to allow them to enter the capital. The agitation reached its zenith in the sectional assemblies on 30 Floréal (19 May). That evening the pamphlet, *Insurrection du peuple pour obtenir du pain et reconquérir ses droits*, gave the signal for the popular rising and decided on its rallying slogan: 'Bread and the Constitution of 1793!'

At five o'clock on the morning of 1 Prairial Year III, the tocsin rang out in the Faubourgs Saint-Antoine and Saint-Marceau. Soon the call to arms was resounding in all the sections of Eastern Paris, while women ran through streets and workshops and men took up their arms. Towards ten o'clock, outstripping the speed of the National Guard's mobilization, the first crowds of women marched, with drums beating, on the Convention. In the early afternoon, the battalions of the Faubourg Saint-Antoine moved off in turn, and were reinforced *en route* by battalions from other sections. At the same time, a crowd of women, aided by a few men, were attempting to invade the hall of the Convention. When, at about three o'clock, the battalions appeared on the nearby Carrousel bridge, the pressure became irresistible, the Convention was overrun, and the deputy Féraud was murdered and his head fixed on the end of a pike. A long riot broke out, in the midst of which a gunner, Duval, managed to read aloud the programme of the uprising, the *Insurrection du peuple*. The rebels did nothing, however, to secure the Committees of government, who prepared the counter-attack at their leisure, waiting, incidentally, for the Montagnard deputies to compromise themselves with the uprising. About seven in the evening, debates restarted in the hall of the Convention: Duroy and Romme obtained decrees setting up the sections *en permanence* and freeing gaoled patriots, Soubrany managing to have a decree passed dismissing the

Committee of General Security and replacing it by a provisional commission. By this time it was half past eleven at night. The National Guard from the western sections of Paris was now launched against the hall, and drove back the rebels, who soon took to flight. The fourteen Montagnard deputies who had been compromised assisting the rebels were put under arrest.

On 2 Prairial Year III (21 May 1795), the insurrection formed up again in the Faubourg Saint-Antoine with illegal assemblies being held in those sections where the popular movement held sway. A crowd seized the Maison Commune and at about three in the afternoon the faubourg's battalions marched on the Convention once again. The gendarmerie came over to their side. As on 2 June 1793, the rebels' gunners, at seven in the evening, trained their cannons on the Assembly, with fuses lit. The gunners from the moderate sections now came over to the rebels. Legendre urged deputies to accept their death stoically on the benches of the Convention. However, instead of routing the forces loyal to the Convention, the rebels wavered, and when ten deputies dispatched by the Committees of government came out to negotiate, they allowed themselves to be tricked by a phoney 'fraternization'. A deputation from their number was admitted to the bar of the Convention, where they reiterated menacingly the sans-culottes' demands for bread and for the Constitution of 1793. The Convention's President gave the official embrace, and the rebel battalions retraced their steps to their sections. The popular movement had let slip its final opportunity. 'Our attempt has failed,' said one rebel. 'The people has been taken in by speeches.'

The military reduction of the Faubourg Saint-Antoine was prepared as swiftly after the *journées* as the 3 Prairial (22 May). Three thousand cavalry, reinforced the following day by numerous detachments, entered Paris. These, together with the *bons citoyens* who were mobilized by word of mouth, meant that the government had about 20,000 men at its disposal. Menou was appointed commanding general of the government's forces. 'Paris resembles a camp,' wrote the *Journal des Hommes libres*. The exhausted Faubourg was sleeping quietly while the government troops surrounded it during the night. On the morning of 4 Prairial, the *jeunesse dorée* gangs invaded the Faubourg, but were obliged to beat a rather inglorious retreat. The battalions of the three sections were soon on their feet, with their cannons trained on the city, and supported by women who were, according to the report of a police informer, 'crowded together in mobs on every corner'. 'Bread is the material basis of their insurrection,' the report continued, 'but the Constitution of 1793 is the moving spirit. In general they have a doleful appearance.' The rebels, leaderless and virtually without cadres, had only their despair to fall back on. At about four o'clock in the afternoon, the troops received the order to advance. The Faubourg was called upon to hand over its arms, and it immediately capitulated without putting up a fight. By eight o'clock it was all over.

The repression was organized at once, and evolved on two levels, in the tribunals and in the sections. By 4 Prairial, the Committee of General Security was announcing that the prisons were full.

The judicial repression was directed by a Military Commission which the Convention set up on 4 Prairial. It passed sentence on 149 men, freeing 73, but sentencing 36 to death, 18 to imprisonment, 12 to deportation, and 7 to be put in irons. Notable among those sentenced to death were 18 of the 23 gendarmes who had gone over to the rebels; 5 of the insurrection's leaders, including the courageous and strong-minded Duval and Delorme – the latter captain of artillery in the Popincourt section; and 6 of the Montagnard deputies who had been compromised by their support for the rising. This latter group stabbed themselves as they left the court-room: Duquesnoy, Goujon and Romme fell down dead, while Bourbotte, Duroy and Soubrany were finished off by the guillotine. These men came to be known as the 'martyrs of Prairial'.

Because of its long-term consequences, the sectional repression was even more important than the judicial repression. On 4 Prairial, the Convention decreed the disarming and, if necessary, the arrest of *mauvais citoyens* by the sections themselves. The vast sectional purge which ensued took place between 5 and 13 Prairial, and involved about 1,200 arrests and 1,700 disarmings. The victims were mainly the Prairial rebels and the militant sans-culottes of Year II, even if they were unconnected with the insurrections of Year III. They also included former terrorists and Jacobins. The social and psychological effect of the repression was considerable, while the prolonged incarceration of the men meant destitution for a good many families. In wider terms, this repression destroyed the two forces by which the Thermidorian régime had felt itself temporarily threatened.

The Prairial *journées* were crucial. The popular movement, in a state of exhaustion and disorganization, with its leaders and cadres removed by the repression, had seen ranged against it in a monolithic block the entire range of the bourgeoisie from republicans to supporters of the Ancien Régime, backed moreover by the army. In these Prairial *journées*, the Revolution's mainspring was smashed: the Revolution was at an end.

In the final analysis, the failure of the popular insurrections of Germinal and Prairial Year III proved the most dramatic episode in the conflict of classes within what had formerly been the Third Estate. Because the French bourgeoisie held the whip hand, there was no question of the popular movement being able to achieve its own ends. Just as the antagonisms between the Revolutionary Government and the popular movement had destroyed the régime of Year II, so the deep-rooted opposition between the bourgeois revolution and the popular movement doomed the latter to failure. This process was facilitated by the fact that the internal contradictions of the movement were bearing it towards disintegration.

The sans-culotterie did not form a class, nor was the popular movement a class party. Artisans and shopkeepers, *compagnons* and day-labourers joined with a minority of bourgeois to form a coalition which unleashed an irresistible force against the aristocracy. Antagonisms within the coalition emerged, however, between artisans and shopkeepers on the one hand, who lived off the profits they derived from their ownership of the means of production, and *compagnons* and day-labourers on the other hand, who merely received wages. The exigencies of the revolutionary struggle had cemented the unity of the sans-culotterie, and thrust into the background those conflicts of interests which set its component parts at loggerheads with one another. There was no chance, however, of these conflicts being dissolved altogether. Certain aspects of the differing social attitudes of the groups made the interplay of antagonistic forces even more complicated. The contradictions within the ranks of the sans-culotterie were not simply those apparent between property owners and producers on the one hand, and wage-earners on the other. We find among the latter group that artists and members of the clerical and teaching professions, because of their way of life, regarded themselves as bourgeois, and had no intention of being taken for *bas peuple*, even if they espoused their cause.

448 Revolutionary Government and the Popular Movement

Their heterogeneous social composition, then, produced a lack of class-consciousness among the sans-culottes. Even though they were united in their general hostility towards nascent capitalism, the motives behind their attitudes often diverged. The artisan was afraid of seeing himself reduced to the level of a wage-earner, while the *compagnon* detested the hoarder who made life dearer for him. Though they were wage-earners, the *compagnons* were not at all aware of themselves as a distinct social entity, since capitalist concentration had not yet awoken a sense of class solidarity in them, and their attitudes were more conditioned by their artisan masters. One cannot fail to note, however, a certain consciousness among the wage-earning sans-culottes of their unity, emphasized by the manual nature of their jobs, their position in the process of production, and also by the way they dressed and their whole way of life. This also came out in their lack of education, which created among the ranks of the people a feeling of inferiority and sometimes of powerlessness. Thus when the sans-culotte movement started to lose contact with the *hommes à talent* from the Jacobin middle bourgeoisie, it was lost.

Despite a few hesitant attempts at coordination, the Paris sans-culottes were always lacking an effective weapon of political combat: a disciplined party, based on recruitment along class lines and on drastic purges. Though a great many militants endeavoured to bring discipline into the popular movement, an equally great number had no sense whatever of the need for social and political discipline. The social and economic conditions of the era precluded the masses themselves having any developed political sense apart from their hatred of the aristocracy: they waited confusedly for the Revolution's benefits to accrue to them. Thus they demanded the maximum so as to maintain their standard of living, and then broke with the Revolutionary Government when it geared the directed economy round the policies of national defence, without realizing that the fall of the Revolutionary Government would entail the destruction of the sans-culottes.

The disintegration of the popular movement was part and parcel of the dialectical advance of history. Five years of continual revolutionary struggles had made the movement lose, in the long run, its enthusiasm and its bite; the constant deferring of the 'Great Hope' gradually produced the demobilization of the masses. 'The people is growing weary,' Robespierre had noted, and the sans-culottes of the Faubourgs Saint-Marceau and Saint-Jacques had stated on 27

Ventôse Year III (17 March 1795): 'We are on the verge of regretting all the sacrifices we have made for the revolution.' Month after month, the war effort had weakened the sans-culotterie to the point of exhaustion by constantly draining off manpower. The levies, moreover, were borne most by the youngest and the most combative sans-culottes, who would also have been the most aware and the most enthusiastic, regarding the defence of their new country as their first revolutionary duty. Even in Year II, a considerable proportion of the battalions of the Paris sections were men aged fifty or even sixty years old. The irremediable ageing effect this produced on the popular movement severely inhibited the fighting flair of the masses.

It would be wrong, however, to draw up a purely negative balance-sheet of the popular movement so effectively scuttled by the repression of Prairial Year III. Since July 1789, and more particularly since 10 August 1792, it had helped to promote historical advance by the decisive assistance it had lent to the bourgeois revolution. From 1789 to Year III, the Paris sans-culotterie had comprised the key component in the forces fighting for the Revolution and for national defence. The popular movement enabled the Revolutionary Government to be established, and thus counter-revolution to be defeated at home, and the coalition abroad. Its victory during the summer of 1793 had led to the Terror – whose grim blows had completed the destruction of the old society – becoming the central plank in the programme of the Revolutionary Government. Thermidor had brought a general reaction in its train; yet by that date, the Terror had already paved the way for the establishment of new social relationships in French society.

By removing the people from the political stage for long afterwards, and by destroying the popular hope for an egalitarian social democracy, the defeat of the popular movement in Prairial Year III allowed the Thermidorians and then the Directorials to revive the link with 'Eighty-nine' and the work of the Constituent Assembly. The foundations of economic freedom and the property franchise had been regained, and on them was starting to be erected the system of the reign of the notables.

Part Three

'A Country Governed by Landowners': Bourgeois Republic and Social Consolidation

1795–1799

Continuity with 'Eighty-nine' was reestablished in 'Ninety-five'; Year III of the Republic linked up with Year I of Liberty. The sans-culotterie and the popular movement, decisive factors in political and social struggles since 1789 and especially since 10 August 1792, were now removed from the stage. For a short while, the exigencies of the war against the aristocracy, internal counter-revolution and the Coalition outside France had compelled the Montagne to take on the sans-culottes as their allies, obliging them moreover to allow an attempt at a social democracy. The propertied classes long kept the terrified recollection of this endeavour, which had cut back on their freedom, limited their profits, and which had actually made those lesser than themselves their political masters. Toughened by the experience, and with their class-consciousness strengthened, the bourgeoisie was now determined to prevent at all costs the revival of the experiment of Year II. They organized power in such a way that they were its sole beneficiaries. The hegemony of the notables was restored: once again, the character of the nation was being determined within the narrow confines of the bourgeois property franchise.

In his preamble to the draft of the new Constitution, 5 Messidor Year III (23 June 1795), Boissy d'Anglas lucidly expounded the tenets of the new order:

Finally, you must guarantee the property of the wealthy.... Civil equality is the sum total of what a rational man may demand. ... Absolute equality is a chimera: its existence would posit a complete equality in intelligence, virtue, physical strength, education and fortune in all men.

In a speech which reveals remarkable continuity between the Girondins and the Thermidorians, Vergniaud had before used exactly the same argument, on 13 March 1793:

For man in society, any equality must necessarily be an equality of rights. It can no more be an equality of wealth than an equality of height, strength, intelligence, enterprise, industry or work.

We must be ruled by the best citizens [Boissy d'Anglas continued]. The best are the most learned and the most concerned in the keeping of the laws. Now, with very few exceptions, you will find such men only amongst those who own some property, and are thus attached to the land in which it lies, to the laws which protect it and to the public order which maintains it; men who owe to their property and to the affluence that it affords, the education which has fitted them to discuss widely and equitably the advantages and disadvantages of the laws which determine the fate of their country. . . . A country governed by landowners is in the social order; a land where non-landowners govern is in the state of nature.

Economic freedom, Boissy d'Anglas went on to say, is necessarily linked to property rights:

If you grant unreserved political rights to men without property, and if these men ever find themselves seated among the legislators, then they will rouse up agitations, or allow them to be roused up, without fearing their consequences; they will establish, or allow to be established, harmful taxes on commerce and agriculture; for they will not have felt, nor feared nor foreseen their dangerous consequences. In the end, they will precipitate us into the violent convulsions from which we have barely emerged.

This was tantamount to condemning irremediably the experiment of Year II and precluding any hope on the part of the popular classes. Thus the entente between Thermidorians and Constitutional monarchists, fully in line with the traditions of 'Eighty-nine', bore witness to the developing framework of a nation of 'notables', that is, of all property owners who were at least fairly well-off. 'The man without property,' Boissy d'Anglas had made plain, 'needs a constant effort of virtue to involve himself in a social order which preserves nothing for him.'

The bourgeoisie wanted jealously to reserve for themselves this right attaching to property. They now invoked the requirements of the liberal economy to deny the non-propertied classes – especially the small peasantry – access to property which Montagnard legislation had temporarily facilitated. The same requirements were stressed by Lozeau, deputy for the Charente-Inférieure, as early as 22 Fructidor Year II (8 September 1794), when he brought before the Convention his report 'on the material impossibility of transforming all Frenchmen into landed proprietors, and on the sorry consequences which would moreover flow from such a transformation'. It was sheer fantasy, Lozeau upheld, to want to suppress indigence by distributions of land; indeed the Republic would have nothing to be pleased about even were it to be allowed that the transformation of all peasants into independent farmers was a possibility: for where then would the big farmers, the merchants and the industrialists find the labour-force indispensable to their enterprises? The existence of a proletariat, Lozeau was maintaining, is the necessary condition of bourgeois social and economic order.

The aristocracy, however, was still intransigent and, after an ephemeral attempt at peace, war restarted. The delicate stability of the bourgeois nation and the 'Landowners' Republic' – which its liberal form made excessively vulnerable – was once again put in the balance. In 1799 as in Year II, danger to France compelled a recourse to authoritarian methods. But there was now no question of the social and political predominance of the bourgeoisie being put out of gear by the masses. Once the option of a revolutionary dictatorship had been ruled out, there only remained the solution provided by a military dictatorship. This was indeed the real meaning of the coup of 18 Brumaire Year VIII: it enabled the legal nation to remain within the narrow property franchise limits of the Landowners' Republic which the notables had set down for it in Year III.

Chapter 1

The End of
the Thermidorian Convention,
the Treaties of 1795
and the Constitution of Year III

After the crushing of the Paris sans-culottes in the Prairial *journées* of Year III, the reaction speeded up. However, the excesses of the White Terror and still more the attempted Quiberon landing – which underlined the émigrés' treason – proved ultimately to be to the advantage of the Revolution. At the same time, the Thermidorians reaped the fruits of the Revolutionary Government's endeavours: the Coalition disintegrated.

The Thermidorians did not overstep the limits of their policy of compromise and of the *juste milieu*, however. Abroad, they returned to traditional diplomacy and, continuing the war, came out strongly for a peace which would secure France annexations and conquests. Inside France, in order to complete their self-assigned task, they came to an understanding with the Right. In the Constitution of Year III, moderate republicans and constitutional monarchists laid the foundations for the régime of notables. Even before getting under way, however, the new constitutional experiment had been compromised by the Royalist opposition and by the conduct of the war.

I. AFTER PRAIRIAL: THE WHITE TERROR AND QUIBERON (MAY TO JULY 1795)

The *journées* of Prairial Year III, the effect of which had been the removal of all popular opposition, led to a general sharpening of reaction in all spheres of public life.

The first consequence of this was the revival of religious worship.

On Lanjuinais's proposal, 11 Prairial (30 May 1795), the churches were returned to the faithful, though external religious demonstrations were still prohibited. Under the *simultaneum* clause, the republican form of worship, Constitutional Catholicism and Roman Catholicism shared the use of the churches – which led to a continual stream of conflicts. All priests were required to swear an oath of allegiance to the laws of the Republic. The Constitutional clergy took advantage of this legislation to reform their church under Grégoire's direction. The Roman Catholics, who before had been non-jurors, were split, as they had been over the 'small oath' of 1792. Those who agreed to take the oath – the *soumissionnaires* – took their lead from abbé Emery, former head of the Seminary of Saint-Sulpice, while *non-soumissionnaires* continued to worship clandestinely. Religious disturbances persisted.

The crushing of the sans-culottes led to the ruin of the *assignat*, which the Thermidorian bourgeoisie abandoned to its fate. In the end, the Convention sanctioned the collapse of paper currency by establishing, on 3 Messidor Year III (21 June 1795) a scale of depreciation corresponding to successive issues. On 2 Thermidor (20 July), the deputies decreed that half the land tax should be paid in grain. Finally it accorded public officials a sliding scale of salaries. The Treasury remained empty, however, with issues of *assignats* continuing at the rate of nearly 4 billion *livres* per month. The value of the *assignat* fell from 8 per cent of its nominal value in Germinal (April) to 3 per cent in Thermidor (July 1795).

The White Terror received an important boost from the defeat of the popular movement in Prairial. In the Convention, all the members of the old Committees of Year II, with the exceptions of Carnot and Prieur of the Côte-d'Or, were arrested, along with a dozen Montagnards, including Ruhl and Maure, both of whom threats drove to suicide. On 12 Prairial (31 May 1795), the Convention suppressed the Revolutionary Tribunal and quashed convictions for federalism.

In the departments, the former terrorists were brought to trial. The members of the Orange Commission and Lebon in the Somme were executed. On 20 Floréal (9 May), the Convention had authorized the administrative bodies, which were now in the hands of ex-federalists and avowed Royalists, themselves to denounce terrorists to the police officers attached to the Tribunals. Trials proliferated. In all regions, the men of Year II were harassed: even if they were not found guilty they were so remorselessly pestered as to make their life impossible. Most towns now had their own *jeunesse dorée* which with the complicity of the authorities, ruled the streets. Gangs of assassins – the Companies of Jesus, of Jehu and of the Sun – terrorized the South-east. Prisoners were butchered at Lons-le-Saulnier and at Bourg. At Lyons, the prisons were broken into on 5 and 15 Floréal (24 April, 4 May), and the prisoners put to death. There were also massacres at Montbrison and Saint-Etienne. The Marseille detachment of the Company of the Sun massacred the prisoners at Aix on 22 Floréal (11 May) and again on 27 Thermidor (14 August). The sans-culottes of Toulon, the last bastion of Jacobinism, revolted, but were crushed on 4 Prairial (23 May), and the White Terror in the region intensified. The Company of the Sun assassinated the political prisoners at Fort-Saint-Jean in Marseille on 17 Prairial (5 June). At Tarascon, the Jacobins were hurled into the Rhône from the walls of the Château du roi René, under the eyes of and to the applause of the local aristocracy. There were massacres too at Salon, at Nîmes and at Pont-Saint-Esprit. 'Wherever you look there is throat-cutting,' wrote a deputy on 13 Prairial (1 June 1795).

Parallel to the amplification of the White Terror, the Royalist party staged a revival. Those Thermidorians who were still republicans became alarmed when they saw the supporters of the Revolution threatened indiscriminately by the growth of royalism. The Paris press was generally favourable to it. 'The most insane hopes are everywhere in evidence', the *Moniteur* reported on 17 Prairial (5 June 1795). 'It seems that there is nothing left for the Convention to do but proclaim the restoration of the monarchy.'

In Paris, non-juring priests and returned émigrés, lavishing English money to right and left, were intriguing with impunity. In the departments, trees of liberty were cut down and the tricolour cockade trampled underfoot. The Royalists were split, however. Constitutional monarchists counted on governing under the aegis of the child king, Louis XVII, who was still a prisoner in the Temple gaol. The child died on 20 Prairial (8 June), however, and the absolutists emerged triumphant. The Comte de Provence took the title of Louis XVIII and issued a manifesto from Verona on 24 June 1795 in which he undertook to reestablish the three orders, the *parlements*, the predominance of the Church and also to punish all regicides. His entourage were even urging that all members of the Constituent Assembly should be hanged, and all purchasers of national lands shot. Royalists of the absolutist leaning now set to work to rekindle insurrection in France: they reformed their cadres in Franche-Comté, in the Ardèche, in Haute-Loire and in the Lozère, and deployed corruption through the intermediary of the 'Royal Agency' in Paris. In May and June 1795, the Agency made overtures to Pichegru, who was the general commanding the Rhine Army. From early Prairial, the Chouans had taken to arms again. Faced with the threat of Royalism, the Thermidorians forgot their differences and formed serried ranks against the danger.

The Quiberon expedition which – if there was still any need – demonstrated Royalist collusion with England, managed to re-awaken revolutionary enthusiasm. Mallet du Pan had emphasized in his clear-sighted way, on 21 June 1795, the danger that this collusion presented for the Royalist cause:

Civil war is a chimera. The alternative strategy of foreign war is just as decrepit. The scorn which Frenchmen bear towards the arms and the policies of the allies is only matched by the equally general hatred these have inspired.

The Convention's concessions to the rebels in the West, the repression which had followed Prairial and the general weakness of the government encouraged those who advocated recourse to arms. Puisaye prepared an armed landing, for which the English government provided money, a naval squadron and uniforms for two divisions of émigrés under the command of d'Hervilly and Sombreuil. The landing took place on 9 Messidor (27 June 1795) in the Quiberon peninsula on the southern coat of Brittany. Although some bands of Chouans under Cadoudal took up arms, the mass of the people remained immobile. Dissension between d'Hervilly and Puisaye crippled the Royalist high command. The government, which had been forewarned of the landing in early Prairial, had had time to concentrate forces under the command of Hoche. The Republic's troops forced the Chouans back into the Quiberon peninsula and blockaded them in by building a solid line of trenches. The Royalists attempted to break out on 19 Messidor (7 July) and again on 28 Messidor, but both attempts were bloody failures. Hoche's troops took to the offensive on the night of 2–3 Thermidor (20–21 July 1795), pushing the émigrés back into the very tip of the peninsula. Although Puisaye managed to rejoin the English naval squadron, Sombreuil surrendered. Under the decrees in force, 748 émigrés captured in arms and wearing English uniforms were shot as the Coalition's allies and for high treason.

The failed landing of émigrés at Quiberon intensified hatred of England throughout France. It consolidated the Republic, at the very moment that the Coalition was disintegrating for good.

2. THE VICTORIOUS PEACE (1795)

The Thermidorians had destroyed the work of the Revolutionary Government, yet they managed none the less to enjoy the benefits produced by the policies of national defence in Year II. They benefited in addition from the breakdown of the Coalition under the pull of divergent interests.

The supremacy of the republican armies had been asserted at Fleurus on 8 Messidor Year II (26 June 1794). By 9 Thermidor, Belgium had been reconquered. During the summer, military operations underwent a lull. The armies continued to advance in September, Jourdan's Sambre-et-Meuse Army forcing its way over the Roer on 11 Vendémiaire Year III (2 October 1794), and driving Clerfayt's Austrians across the Rhine, while the Moselle and Rhine Armies occupied the Palatinate. The Army of the North under Pichegru took the Dutch positions, notably at Maestricht, and in late December crossed the Meuse and the ice-covered branches of the Rhine: Holland was occupied and the Dutch fleet, trapped by the ice off the island of Texel, was taken by the hussars. In January 1795, the Batavian Republic was proclaimed. In the South, although the armies kept to the defensive on the Alps front, Moncey's troops in the Pyrenees invaded Catalonia, and, to the West, San Sebastian was occupied in August 1794.

French national territory was thus liberated. Moreover, the conquest of the Low Countries procured the Republic enormous economic advantages. At the very moment when the Coalition was splitting, the Thermidorians found themselves in a strong position.

Thermidorian diplomacy and the Coalition

In the diplomatic sphere as in others, the Thermidorians were shackled by the forces of reaction. The Committee of Public

Safety of Year III, bereft of authority, had to reckon with a distrustful Assembly and with a counter-revolutionary opposition who were campaigning for an immediate peace and the return of conquests. On 14 Brumaire (4 November 1794), Tallien proposed peace terms which would involve France withdrawing to 'within her former limits'. Ten days later, Barère expressed Montagnard indignation by launching an attack on those who were supporting 'a patched-up peace'. 'There are some people who want to squander the success of our armies,' cried Bourdon on 8 Nivôse (28 December 1794), and then again, on 11 Pluviôse (30 January 1795): 'We shall confine ourselves within the limits that nature has set down.' Natural frontiers thus became the bone of contention between the parties, and the touchstone of republicanism.

There were other influences at work. The feelings of the army – which had become, in the crisis of Year III, a political force which could no longer be neglected – were plainly apparent. The economic role of the army was just as important as its political one: not only was war beginning to nurture war, but also to provide for the needs of the whole nation. Although the Thermidorian government abolished the evacuation agencies created in Floréal Year II which were destituting the occupied countries, the French administrations established at Brussels (for Belgium) and at Aix-la-Chapelle (for the Rhineland) obliged local farmers to accept *assignats* for requisitions. In negotiations with the Batavian Republic, the French government insisted on a war-indemnity which would allow it to finance the forthcoming campaign.

The Thermidorians were divided, however, over the question of annexations. The areas in dispute were Belgium and, especially, the left bank of the Rhine – the future of Nice and Savoy was never even broached. Carnot, readopting the policy of the Committee of Year II, would have been satisfied with a strategical rectification of the old borders – an opinion he shared with the moderates and the constitutional monarchists. In the end, the republicans agreed on Belgium's annexation, but hesitated over the future of the Rhineland. Merlin de Douai and Merlin de Thionville were opposed to its annexation, while Reubell and Sieyès, who had both entered the Committee of Public Safety on 15 Ventôse (5 March 1795), declared themselves fervent annexationists, the former in order to include in France his native Alsace, the latter in order to have one more bargaining-counter, when it came to the final reckoning. Such considerations were far removed from the policies of the Committee of Year II: the Thermidorians had returned to the practices of traditional diplomacy.

However, torn between divergent interests, the Coalition was breaking up. Committed apparently reluctantly in the West, and defeated at Valmy, Prussia had sought compensation in the East, and along with Russia had performed the Second Partition of Poland on 23 January 1793. Following Kosciuszko's Polish uprising in March 1794, the Prussians besieged Warsaw, but were unable to capture it by their attack of 6 September 1794. On 6 November, the city surrendered to the Russian army under Suvarov, just as the Austrian government, reconciled with Catherine II of Russia, was preparing to occupy Cracow. The Third Partition of Poland was in gestation. In order to forestall the temporary alliance of Austria and Russia, Prussia determined to push her troops east and compel the two powers to admit her to the negotiations. The Prussian troops crossed back over the Rhine. In November 1794, Frederick William II of Prussia decided to send representatives to Switzerland to open negotiations with Barthélemy, on the French side. On 3 January 1795, the Third Partition of Poland was agreed on: Prussia had not been consulted and was not allowed the best pickings. Thus the Polish crisis had helped to cause the break-up of the Coalition.

The peace treaties of 1795

French negotiations with Prussia, which had started in Basle in November 1794, became more active when Frederick William II sent the Francophile, Goltz, to join the Prussian delegation. Barthélemy, for his part, had been instructed to obtain Prussia's agreement to the eventual annexation of the left bank of the Rhine, in return for compensation. However, Goltz died in February 1795, and his replacement, Hardenberg, displayed less alacrity, demanding the neutralization of Northern Germany under Prussian guarantee. In the end, the King, anxious to send his Westphalian army swiftly into Poland, ceded over the question of the Rhine, and ordered his minister to come to terms. In return, Barthélemy agreed that Northern Germany should be neutral, and assumed responsibility for signing the treaty on the night of 15–16 Germinal Year III (4–5 April 1795).

The Treaty of Basle with Prussia predicated 'peace, friendship and mutual understanding between the French Republic and the King of Prussia'. French troops would evacuate Prussian possessions on the right bank of the Rhine, but would continue to occupy those on the left bank until a general peace was made. In secret articles, the two powers undertook to observe a strict neutrality in regard to each other:

If, on the drawing up of a general peace between the German Empire and France, the latter keeps the left bank of the Rhine, H.M. the King of Prussia will come to an understanding with the French Republic over the mode of cession of the Prussian states on the left bank of the river, in return for such territorial indemnification as shall be agreed upon. . . .

The Treaty of The Hague was signed with Holland by Reubell and Sieyès on 27 Floréal Year III (16 May 1795). As Prussia had already come to terms, the Batavian leaders, who were well-disposed towards France, had no option but to surrender to Thermidorian demands. France received Dutch Flanders, Maestricht and Venloo, which she could not retain without occupying Belgium. The office of Stadtholder was abolished. A defensive and offensive alliance was concluded between the two Republics, to last until the end of the war. The Batavian Republic agreed to maintain an occupying force of 25,000 men; and furthermore to pay an indemnity of 100 million florins, 'Holland's currency, either in coin or in valid foreign bills of exchange' (article 20).

The Treaty of Basle with Spain was signed on 4 Thermidor Year III (22 July 1795) by Barthélemy for France and by the Spanish envoy Yriarte. The victories of Moncey, who had occupied Bilbao and Vittoria and reached Miranda on the Ebro, had hastened negotiations. Under the Treaty, France abandoned her conquests, but received in return the Spanish part of Santo Domingo in the West Indies. This treaty was to be complemented a year later by a defensive and offensive alliance, signed at Saint-Ildefonse on 2 Fructidor Year IV (18 August 1796).

No conclusion was reached in the negotiations with Austria, however. On the news of the Peace of Basle, Austria's position was strengthened by her bonds of alliance, with first England and then Russia being drawn more closely together – illustrated most strikingly by the English subsidies which enabled her to maintain a force of 200,000 men on a war footing (20 May 1795). The Committee of Public Safety, in which the annexationists held a majority after

Thermidor, wanted to retain Belgium and to offer Austria Bavaria as compensation. This conflicted with Austria's refusal to recognize the Rhine as France's Eastern frontier. On 9 Vendémiaire (1 October 1795), Belgium was annexed. By this date, the break was already absolute, and war had begun again. By now, moreover, the French army was in a sorry state.

The army and the war in Year III

The disorganized state in which national defence now found itself was largely consequent on the dismemberment of the Revolutionary Government, the abandonment of the directed economy and the collapse of the currency. Their effects were disastrous first and foremost for the war industries and for the system of supplying the armies. The output of the national arms factories was gradually run down, in order to benefit private firms, for whom a decree of 21 Frimaire Year III (11 December 1794) supplied the labour force they required, 'even by means of requisitioning'. On 17 Germinal (6 April 1795), the manufacture of saltpetre organized by the Revolutionary Government was returned to the private sector. Finally, on 25 Prairial (13 June), the workshops in the Paris sections for army uniforms were liquidated, so that individual entrepreneurs might benefit.

The supplying of the armies was severely impaired by the monetary crisis and the government's financial incompetence. Because requisitions were no longer being supplied in the specified amounts, the soldiers went short of bread. Since they only received their wages irregularly and in *assignats*, they were unable to obtain anything for themselves. 'With the 170 *livres* that the Republic gives me each month,' wrote a lieutenant on 26 Messidor Year III (14 July 1795), 'I cannot afford to shoe my horse or wash my clothes. . . . However, I cannot manage without breeches, boots or shirts, all of which I am on the verge of being completely without.' War manufactures, war provisioning and transports – all now relinquished to private enterprise – constituted an important source of profits for finance companies like the Lanchère Company, or the Michel and Roux Company which took over transports for the Italian and Alps Armies.

The army's penury caused a dwindling in the numerical strength of the army, which was partly also due to the fact that the measures

against deserters and *insoumis* were no longer being applied as they
had been in Year II. In March 1795, there were only 454,000 soldiers
in the army, whose theoretical strength stood at 1,100,000. This loss
of manpower increased throughout the spring, resulting in the
republican armies on the Rhine losing their numerical superiority.
Government incompetence worsened matters. They had allowed
the year following the *levée en masse* to pass without calling up
single men who had since reached their eighteenth birthday. Thus
only those called up in 1793 continued to serve – and to serve
indefinitely. Civic feeling and discipline were maintained, however,
for hostility towards the *ci-devants* and the priests, and hatred of
monarchy were still as keenly felt as ever. The Jacobin spirit in fact
persisted more strongly in the army than among the population at
large, and was mixed with a certain contempt for the Thermidorian
government on account of its inability to master the reaction.

In these circumstances, the 1795 Campaign could hardly be
decisive. It opened late. The Sambre-et-Meuse Army under Jourdan
and Pichegru's Rhine Army, short of all essentials, had remained
immobile throughout the winter. Only on 20 Fructidor Year III
(6 September 1795) did Jourdan cross the Rhine, forcing Clerfayt's
Austrian troops to retreat. Pichegru, however, had been won over
by the Duc de Condé's agents and by English gold, and gave his
colleague poor support. In early October, Clerfayt counterattacked, and forced Jourdan back over the Rhine. In November,
the Austrians invaded the Palatinate. An armistice in December 1795
brought the campaign to a close.

Hopes for a general peace were slipping away. The Thermidorians
had been unable to impose one by force. Indeed, their annexationist
policies had only strengthened the Anglo-Austrian coalition which
Russia had joined on 28 September. When the armistice brought the
campaign to a close in December 1795, the Convention had already
broken up. The Thermidorians had transmitted to the régime which,
in the Constitution of Year III, they had organized, the grave legacy
of war.

3. THE ORGANIZATION OF THE POWER OF THE BOURGEOISIE

The alliance of the Centre and the Right – conservative republicans
and constitutional monarchists – held sway in the Convention when

the new Constitution was being debated and voted upon. It might well have been thought that the grave threat of royalism, apparent in the excesses of the White Terror and the Quiberon expedition, would provoke a split among republicans. In fact, it did the contrary, rekindling the revolutionary spirit for the whole of the summer of 1795. The anniversary of the fall of the Bastille was celebrated amid great pomp on 26 Messidor Year III, when the 'Marseillaise' rang out again. 'It would be impossible to describe,' the *Moniteur* reported, 'the effect that this unexpected and long-forgotten sound produced.' The sans-culottes reappeared, and, assisted by soldiers, hunted down the *jeunesse dorée* in what came to be called the 'War of the Black Collars'.

The government displayed some energy against deserters and *insoumis* and also, by subsidies, revived a republican press: on 6 Messidor (24 June 1795), Louvet, a former Girondin and a staunch republican, launched his *Sentinelle*. However, the Plain needed the support of the Right to vote in the new Constitution, and therefore had no intention of making anything more by way of concessions to the Left. This led to some revealing compromises: on the commemorative festivals of 9 Thermidor and 10 August, the 'Réveil du peuple' was played alongside the 'Marseillaise'. So too, on 21 and 22 Thermidor (8–9 August 1795), the Convention decreed the arrest of six former Montagnards, including Fouché. It was in this political atmosphere that the debate on the Constitution of Year III took place.

The Constitution of Year III

The debate on the draft Constitution which Boissy d'Anglas presented to the Convention lasted two months, from 5 Messidor to 5 Fructidor (23 June to 22 August 1795). The draft had been drawn up by a Commission of Eleven, appointed on 29 Germinal (18 April), which included some republicans, such as Daunou, La Revellière, Louvet and Thibaudeau, but also some monarchists, like Boissy d'Anglas and Lanjuinais. Moderate republicans and constitutional monarchists were as one man in demanding that the way be barred to both democracy and dictatorship, and that a return be made to the principles of 1789, now interpreted and inflected in the direction of bourgeois interests. The country's political and economic leadership was to be returned to the 'notables' – that is, all landowners who were at least fairly well-off. In his report of 5 Messidor (23 June), Boissy d'Anglas made his meaning quite clear: 'Absolute equality is a chimera.'

The Declaration of Rights of Year III marks a definite regression compared with the 1789 Declaration. In the debate, on 26 Thermidor (13 August), Mailhe had stressed the danger inherent in putting 'in this declaration principles contrary to those encompassed in the Constitution'. 'We have been through a cruel enough test of the abuse of words,' he continued, 'for us not to use words which do not serve our purpose.' The first article of the 1789 Declaration was therefore abandoned ('Men are born and remain free and equal in rights').

If you say that all men remain equal in rights [Lanjuinais had declared on 26 Thermidor], then you are inciting all those men to whom, in the interests of the security of all, you have denied or suspended rights of citizenship, to rebel against the Constitution.

In much the same way as the Constituent Assembly, only even more cautious, the Thermidorians were in favour of only civil equality. Thus, according to article 3, 'Equality consists in the fact that the law is the same for all.' No consideration was given to either the social rights recognized by the 1793 Declaration, or the right to insurrection. The right of property, on the other hand, which the 1789 Declaration had not defined at all exactly, was defined as in the 1793 Declaration:

Property comprises the right to enjoy and dispose of one's goods, revenues and the fruits of one's labour and industry (article 5).

This was equivalent to sanctioning the full exercise of economic freedom. The Declaration of the Duties of Citizens, which the Thermidorians saw fit to add to the Declaration of Rights, further elucidated this question in article 8:

The cultivation of the soil, all production, every means of work, and the whole social order rests upon the maintenance of property.

Voting rights were restricted:

A country governed by landowners is in the social order [Boissy d'Anglas had declared], a country where non-landowners governs is in the state of nature.

Electoral qualifications were, however, wider than in 1791. An active citizen was defined as any Frenchman over twenty-one years of age, domiciled for more than one year and who paid taxes of any kind at all. Active citizens were to be convened in 'primary assemblies' in the main town in each canton, where they were to appoint electors from those Frenchmen over twenty-five years old who either, in those communes with more than 6,000 inhabitants, owned property yielding a revenue equivalent to the value of 200 days' work, or else, in all other communes, who were tenants of a house with a rent equivalent to 150 days' work, or of a piece of landed property with a rental equivalent to 200 days' work. The electors, who numbered about 30,000 in the whole of France, met in 'electoral assemblies' in the departmental capitals, and there elected the legislature, for which no further qualifying conditions were necessary.

The organization of the public powers followed extremely scrupulously the principle of the separation of powers. Under article 22 of the Declaration of Rights, 'without the separation of powers, there can be no real safeguard for the individual in society'. It was held that all threat of dictatorship would be avoided if this separation was properly enshrined in the Constitution.

Power to legislate was entrusted to two Councils, both of which were to have one-third of their membership renewed annually. The Council of Ancients comprised 250 members over forty years old, either married or widowers, while all members of the Council of Five-Hundred were to be over thirty years old. The latter had the right to initiate laws and to frame resolutions, which the former scrutinized and could make into laws.

Executive power was entrusted to a Directory, composed of five members, who were appointed by the Ancients from a short list of ten names drawn up by the Five-Hundred. Directors were to be over thirty years old, and were to be renewed at the rate of one a year. The Directory, which was to safeguard the internal and external security of the Republic, had the armed forces at its disposal, though it was not allowed to command them. By means of commissioners which it named itself, it supervised and ensured the execution of the laws within the administrative and judicial systems. The old Executive Commissions were abolished, and replaced by six Ministers, appointed to their posts by the Directory, and responsible to it; the Ministers did not form a separate council. The Directory had no power over the Treasury, which was entrusted to six elected commissioners; it had no initiative in framing laws; and it could only communicate with the Councils in 'messages'.

Administrative organization was simplified and once more decentralized. Each department was given a central administration of five members, who were appointed by the electoral assembly. The district – in Year II the most thoroughly revolutionary administrative division – disappeared. Small rural communes were grouped together under the leadership of cantonal municipal administrations, while the big towns, Paris most notably, lost their autonomy along with their Commune and their mayor, by being split into several municipalities. This administrative organization was still more centralized than has often been maintained. The administrations were structured into a hierarchy, with municipal subordinated to departmental administrations, and the latter subordinated to the Ministers. An important feature of the centralization was the way in which the government was represented by an appointed commissioner attached to each municipal and departmental administration. These Directorial commissioners supervised and enforced the execution of the laws, sat in on the debates of the municipal and departmental administrations, and kept an eye on public officials; they also corresponded directly with the Minister of the Interior. Because they were dealing with administrations, a fraction of which were annually renewable, these commissioners ensured a degree of stability in local government. Another way in which centralization was asserted was in the Directory's right to intervene directly in the administration. Under article 196 of the Constitution, the Directory could annul the transactions of the administrations, suspend or dismiss administrators and supply replacements for them until the following election. Although there was of course no real comparison with the Jacobin centralization of Year II, this system was nevertheless far removed from the complete decentralization mapped out in the Constitution of 1791.

The enforcement of the Constitution was fraught with dangers: the Revolution was not yet stabilized (emergency legislation against émigrés and non-juring priests, for example, still existed); bankruptcy was at hand; the war was still under way. Above anything else, however, the Thermidorians feared the return to power of the sans-culottes, the dictatorship of an assembly or of a single man. This fear was the main impulse behind the many precautions and safeguards with which they surrounded the Constitution. Actually, these precautions left the central power defenceless and unstable – half the municipalities, for example, one-third of the Councils, and one-fifth of the departmental administrations were renewable annually. Yet no expedient had been devised to resolve the conflicts which were always possible between the executive and the legislature. For the moment, the persistence of the crisis and the fear of delivering the new régime into the hands of their enemies led the Thermidorians, from the very outset, to rig the liberal system they were wanting to establish.

The beginnings of the new régime

This crisis deepened dangerously throughout the summer of Year III. Inflation continued to wreak havoc, prices rose daily, speculation acquired a frantic rhythm and the extravagance of the minority who had shamefully enriched themselves affronted popular distress more than ever. The number of *assignats* in circulation rose from 8 billion *livres* at the time of the abolition of the maximum to 20 billions on 1 Brumaire (23 October 1795). Economic life had come to a halt, social intercourse was in a state of utter confusion, with those farmers and tenants who owed money discharging their debts in the devalued paper currency. As wages were unable to follow the upward spiral of prices – the price of meat rose during the summer from 8 to 20 francs a pound – and as the harvest was not outstanding in most regions, recourse was had to the coercive measures of Year II, price-fixing apart: requisitioning, the enforced selling of agricultural produce on the market (reestablished on 4 Thermidor (22 July 1795)), and arrangements for trade-control (codified by the law on the grain trade of 7 Vendémiaire Year IV (29 September 1795) which remained in force until 1797. The price of bread in Paris was artificially fixed at 3 *sous* a pound, whereas in early summer it was costing 16 francs a pound on the open market. Even in Paris, however, the bread ration fell to a quarter of a pound at the time of shortage just preceding the harvest, and only rose to three-quarters of a pound afterwards. The cost of living index, using 1790 levels as 100, seems to have risen in Paris to no less than 2,180 in July 1795 and to 3,100 in September; by November, it stood at 5,340. It was hardly surprising in these circumstances, therefore, that the Festival commemorating 10 August, the fall of the monarchy, should have passed off, according to the police, 'in a state of apathy'.

Aware of their enormous unpopularity and of the intrigues of the constitutional monarchists, who were hopeful of achieving their ends by the legal means of the ballot-box, the Thermidorians resolved to keep themselves in power. The Two-Thirds Decree of 5 Fructidor Year III (22 August 1795) aimed to forestall the success of the royalist opposition in the elections. 'Into whose hands shall be committed the sacred trust of the Constitution?' one of the members of the Constitutional Committee had asked. The Decree provided the answer: the electoral assemblies were to elect two-thirds of the new deputies – 500 out of a total of 750 – from among the deputies now sitting in the Convention. A further decree of 13 Fructidor (30 August) went on to specify that if this number were not attained, then the deputies from the Convention who had been elected would fill out their numbers by cooptation. These two measures would be more or less equivalent to the simultaneous removal from the new Assemblies of both the ex-Montagnard and the Constitutional monarchist oppositions, to the advantage of the Thermidorians.

Although the Constitution had established a régime grounded in the property franchise, a plebiscite by universal suffrage was held – which included votes for the army – in order to ratify the Constitution and the supplementary decrees. The primary assemblies began to meet after 20 Fructidor (6 September 1795). The Convention had introduced a certain number of decrees against émigrés and non-juring priests: those whose names had not definitively been deleted from the lists of émigrés lost their civil rights, and their relatives were barred from holding public office; former priests who had been deported were allowed just fifteen days to return into exile. On the other hand, voting rights were returned to the now disarmed ex-terrorists – though the clubs had been suppressed by a decree of 6 Fructidor (23 August 1795). On 1 Vendémiaire (23 September), the Convention announced that the new Constitution had been ratified: according to the figures published on the 6th, by more than a million votes against 50,000. These figures are eloquent of the mass of abstentions. The Two-Thirds Decree, however, to which the plebiscite did not specifically refer, was accepted by only about 205,000 votes to 108,000. In fact, more than 250 primary assemblies had proffered comments concerning the Constitution, while 19 departments, and all except one of the Paris sections, had rejected the Two-Thirds Decree outright.

The royalist insurrection of 13 Vendémiaire (5 October 1795) was the culmination of an agitation which had asserted itself in

Paris from the previous month, and preceded the meeting of the electoral assemblies, which had been arranged for the 20 Vendémiaire. On 20 Fructidor (6 September 1795), the Lepeletier section – the home of the Paris stock-exchange and thus of speculation – had voted an 'act of guarantee', while the Fontaine-de-Grenelle section had declared itself *en permanence*. The royalist-dominated primary assemblies in Paris refused to admit sans-culottes and former terrorists. The storm increased after the results of the plebiscite had been announced. Eighteen of the Paris sections contested the result. On 3 Vendémiaire (1 October), news came in of royalist rebellions at Châteauneuf-en-Thimerais and at Dreux the previous week, and was accompanied by news of their suppression. Thereupon, the Lepeletier section issued a call to insurrection. By 11 Vendémiaire, at least seven sections were in a state of revolt. The Convention declared itself *en permanence*, appointed an extraordinary commission to deal with the crisis, the five members of which included Barras, and issued an appeal to the sans-culottes. A decree of 12 Vendémiaire (4 October) repealed the former disarmament of former terrorists, and three battalions of 'Patriots of Eighty-nine' were formed. The uprising developed on the night of 12–13 Vendémiaire, with the complicity of General Menou, commander of the army. An insurrectionary central commission was set up. The majority of the capital fell to the rebels, the Convention was besieged. At dawn on 13 Vendémiaire, Barras, who had been appointed to lead the resistance, collaborated with several generals, including Bonaparte. General Murat managed to seize the canons from the Camp of the Sablons, and the rebels, some 20,000 strong, but lacking any artillery, were thrown back and dispersed. Only moderate repression ensued. The failed insurrection of 13 Vendémiaire had nevertheless completed the split between the Thermidorians and the royalists. Once again, the dangers that had been run rekindled a degree of the old republican spirit. Fréron was sent to the Midi to repress the White Terror, and the Convention decreed the arrest of three deputies from the Right. Finally, on 4 Brumaire Year IV, just before breaking up, the Convention voted a general amnesty for 'deeds exclusively connected with the Revolution'.

The calculations of the Thermidorians were thwarted, however, in the elections which had begun on 20 Vendémiaire (12 October 1795). Only 379 Convention deputies were reelected, including 124 substitute deputies. Moreover, most of these were moderates or crypto-royalists like Boissy d'Anglas or Lanjuinais. The new third was composed for the most part of royalists and Catholics. The turncoat Montagnards who had been largely responsible for the Thermidorian reaction, such as Fréron and Tallien, had been defeated. The latter sounded the alarm: 'If we don't get rid of the royalists in the administrative and legal systems, then the counter-revolution will be completed through constitutional channels before three months are out.' The moderate republicans, however, refused to annul the elections. Under such auspices, the new constitutional experiment opened and the Directory settled in.

On 4 Brumaire Year IV (26 October 1795), the Convention broke up to cries of 'Long live the Republic!' In its more than three years of existence, its political line may appear somewhat tortuous. Yet in fact, from September 1792 to October 1795, one and the same idea informed its endeavours: the desire to break completely with the aristocracy and to prevent for ever a return to the Ancien Régime. Hence, once the democratic episode of Year II was over, the Thermidorian Convention resumed the policies of the Constituent Assembly in order to ensure the rule of the bourgeoisie which, in its own eyes, its social preponderance and intellectual ability justified. Both the democratic model of 'Ninety-three' and the aristocratic model of 'Eighty-nine' were swept aside. Government and administration were now to be considered the realm of the 'notables', a social category which equality before the law made remarkably open in recruitment.

The Thermidorians wanted to guarantee the bourgeoisie social preeminence and political authority, but within the framework of a liberal régime and in a land where civil and foreign war still held sway. The Vendée was still a source of trouble and the Coalition had not been forced to terms. By insisting, in the Constitution of Year III, that the new régime safeguard and maintain the 'constitutional borders' which were held to include the nine departments of annexed Belgium, and by gearing their diplomacy round the idea of 'natural frontiers', the Thermidorians determined, to a large extent, the policies of the Directory. The campaign was going to resume in spring 1796, and to conduct the war, the new régime inherited a devalued *assignat* and a disorganized army. The enforcement of the Constitution of Year III, one of whose main features was the holding of annual elections – which thus would have necessitated peace both at home and abroad – could only be severely impaired. Since any recourse to the people along the lines of Year II was precluded, the Thermidorians, and after them the Directorials, were therefore driven, in their attempts to ward off the renewed attacks of the aristocracy, to load the constitutional dice, and before very long to call in the army.

Chapter 2

The First Directory:
the Failure of
Liberal Stabilization (1795–1797)

The narrowness of the range of social classes to whom the vote was allowed by the new Constitution meant the exclusion from the new Republic of both the aristocracy and the popular classes. In fact the bourgeois nation was doomed to instability not only because of the new property franchise, but also because the régime's liberalism proved ineffective in practice. The Thermidorian notables' fear of royalism and of democracy had led them to increase the number of safeguards against the omnipotence of the State. Consequently, the skilfully-contrived Constitutional equilibrium of Year III allowed of no other alternatives than government impotence or a recourse to violence. To be effective, the Directory's stabilizing policies, already deeply compromised by the exclusion of aristocracy and popular classes from the legal nation, and thus by the twofold opposition it had to face within France, would have required a swift return to peace abroad. However, war persisted and conquest became the general rule of policy. The part of Robespierre's speech against the war, on 2 January 1792, when he attacked the generals – who would become 'the hope and idol of the nation' – was thus coming true. Robespierre might have been addressing the Directorials when he warned: 'If one of these generals is destined to achieve some degree of success . . . will it not give his party a dangerous ascendancy?'

I. THE IMPOSSIBLE TASK OF INTERNAL STABILIZATION (1795–1797)

The social base on which the Directorials, following the Thermidorians, set about stabilizing the régime seems extremely small. It excluded, of the property-owning classes, not only the aristocracy

but also a fraction of the bourgeoisie. The law of 3 Brumaire Year
IV (25 October 1795) prohibited the relatives of émigrés from holding public office. This law was repealed by the royalist majority in
Year V, but re-established on 18 Fructidor. Shortly after the Brumaire law, Sieyès put forward a proposal that nobles who had held
high office or enjoyed high rank under the Ancien Régime should
be banished, and that all other nobles should be reduced to the status
of aliens. The law of 9 Frimaire Year VI (29 November 1797)
restricted itself to the latter measure. Although this law was never
implemented, the intention of doing so is particularly revealing.
Directorial exclusivity extended even further. The Directorial
bourgeoisie, men of the middle rank, mistrusted the Ancien Régime
bourgeoisie, whose social level was higher and nearer the aristocracy's. Moreover, the Directorials also rejected the constitutional
monarchists as absolutists. They wanted the Republic to be bourgeois and conservative, yet they refused the support of a portion of
the bourgeoisie because they feared it would sweep them along
towards the restoration.

In regard to the popular classes, the recollection of Year II and
social fear remained throughout the Directorial period a powerful
incentive to reaction, and ultimately justified the coup of 18 Brumaire. The Conspiracy of Equals showed, however, that the most
conscious of the popular classes did not accept their expulsion from
the political nation and from the Republic for which they had striven,
without putting up a fight. But while the revolutionary movement was adjusting itself, still very tentatively, to new methods, the
bourgeoisie's fear comprised a powerful lever in the hands of
the government in their attacks on the *exclusifs*, the *terroristes*, the
brigands and the *buveurs de sang*. More than anything else, the
notables, the *honnêtes gens*, feared a return to the system of Year II,
when the wealthy man had been held suspect, the lower classes had
laid down the law, when traditional social values had been overthrown and political democracy had brought social levelling in its
train. The spectre of the *loi agraire*, of the division of property,
was still as potent as ever. Proclaiming his opposition to the establishment of a graduated tax, the little-known Dauchy, on 10 Frimaire
Year IV (1 December 1795) maintained before the Council of Five-
Hundred that:

The State can only prosper if it attaches its citizens to property as much
as it can.... The graduated tax is a piece of special legislation directed

at well-to-do citizens. . . . Its effects would inevitably be the breaking up of properties to the most extreme degree, a system which has already been followed with lamentable effects in regard to the alienation of national lands. . . . To put it in a single phrase, the graduated tax is nothing less than the seed of the *loi agraire*: we must crush it at birth. . . . It is the duty of the legislature to declare itself strongly against any principle destructive of social harmony, and in this case against a principle which tends patently towards incursions against property. It is only by having a religious respect for property that we shall be able to attach all Frenchmen to liberty and to the Republic.

The social thinking of the Directorials thus tended towards the exclusion from the Republic of all those who were not landowners, even if they had helped to found it. In the end, however, it proved impossible to stabilize the Directorial régime on the narrow base of property – on the enfranchised bourgeoisie, and the republican notables.

Directorials, Jacobins and royalists

As there was considerable continuity between the Thermidorian Convention and the Directorial Councils in terms of personnel, the bulk of the early period of the new régime was spent in getting the institutions established by the Constitution of Year III under way.

Thanks to the Two-Thirds Decree, the new Councils contained 511 deputies from the Convention. Of these, 413, all moderates or reactionaries, had actually been elected: 379 had been elected by 6 Brumaire Year IV (28 October 1795), and these were later joined by 15 others chosen by the departmental electoral assemblies, and 19 representatives for Corsica and the colonies, whose mandate had been extended. Lanjuinais had been elected by 39 departments, Boissy d'Anglas by 36. Formed into the 'Electoral Assembly of France', the elected deputies from the former Convention proceeded to fill out the prescribed two-thirds of the new Councils by co-optation, and indeed, even went beyond that fraction. The new third, for its part – constitutional monarchists like Barbé-Marbois, Dupont de Nemours, Portalis, or avowed counter-revolutionaries like Boissy d'Anglas, Henry Larivière and Isnard – strengthened the forces of the Right. The Directorial majority ranged from former Girondins like La Revellière or Louvet, to men of the Plain, like Letourneur, and Sieyès, to ex-Montagnards such as Barras and

Tallien. The Councils included 158 deputies who had voted for the execution of the King, though the political opinions of some of these had evolved since then. In so far as we can tell what the opinions of the deputies were, there seem to have been 158 royalists present – most of whom were liberals – 305 republicans, who were mainly Thermidorians, and 226 supporters of the Constitution of Year III. It was this last group which swayed the election of the Directors.

The Directory was chosen from a list of names put forward by the Five-Hundred. The Ancients designated Barras, La Revellière, Letourneur, Reubell and Sieyès, all of whom had voted the King's death. Sieyès declined the appointment and his place was taken by Carnot. La Revellière had been a deputy in the Constituent Assembly and in the Convention, and was an ex-Girondin. Violently anti-Jacobin, he was, while only a figure of the second rank, staunchly republican and anti-clerical. Usually he followed the lead of the Alsatian Reubell, who had also sat in both the Constituent Assembly and the Convention, but on the Montagnard benches. An authoritarian figure, Reubell was an active and fervent supporter of the principle of natural frontiers. Carnot kept Letourneur under his wing: both had been officers in the Engineers. Carnot still retained his reputation as a former member of the Committee of Public Safety – though his firmly conservative political career from this time on would soon erase it. Between these two groups of decent and diligent men, who together cast a fairly faithful reflection of the republican bourgeoisie, stood Barras, the strong man of 9 Thermidor and 13 Vendémiaire. A *ci-devant* viscount and army officer, who had turned cold-blooded terrorist, he was doubtless attached to the Revolution, but was ready to sell himself to the highest bidder.

The Directory established itself in the Luxembourg Palace, which under the Terror had been a prison, and there created a secretariat which was to become Bonaparte's state secretariat. The six ministerial appointments were as follows: Bénézech to the Ministry of the Interior; the 'regicide' Ramel-Nogaret to the Finance Ministry, which he was to keep until Year VII; Merlin de Douai, who had drawn up the Law of Suspects, to the Ministry of Justice; Delacroix, another regicide, to the Foreign Affairs Ministry; plus two less important military figures in the War and Navy Ministries. A seventh ministry was later to be created, the Police Ministry, shortly afterwards entrusted to Cochon.

On 14 Brumaire Year IV (5 November 1795), 'in order to publicize its establishment', the Directory issued in a proclamation a veritable governmental programme. In the political sphere it intended

to wage an active war on royalism, to revive patriotism, vigorously to suppress all factions, to extinguish all party spirit, to destroy all desire for vengeance, to make harmony reign and to restore peace.

In the economic sphere, the aim was

to reopen the sources of production, to resuscitate industry and commerce, to stamp out speculation, to revitalize the arts and sciences, to re-establish public credit and to restore plenty.

In short, 'to replace the chaos which always accompanies social revolutions by a new social order'. Although it is the spirit of stabilization, of balance and of the *juste milieu* which informs this programme, the Directory did allow itself one pungent remark against the Right: while no allusion is made to the Jacobins, the proclamation puts the people on its guard against 'the treacherous suggestions of royalists who are reviving their intrigues, and of fanatics who ceaselessly inflame imaginations'. Such a warning is clearly influenced by the prevailing atmosphere in the aftermath of Vendémiaire: at the outset, the Directory appealed to all Republicans.

At the political level, it was essential for the stability of the régime that no serious dispute arise between the legislative and executive powers to upset the skilfully-contrived balance established by the Constitution of Year III. The Directors began by ruling in accordance with the wishes of the majority who had elected them and who had an interest in maintaining them in office. They gave their approval to the local administrative figures and the judicial officials taking up their posts. They provided stop-gaps in those cases where electoral assemblies had broken up without performing their task, assuming the right to choose the replacements themselves. Thus from the very outset, the powers of the Directory were on the increase. It was not, however, very strictly obeyed, not least because wages were never paid with much exactness. The majorities in the Councils and the Directory soon came into conflict, however, with the same forces of opposition as the Thermidorian Convention before it: first and foremost, with royalism.

Although they had been defeated in Paris in Vendémiaire, the royalists were continuing to foment disturbances in the West, in Languedoc and in Provence. They were aided by the arms and the false *assignats* provided by England. In January 1796, Stofflet resumed the struggle in the West. Hoche saw fit to abandon the strict enforcement of legislation against non-juring priests, he deployed his troops over the whole of the affected region, increased military outposts and ended up disarming the peasants. Stofflet and Charrette were captured and shot, the former at Angers on 25 February 1796, the latter at Nantes on 29 March. To the North of the Loire, Cadoudal surrendered shortly afterwards in the Morbihan, as did Frotté in the Normandy bocage, and Scépaux in the Maine. The end of the uprising in the West was in sight. In June, the Army of the West was disbanded, although banditry continued sporadically. The royalists were now divided over the tactics they should employ. The émigrés had lost their courage, and supporters of violent action now ceded to those who proposed constitutional methods, urging royalists to pool all their efforts in an attempt to win the majority in the forthcoming elections, and to overthrow the republican government legally. General Pichegru, who had not dared to act as the royalists wanted, and who had resigned his command, threw in his lot with this tactic.

The Jacobins benefited momentarily from the goodwill of the government. The Directory staffed some administrative posts with them, and tolerated their press, even going so far as to subsidize Duval's *Journal des hommes libres*. The clubs reappeared: on 25 Brumaire Year IV (16 November 1795), the Panthéon Club, for example, was opened and soon had more than a thousand members, including some former deputies in the Convention, such as Drouet. On 15 Brumaire (6 November), Gracchus Babeuf had restarted to publish his *Tribun du peuple*, in which he had asked:

What is political revolution in general terms? What is the French Revolution in particular? Open warfare between patricians and plebeians, rich and poor.

Babeuf directed his criticisms against the anti-democratic character of the Constitution of Year III:

All the Declarations of Rights with the sole exception of that of 1795 have had as their starting-point this most important maxim of eternal justice: 'The aim of society is the common happiness.' We have made great strides and great and rapid progress towards this aim until the present time, since when we have gone back on our tracks, moving away from society's aim and the Revolution's aim, and towards the common misfortune and the happiness of only a minority. Let us venture to say that the Revolution, despite all obstacles and oppositions, advanced up to 9 Thermidor and has retreated since.

With support from some former members of the Convention, such as Amar and Robert Lindet, the Left onslaught spread, and ultimately alarmed the Directory. On 14 Frimaire (5 December), Babeuf's arrest was ordered, and he went underground. Reubell countered for the Directory when on 1 Pluviôse (21 January 1796), in the ceremony commemorating the execution of the King, he not only assailed royalism, but also inveighed against 'that time when anarchy and terror came even into the midst of the Senate to lay down its laws. . . . May good citizens be reassured.'

The success or failure of the attempt to stablize the régime actually depended on the solution to be found to the deep-seated problems inherited from the Thermidorian period, most important of all the economic and financial problem. The currency was in a state of collapse, the economy was run down. A fiscal crisis had been superimposed over the monetary crisis: taxes were not coming in, the Treasury was empty. In vain Reubell invited 'even the apathetic . . . to adhere to the Republic and to join with the vast mass of republicans, before whom all faction will vanish'.

The monetary crisis augmented popular distress and disqualified policies of unity as soon as they had been proposed, however. Fearing that the Left Opposition would avail itself of the opportunity to stage an uprising, the Directory veered towards the Right.

The end of the revolutionary paper currency

Even as the Directory was establishing itself, the inflation had reached its peak: 100 *livres* in *assignats* were worth only 15 *sous*. While the Treasury remained empty, the *assignat* presses continued to pour out a currency whose value was soon less than the paper it was printed on. In less than four months, the volume of paper money doubled, reaching 39 billion *livres* on 30 Pluviôse Year IV (19 February 1796). Even the introduction of a tax on capital – the forced loan levied according to a sliding scale (19 Frimaire [10

December 1795]) – was unable to cope with the crisis. Payable in metal currency, in grain or in *assignats* at 1 per cent of their face value (although their quoted level was three to four times less), the loan brought in only 27 billion *livres* in paper money and 12 millions in cash. Moreover, it aroused lively discontent among the ranks of the bourgeoisie who had been obliged to bear the brunt of it. Finally, on 30 Pluviôse (19 February 1796), the government had to suspend issues and to abandon the *assignat*.

A return to a metal currency appeared to be impossible. Only 300 million *livres* in coin were then in circulation, contrasted with $2\frac{1}{2}$ billions at the end of the Ancien Régime. The idea of a national issue bank was deliberately ignored, and the law of 28 Ventôse Year IV (18 March 1796) instituted *mandats territoriaux*, 2,400 million *livres* of which were to be issued immediately. Thus the *assignat* was replaced by a new form of paper currency. The law, moreover, marked a return to the idea which had been uppermost at the creation of the *assignat*: the *mandats* were backed by unsold national lands. They were exchanged against the *assignat* at the rate of 30 to 1, even though at that very moment the *assignat* was being accepted as payment for the forced loan at the rate of 100 to 1. The *mandats* had a compulsory quotation, and were valid for acquiring national lands at their evaluated price, without auction. The history of the *mandat* was to prove identical to that of the *assignat*, only it covered in six months the ground which the *assignat* had covered in five years.

The monetary catastrophe was instantaneous. The value of the *mandat* had been legally fixed at the value of gold, but also at thirty times the value of the *assignat*, which itself was only worth 0·25: thus the law itself gave a-100 franc *mandat* a value of 7·50 francs. From the very first issues, the *mandat* lost up to 65 or 70 per cent of its face value. Depreciation had reached 80 per cent by 15 Germinal (4 April 1796) and 90 per cent by 1 Floréal (20 April). After this, commodities had three different prices, which could only add to exchange and provisioning difficulties. Thus on 27 Germinal (16 April 1796), when the price of a pound of bread stood at 3 *sous* in cash, the Central Bureau in Paris fixed the price at 35 *livres-assignats* and 1 *livre*, 3 *sous*, 4 *deniers* in *mandats*. The extravagant running down of national lands further helped to ruin the *mandat* by reducing its material backing. The law of 6 Floréal Year IV (25 April 1796) had provided for the sale of national lands to recommence;

sale was not to be by auction; the *mandat* would be accepted at its face value. This law sanctioned a veritable stampede of plunder, which benefited those who had amassed *mandats*, particularly government contractors. One man who had acquired a château for 20,000 in *mandats* derived 8,000 *livres* solely from the sale of its iron gates and handrails. By Prairial, bread was costing 150 francs a pound in *assignats*, and even beggars were refusing the paper money they were handed.

The disappearance of revolutionary paper currency sprang from this ill-starred experiment of *mandats*. Apart from the fact that it lasted only two months, the winding-up cycle was the same as for the *assignat*. First, on 29 Messidor (17 July), the compulsory quotation was abolished. Then, under the law of 13 Thermidor (31 July) – too late to prevent the nationalized estates from being frittered away – national lands were to be paid for in *mandats* at their market value. This rule was gradually extended to wages, government stocks, taxes and rents. By the end of Year IV (mid-September 1796), the fiction of paper currency had come to an end, although it was only finally withdrawn from circulation a few months later. Metal currency was reappearing, though the State, which received only paper money, did not derive any advantage from it. Finally, the law of 16 Pluviôse Year V (4 February 1797) withdrew the *mandat*, whose value was fixed at 1 per cent of its face value, thus ending the history of revolutionary paper currency. It was above all the profits flowing from the military victories of Year IV which had enabled the Directory to return to metal currency: on 5 Germinal Year V, it had drawn 10 million *livres* in coin from the Sambre-et-Meuse Army, and more than 51 millions from the Army of Italy. The régime was coming to be nurtured by the war.

The social consequences of the monetary crisis were, as one might expect, catastrophic for public officials, rentiers and the mass of the popular classes. On 22 Messidor Year IV (10 July 1796), the administration of the department of the Isère wrote that, because of the insufficiency of wages paid by the government, it was preferable to be a convict rather than a *chef de bureau*:

Each convict, detainee and prisoner costs the government more than four times the salary of one of our departmental heads, whose wages are now down to 6 *livres*, 2 *sous*, 8 *deniers* per day. The pressing need to provide for their own subsistence has long since compelled them to sell their furniture and those of their belongings which are the most essential to a man's existence, and they are now having recourse to the bread distributed solely to indigents.

The winter of Year IV was a terrible one for wage-earners, who were overwhelmed by the breathtaking rise in prices. Moreover, the markets remained empty; the 1795 harvest had not been good, the peasants were only accepting metal currency, and requisitioning was no longer being enforced. The Directory was forced to initiate buying from abroad and to impose severe restrictions on consumption within France.

The daily bread ration in Paris fell from one pound to 75 grammes, and was supplemented by rice which, because of the shortage of wood, housewives were unable to cook. Throughout the winter, police reports refer with wearying regularity to popular distress and discontent, which seemed to be emphasized by the brazen extravagance of those who were making their fortunes from the shortage.

Paris seems calm, but opinion is acutely distraught [noted the Central Bureau's report of 28 Pluviôse (17 February 1796)]. The extreme dearness of all goods is invariably believed to be the inevitable consequence of the illicit commerce of those contemptible creatures called speculators. This cruel and disastrous crisis which has for a long time now been destroying private and public fortunes weighs most heavily upon the indigent classes, whose complaints, grumblings and hot-blooded speeches are heard everywhere.

This popular discontent, which turned naturally against the Directory, benefited the Jacobin opposition which, in the Pantheon Club, debated the re-establishment of the *maximum*. In early Ventôse, police reports stressed the progress which the agitation among the popular classes and the demand for price-fixing had made:

The workers are contemplating having their wages raised [the report of 5 Ventôse (24 February) maintained], but say that the next bout of price-fixing will decide them. . . . By 'price-fixing', the people mean a lowering of the fixed price on bread.

Fearing that popular discontent would crystallize round the Jacobin opposition, the Directory ordered the closure of the Pantheon Club on 7 Ventôse (26 February 1796), took legal action against journalists from the Left and dismissed public officials with a reputation for Jacobinism. The Left Opposition assumed a new form, however, with Babeuf's organization of the Conspiracy of Equals.

Babeuf and the Conspiracy of Equals (1795–1796)

Babeuf was the first person in the whole French Revolution to overcome the contradiction which all politicians dedicated to the popular cause had run up against, between the assertion of the right to existence on the one hand, and the maintenance of private property and economic freedom on the other. Babeuf followed the sans-culottes and the Jacobins in declaring that the aim of society was 'the common happiness' and that the Revolution was to ensure *égalité des jouissances*. But since private property necessarily entailed inequality, and since the *loi agraire*, that is, the equal division of property, could 'last but one day' (for 'the day following its establishment', he held, 'inequality would reappear'), the only way of attaining practical equality, he maintained, was

to establish a common administration; to suppress individual property; to attach each man to the employment or occupation with which he is acquainted; to oblige him to place the fruits of his labour in kind into a common store; and to establish a simple administration for food supplies, which will take note of all individuals and all provisions, and will have the latter divided up according to the most scrupulous equality.

Compared with Jacobin and sans-culotte ideologies, both of which had been marked by their attachment to small property based on personal labour, this programme, set forth in the 'Plebeians' Manifesto' which appeared in the *Tribun du peuple* of 9 Frimaire Year IV (30 November 1795) constituted a modulation, or, to be more exact, an abrupt transformation: the 'community of goods and of labour' was the first form of the revolutionary ideology of the new society which was the product of the Revolution itself. Through Babouvism, communism, till then only utopian reverie, was formulated in an ideological system; through the Conspiracy of Equals, it entered political history.

Babouvism inevitably bears the imprint of its age. The self-taught Babeuf doubtless conceived his communist ideal by reading Rousseau, Mably, and Morelly's *Code de la nature*, still then attributed to Diderot. But he went beyond the stage of utopian dreaming. Throughout the Revolution, Babeuf was a man of action. It was in contact with the social realities of his native Picardy, and in the course of his revolutionary struggles, that his ideological system took shape.

Babeuf's experience of peasant life in Picardy determined certain elements in his agrarian communism. The son of an excise officer and of an illiterate servant girl, he was born at Saint-Quentin in 1760, and later settled at Roye in the Santerre, a region of large-scale farming. The rural communities here, which had their own collective rights and community customs, and which were struggling obstinately against the concentration of farming units in the hands of the big capitalist farmers, made a deep and long-lasting impression on him. As seigneurial rent-collector and as a specialist in feudal law, and then as the registrar of a community, Babeuf gained an intimate knowledge of the peasantry of Picardy, its problems and struggles, which was doubtless instrumental in leading him, even before the Revolution, towards practical equality and communism. In his *Cadastre perpétuel* of 1789, he showed himself sympathetic towards the *loi agraire*, that is, the socialism of the *partageux*, as it was to be called in 1848. Yet in 1785, in an article on the 'farms', and in a letter dated June 1786 to Dubois de Fosseux, the secretary of the Academy of Arras, he envisaged the organization of 'collective farms', veritable 'fraternal communities':

If fifty, forty, thirty or even twenty individuals come to live in association on a farm around which they had previously been scattered and cut off from each other, virtually inert in their distress, then they will quickly become well-to-do.

Here already is the idea of the community of labour. It seems therefore that, ten years before the Conspiracy of Equals, Babeuf was posing the problem, not only of the real equality of rights, and thus the redivision of property, but also, glimpsing as he did the need for collective cultivation, the problem of production:

Breaking up the land among all individuals into tiny but equal plots is tantamount to destroying the greatest sum of resources which could be derived from it through combined labour.

Babeuf's revolutionary experience was decisive in the development of his system. It soon became apparent when in the middle of the revolutionary ferment the problems of food supplies and of daily bread were raised, that the equality of rights proclaimed by the 1789 Declaration of Rights was merely an empty phrase. 'Who can set store by a nominal equality?' Babeuf wrote on 20 August 1791 in a letter to Coupé of the Oise. Again, on 10 September 1791, in another letter to Coupé, who had been elected a deputy to the Legislative Assembly:

This leads us on to the obligation and the necessity of giving subsistence to this enormous majority of the people who, for all their willingness to work, cannot. Only the *loi agraire* has real equality as its corollary.

Babeuf was admittedly anti-Robespierrist after 9 Thermidor. Yet the havoc wrought by inflation and the appalling distress of the people showed him, after the event, the value of the *maximum* and of the directed economy, of the nationalization, albeit only partial, of production, and also the importance of the experiment of Year II especially where this affected the armies of the Republic.

Experience demonstrates the viability of this government [wrote Babeuf of the common administration, in his 'Plebeians' Manifesto'], for it is this which is applied to the 1,200,000 men in our twelve armies. What is possible on a small scale, is possible on a larger one.

Babeuf was by now rejecting the *loi agraire*, on the grounds that it could only be ephemeral, and was declaring for the abolition of the private ownership of land. In his letter to Germain, dated 10 Thermidor Year III (28 July 1795), he made clear how his system would work. Each man would be

attached to the employment or occupation with which he is acquainted. ... All productive and manufacturing agents will work for a common storehouse, to which each will send in kind the fruits of his labour, and distribution agents – no longer working solely for their own interests, but rather for those of the great family – will allot to each citizen his equal and varied portion of the whole mass of the product of the entire association.

This is essentially, as Georges Lefebvre has emphasized, a communism of distribution. Yet, inspired by the example of his native Picardy, Babeuf had glimpsed, in the sphere of agriculture, the need for a communism of production, and for the collective organization of agricultural work. However, he overlooked the essential factor of capitalist concentration and of the expansion of industrial production. Indeed, his partiality for the old economic forms, especially the artisanal ones, and the absence from his work of any description of a communist society based upon an abundance of consumer goods,

explains why it has been possible to detect a certain pessimism in his
outlook. The circumstances of the period – the very slight degree of
capitalist concentration, and the total absence of mass production –
and also Babeuf's temperament and his social experience, account
for the way in which he was led to think in terms of the shortage and
the stagnation of the productive forces, rather than their expansions,
and the abundance which would ensue. Thus Babouvism takes its
place between the edifying communist utopias of the eighteenth
century and the industrial socialism of Saint-Simon.

The Conspiracy of Equals constituted the first attempt to bring
communism into the world of reality. During the winter of Year IV
(1795–96), faced with governmental incompetence and the appalling
distress which was weighing heavily upon the people, Babeuf,
shortly before being driven underground, hit upon the idea of overthrowing the whole fabric of society by violence. The core of the
Conspiracy he formed was a minority who had been won over to
communism, and also included Pantheonists and ex-Jacobins,
including Amar, Drouet and Lindet, whose objectives remained
essentially political. Buonarroti, on the other hand, the ex-commis-
sioner of the Committee of Public Safety in Corsica, where rural
communes still retained their vitality, and at Oneglia in Italy, which
was still fervently Robespierrist, had a considerable share in the
formation of the Conspiracy's communist programme, as well as its
political organization. On 10 Germinal Year IV (30 March 1796),
an Insurrectionary Committee, which came to include Babeuf,
Antonelle, Buonarroti, Darthé, Félix Lepeletier and Sylvain Maréchal, was set up. A propaganda campaign was launched, for which an
agent was appointed to each of Paris's twelve arrondissements.
Circumstances were favourable, since inflation was continuing to
wreak havoc.

The political organization of the Conspiracy marked a break
with the methods used till that time by the popular movement. At
the centre of the organization stood the leading group, backed by
a small number of hardened militants; then there came the fringe of
sympathizers, comprising patriots and democrats (in the Year II
sense of the word), who were not involved in the secrecy, and who
seem not to have shared the new revolutionary ideal; finally, there
were the masses themselves, who were to be coaxed into participa-
tion. In sum, Babeuf's was an organizational conspiracy *par excellence*, but one in which the problem of the necessary links with the

masses seems to have been largely unresolved. With this conspiracy, then, beyond the tradition of popular insurrection, the notion of the revolutionary dictatorship, which Marat had glimpsed without being able to define, was taking shape: firstly, it postulated that after power had been seized by insurrection, it would be foolish to return it into the hands of an assembly elected under the principles of political democracy, even along the lines of universal suffrage; and secondly, that the maintenance of the dictatorship of a revolutionary minority was indispensable throughout the period needed to recast society and to establish new institutions. Through Buonarroti, this idea was to be transmitted to Blanqui, and it is arguably to Blanquism that we must trace the Leninist doctrine and practice of the dictatorship of the proletariat.

The Directory split over the issue of Babouvist propaganda. Barras equivocated, taking care not to offend the opposition, while Reubell hesitated to do royalism's dirty work for it by repressing Jacobinism. Carnot, however, whose authoritarian conservatism had turned him resolutely towards reaction, did not hesitate. On his initiative, the Police Ministry was taken from Merlin de Douai and entrusted to Cochon. Then on 27 Germinal (16 April 1796), the Councils decreed the death penalty for anyone wishing to bring about 'the reestablishment of the monarchy or of the Constitution of 1793 . . . or the looting and division of private property under the name of the *loi agraire*'.

Babeuf, however, went ahead with his preparations. He began to communicate with a parallel radical body, the 'Comité des Conventionnels'. He reached agreement with them on 18 Floréal (11 May): they would be included in the new assembly to be elected in accordance with the proposals of Babeuf's Insurrectionary Committee. On 11 Floréal (30 April), however, the Police Legion which had been won over to the insurrection had been disbanded. Moreover, one of Babeuf's military agents, Grisel, had already denounced the conspirators to Carnot. On 21 Floréal Year IV (10 May 1796), Babeuf and Buonarroti were arrested and all their papers seized. Arrests proliferated, fear yet again gripping the political leaders and the bourgeoisie.

The Grenelle Camp's attempt to instigate an army uprising during the night of 23–24 Fructidor (9–10 September 1796) was a failure. The rising was the work of men of Year II, Jacobins and sans-culottes, who were doubtless victims of a piece of police provocation operated by Carnot and Cochon, the Minister of Police, rather than of Babouvists properly so called. Certainly only six of the 131 people arrested in this business had subscriptions to Babeuf's *Tribun du peuple*. A military commission based in the Temple, in a trial which the Appeals Tribunal was later to declare illegal, had thirty of the accused shot.

It was Year V before the trial of Babeuf and the main body of his supporters took place. Barras was in favour of reducing the number of prosecutions, as also were men like Sieyès, who feared playing into the hands of royalism. Carnot, however, was implacable, and prevailed over his fellow Directors. During the night of 9–10 Fructidor (26–27 August 1796), the conspirators were transferred to Vendôme in iron cages; their wives – in Babeuf's case his wife and eldest son – followed the convoy on foot. Eventually, in late February 1797, the Vendôme trial, which lasted three months, opened before the High Court. After the verdict sentencing them to death on 7 Prairial Year V (26 May 1797), Babeuf and Darthé tried to commit suicide. They were conveyed to the scaffold covered in blood the following day.

The Conspiracy of Equals can only be gauged against nineteenth-century criteria. On one level, it was merely a straightforward episode in the history of the Directory, which doubtless had an effect on the political equilibrium. Besides this, however, Babeuf and his efforts are of importance in the history of socialism because through him the idea of communism became a political force for the first time. In his letter of 26 Messidor Year IV (14 July 1796), Babeuf urged Félix Lepeletier to gather together all his 'plans, notes and rough drafts of democratic and revolutionary writings', and to present 'all disciples of Equality . . . with what the corrupt of today call my dreams'. In compliance with this wish, Buonarroti published at Brussels in 1828 the history of the *Conspiration pour l'Egalité dite de Babeuf*. This book exercised a profound influence on revolutionary opinion, and by it, Babouvism was established as a link in the chain of development of communist thought.

The royalist upsurge

The anti-Jacobin repression which followed Babeuf's conspiracy forced the Directory to the right, and helped to worsen the royalist threat.

The royalist campaign developed in the summer of 1796 on several levels. Benjamin Constant, acting on Mme de Staël's advice, urged constitutional monarchists to rally round the Directory and to regard it as a staunch buttress of social conservatism. Meanwhile, in the Midi, where the royalist Willot had been appointed commander of the military division of Marseille, the White Terror recommenced. Although, under pressure from the Right, the councils maintained the amnesty of 4 Brumaire Year IV (26 October 1795) in favour of former terrorists, on 14 Frimaire Year V (4 December 1796) they voted that all those benefiting from the amnesty should be excluded from public office. The same law repealed the article of the law of 3 Brumaire Year IV (25 October 1795) which had retained the terrorist legislation against priests. As the supervision of religion consequently fell into abeyance, public worship restarted in most parishes. The influence of the priests could only promote the reaction. The same was true of the exclusion of Jacobins from public office. With Carnot moving further and further to the right, shared anti-clerical opinions drew La Revellière towards Reubell and Barras. These three – the 'Triumvirs' – began to be rather apprehensive about the progress royalism was making.

At that moment, the Anglo-Royalist plot came as clear proof that the Right had not thrown in its lot with the Republic, but was still working towards the seizure of power. The pretender to the throne, Louis XVIII, an exile in the court of the Duke of Brunswick at Blankenburg, had obstinately refused any concessions. Consequently, the royalist campaign developed according to two strategies, the constitutional and the absolutist. In Paris, the King's representative, abbé Brottier, was running an Agency which colluded widely and secretly. The abbé even numbered among his contacts a few of the Directorial Guard. In the summer of 1796, the Agency formed an association called the 'Amis de l'ordre' which, though confining itself in public to constitutional opposition to the régime, was in fact secretly actuated by the 'Fils légitimes' group, who supported the restoration of an absolute monarchy by insurrectional methods. A former member of the Constituent Assembly and a supporter of legal, non-violent action, Dandré, with a view to the next elections, changed it into a 'Philanthropic Institute'. The Institute had branches in several departments, and here again the duality came out within the organization between constitutional monarchists, who supported legal activity, and the absolutists, who were in favour of violence. The branches in the Sarthe, where the branch of the Institute was organized by a Chouan, and at Bordeaux were two cases in point. Money received from London via Wickham, an English agent established in Switzerland, allowed the press to be subsidized and electoral propaganda to be financed. The royalist propaganda campaign continued, moreover, despite the arrest of Brottier on 11 Pluviôse (30 January 1797) and the confession of one of his accomplices.

The social and political climate was indeed favourable to royalist propaganda. Large numbers of émigrés and deported priests were returning. The religious question in particular was a fruitful soil for reaction. Many republicans, as well as non-juring priests, maintained that Roman Catholicism and the Republic were incompatible. Roman Catholicism's recrudescence was helped by the declining influence of the Constitutional church. Also, Theophilanthropy, a new form of republican worship which had been founded in 1797 and which received the approval of La Revellière, affected only a small number of enlightened bourgeois. More important than the religious question in the advance of the reaction, however, was the financial crisis and the difficulties arising from it.

The situation of the Republic's finances after the collapse of the *mandat* and the return to metal currency was indeed lamentable. After inflation, deflation: metal currency was rare, prices slumped, especially when the 1796 harvest proved to be good. The only positive result of this modulation in the crisis was a slight alleviation in popular misery. The continuance of the war, however, ensured that this advantage could only be ephemeral. The Directory vainly endeavoured to balance the budget. The Councils – with ulterior political motives in mind – stubbornly refrained from making any effective financial exertions. Thus taxes were voted too late – the land tax on 18 Prairial Year V (6 June 1797) for the year then in progress, and the personal *mobilière* tax on 14 Thermidor (2 August). The Directory's proposal to institute in each department a Direct Tax Agency staffed by public officials was not followed up. Although the Council of Five-Hundred agreed to the Directory's plans to re-establish indirect taxes on explosives, saltpetre and salt, the Ancients demurred. In order to turn the sale of national lands to better account, auction sales were reestablished on 16 Brumaire Year V (6 November 1796). Gains from this reform proved minimal, however.

Financial expedients prevailed. Requisitions to supply the armies with grain, fodder and horses were maintained. They were paid for in bonds which could be used to pay taxes or to purchase national lands. Like the Thermidorians, once they had abandoned the directed economy the Directory had to have recourse to the world of finance – bankers, contractors, army suppliers – to whom it lost its independence. After utilizing a fair range of subterfuges – including firstly putting the crown jewels, the famous 'Régent' jewel, in particular, into pledge, and secondly selling off the 'Batavian rescriptions', that is, the bonds owed from Holland's war-indemnity under the Treaty of The Hague – the Directory was finally, in the law of 16 Brumaire Year V (6 November 1796), authorized to make use of national lands as a means of payment. One contractor acquired in this fashion 600 hectares in the Nord department. Before long, the government was reduced to abandoning certain categories of state revenue to creditors – a return, under the name of *délégations*, to the Ancien Régime practice of *anticipations*. This method was resorted to, for example, for wood-cutting rights in the national forests; for the proceeds from taxation in certain departments; and in the sale of English goods, seized at Livorno, from which the Flachat company, suppliers to the Army of Italy, benefited.

Such practices gave a great boost to the development of corruption and peculation. Also instrumental in this were the weakness of the government and the venality of a minority of politicians whose most outstanding figures were Barras – who was working in conjunction with the financier Ouvrard – Fouché and Talleyrand. One man would make his fortune by speculating on salt, another by speculating on national lands. This corruption was accompanied by a licentiousness of morals, which made an even greater impression on observers, because of the contrast it afforded with the Spartan bearing of the Republic of Year II. This licentiousness, however, affected only a moneyed and idle minority, who had made the frenzied pursuit of pleasure their rule and who have been called – in an evident generalization – the 'society of the Directory'. Their world presaged the way of life of Imperial high society, only they were more cynical and sported themselves in less stately surroundings. Two government figures belonged to this dissolute society: Barras, the *ci-devant* viscount, and Talleyrand, the *ci-devant* bishop. Around them gathered the businessmen and the financial promoters – bankers, government contractors, monopolists, speculators – who for all their profiteering at the expense of the system, would readily abandon it for another which would safeguard their fortunes.

The régime came to be generally discredited among all classes of society. Public officials were only being paid very irregularly. Public services, bereft of financial resources, hardly kept going at all. In order to lighten the load of the State, the Directory had obliged local administrations, whose finances were just as run-down as the government's, to assume financial responsibility for the judicial system, the central schools and public assistance. The government paid only a quarter of its debts to bond-holders in metal currency, when it had sufficient liquid assets at its disposal; the other three-quarters it paid in bonds which speculators were redeeming at a very low price, and which could only be used in payment of taxes or for purchases of national lands. By increasing the general discontent, the Directory's financial incompetence played into the hands of the royalist opposition at the very moment that the elections of Year V were approaching.

2. THE WAR OF CONQUEST (1796–1797)

The new features of the war which had tended to become prominent after the fall of the Revolutionary Government and the collapse of its policies of national defence became even more marked under the First Directory. The war-effort was now no longer being run under a directed economy, but under an economy which had been returned to free enterprise and free profit. The material conditions of the army were deteriorating, and it was not long before this had repercussions on the corporate feeling of the troops. A further element promoting change was the fact that the egalitarian standards of the Revolutionary Government and the Terror were no longer acting on the generals, who were beginning to cast off the executive power's tutelage over them and to give free rein to their ambition. Seen in this light, Bonaparte's Italian policies mark a real break: the adventurist perspectives of a private ambition replaced national exigencies as the moving spirit behind policy-making. The change was made even more dangerous by its being hallowed by the glory and prestige attaching to military victory.

The army under the First Directory

The dilapidation of the army continued under the Directory which in the military sphere as in others merely kept up Thermidorian policies. The collapse of the paper currency, the government's financial incompetence and the malpractices of government contractors had serious repercussions on the conditions the soldiers had to face: they found themselves ill-fed, ill-clothed and ill-paid. Poor conditions led to a fall in manpower. The twin diseases of *insoumission* and desertion gnawed at the republican armies from this time on. The Council of Five-Hundred had authorized a commission to draw up the draft of a repressive law against these offences. On 19 Brumaire Year VI (10 November 1795), Dupuis explained their deep-lying causes:

> Your enemies have taken advantage of the aberrations of the accomplices of reaction by making us regard as terrorist activity all the coercive measures which might have stopped the evil at its roots. The mere word 'terrorism' has served Europe better than its most powerful armies. In traversing several departments of the Republic, I have seen gangs of deserters travelling as peacefully as I on the roads, with no one taking it upon themselves to arrest them or to put the laws against desertion into operation. Moreover, I also learnt that mayors and municipal officials were often the relatives of deserters. . . . It was perhaps not safe for them to attempt to have the law executed very strictly, if they were to avoid becoming victims of the frightful reaction which has covered France with so many corpses.

This speech clearly identified the causes of the troubles. Yet the Directory was too much propelled by an ingrained hatred for all memories of Year II for it to act. Also, it was anxious to manipulate the reaction in such a way that it could muzzle the popular movement. Like the Thermidorian Convention before it, the Directory was unable to stave off the problem of losses of military manpower.

The corporate spirit within the army was undergoing change at the same time. The impression left by Year II was still profound, and hostility towards aristocrats and priests, and hatred of the monarchy were still as keenly felt as ever in the ranks. But the flame of revolutionary enthusiasm was no longer being fed, and was diminishing. Though they had been highly responsive to the epochal ideas advanced by the men of Year II, the soldiers were unable to follow the meanderings of the Directorial policy of the *juste milieu*, and could not adhere with any enthusiasm to the middling ideals of the notables. As the gap between the régime and the army opened ever wider, a new scorn for civilians asserted itself, symbolized by the appearance in military jargon of the derogatory term *péquin* or *pékin* to denote civilian. This word had achieved currency by the beginning of the Empire. To a certain extent, however, the feeling for democracy was maintained by the very nature of the military institution. Although democratic practices such as the election of officers and the election of juries in military trials had been suppressed, erudition counted for as little as ever when it came to promotion, the determining factors being intelligence and, still more important, gallantry. Provided that he was brave, the ordinary soldier could still nourish the hope of swiftly attaining the highest ranks. On the debit side, it must be said that this feeling was definitely conducive to encouraging ambition and the spirit of adventure.

National feeling, which had hitherto sustained the morale of the army, was acquiring a new dimension. As there had been no systematic replacement of manpower since the *levée en masse* of 1793, and as conquest was taking the armies increasingly further afield, the soldiers were gradually becoming distinct from the rest of the nation. Because they were stationed abroad, soldiering had inevitably become a job like any other, and this was consequently inclining the troops more towards their generals. Dedication to the nation slowly gave way to fidelity to a chief, the spirit of adventure and, before very long, of plunder. In Year II, no effort had been spared to maintain and strengthen links between the army and the people; from now on, however, every endeavour was concentrated on making the soldier forget that he was also a citizen. Saint-Just, in his speech of 12 February 1793 had declared that he expected victory 'only in so far as it is directly proportional to the progress the republican spirit will have made in the army'. In complete contrast to this was Bonaparte's proclamation on the eve of his Italian campaign on 26 March 1796:

Soldiers, you are unclothed, ill-fed. I want to lead you to the most fertile plains in the world. Wealthy provinces, great cities will be in your power, and you will find in their midst honour, glory and wealth.

Patriotism was fast becoming devoid of all republican and humane content. Nationalism was appearing, as civic feelings and revolutionary enthusiasm were giving way to national vanity, that is, scorn for the foreigner and a partiality for military glory. Marie-Joseph Chénier was soon to celebrate 'the Great Nation to conquest accustomed'. This term, Great Nation – *'la Grande Nation'* – which was so conducive to national self-conceit, and which the Empire was to hallow, was current from the latter period of the Directory.

On the eve of the 1796 Campaign, however, the instrument of war forged by the Committee of Public Safety in Year II was still unparalleled when faced with the Ancien Régime armies of the Coalition powers. In an attempt to strengthen its authority over the generals and the government-contractors, the Directory instituted 'army commissioners' on the lines of the *représentants en mission*. In fact, this was a futile precaution: neither the commissioners nor the Directory possessed any 'coercive force' to employ against the generals. The influence of the generals was coming to predominate; Bonaparte's military genius placed him among the most important in their number. Soon, he would be exercising his genius in the formulation of strategical principles, and in the composition and use of tactical units. Yet for all the apparently innovatory character of Bonaparte's military theory and practice, he still remained faithful to the legacy of the Revolution: he renovated the art of war, utilizing the national army created by the Revolution.

Bonaparte in Italy (1796–1797)

Since the 1795 Treaties, the Coalition comprised only Austria and England. Austria, whose military and financial position was far from outstanding, would certainly have abandoned her claims for the left bank of the Rhine if she had been ensured compensation along the lines of the promises France had made Prussia in the Treaty of Basle. England, for its part, was threatened by an economic and financial crisis which might have had serious social repercussions, and, despite her traditional aversion for seeing the French established in the Low Countries, was unable to sustain a military presence on the Continent.

The Directory's foreign policy, however, was decided in advance by the idea of 'constitutional borders', which were considered sacrosanct. This made settlement with the Coalition practically impossible. Article 332 of the Constitution of Year III forbade 'the alienation of the territory of the Republic'; the annexation of Belgium and, with greater reason, that of Avignon and Savoy were held to have been ratified by the plebiscite on the Constitution. There remained the problem of the left bank of the Rhine. Although Carnot, who was now taking his political cues from the Right, came out for 'the old borders' with slight rectifications in France's favour, Reubell, who was in charge of foreign policy and who prevailed over the Directory in this matter, proclaimed his support for 'natural frontiers', and thus for annexation. His aim was now to secure territories beyond the natural frontiers, which he could use as bargaining counters and which would enable him to negotiate from a position of strength. If these conditions were to be forced on to Austria and England, it was vital that the Directors should not let themselves be led astray by the logic of conquest.

The campaign plans for 1796, prepared by Carnot, allotted a key role to operations in South Germany. The Sambre-et-Meuse Army under Jourdan and the Rhin-et-Moselle Army under Moreau would march on Vienna, while the less important armies of the Alps, under Kellerman, and of Italy, under Schérer, would seize Piedmont and Lombardy, which they would secure as future bargaining counters. An Army of Ireland, to be amassed at Brest under Hoche's command, would provide the threat to England. At the final moment, on 12 Ventôse Year IV (2 March 1796), the Directory replaced Schérer by Bonaparte. In the event, this completely upset its military and political plans.

Napoleon Bonaparte was born in Ajaccio on 15 August 1769. The son of a minor noble family which had accepted French rule, he had taken up a scholarship at the Royal College of Autun in 1779, then until 1784 attended the Brienne College, an offshoot of the Ecole Militaire, where he was a *cadet-gentilhomme* in 1784 and 1785. Bonaparte passed out 42nd out of 58 in his class and, in September 1785, at the age of sixteen, was appointed second-lieutenant. In Valence, then in Auxonne, then in Valence once more, poor and with no prospects, he lived the life of a minor garrison officer. His patriotism in 1789 was Corsican, not French in orientation, and in his frequent stays in his native island from 1789 till 1793, he participated actively in local political life under Paoli's leadership. Paoli became increasingly suspicious of the Bonaparte family, however, and his break with the Convention and his appeal to England finally forced Bonaparte to leave Corsica in June 1793.

By July 1793, the ex-Corsican patriot was a captain in the Army of Italy, had been dispatched to Avignon to organize convoys of explosives and was displaying sincere Montagnard and Jacobin sympathies. In August 1793, his *Le Souper de Beaucaire* was printed in Avignon at national expense. The polemic, which is in the form of a conversation between a soldier – Bonaparte himself – a Nîmes bourgeois, a manufacturer from Montpellier and a businessman from Marseille, revolves around the attempt to convince the bourgeois, who has Girondin tendencies, that the Convention is 'the centre of unity', and that it is necessary to save 'the infant Republic, who is surrounded by the most monstrous of coalitions, threatening to stifle her in the cradle'. Bonaparte had evidently given up his native Corsica and dreams of the island's independence, and was becoming integrated into the revolutionary nation. On 17 September 1793, his compatriot, the *représentant en mission* Salicetti, entrusted him with command of the artillery in the siege of Toulon. He played, in certain respects, a key role in the capture of the town on 19 December. On 22 December, he was appointed brigadier-general. Augustin Robespierre, then *représentant en mission* with the Army of Italy, took him under his wing, speaking highly, in a letter to his brother Maximilien, on 16 Germinal Year II (5 April 1794) of 'the transcendent merit of Citizen Bonaparte'.

The *journée* of 9 Thermidor brought Bonaparte's whole future under review. News of what had occurred reached Nice on the 18th (5 August 1794), and the following day, Bonaparte was relieved of his command by the *représentant en mission* and imprisoned in the Fort-Carré at Antibes as a Robespierrist. He was ultimately freed on 3 Fructidor (20 August) and re-established in his functions. His career now came up against the opposition of the released Girondin Aubry, who introduced reports on military matters in the Convention, and who criticized Bonaparte's 'premature advancement and boundless ambition'. Despite Aubry's attacks, Bonaparte was offered, in March 1795, the command of the artillery in the Army of the West. He refused both this post, and his appointment in June as infantry general in the same army.

From now on, the citizen in Bonaparte gave way to the adventurer, ever watchful for an opening. It was as if his disgrace after Thermidor had broken the continuity of his political evolution. Soon, he would have no other guiding principle than his ambition. He endured a few months of distress, but Vendémiaire put him back in the thick of things. His part in the *journée* of 13 Vendémiaire (5 October 1795) may have won him the nickname 'General Vendémiaire', but it also ensured him advancement thereafter thanks to the good offices of Barras: he was appointed divisional general on 16 October, and then on 26 October General commanding the Army of the Interior. Bonaparte's love-affair with Josephine Tascher de la Pagerie dates from this period. Josephine, six years his senior, the widow of the Viscount de Beauharnais who had been guillotined in 1794, was already jaded according to Barras in his *Mémoires*, though still as seductive and able as ever. Bonaparte's first letter to 'sweet, incomparable Josephine' was on 28 October 1795. The passionate nature of the love-affair is left in no doubt by his letters written during the Italian campaign, which defy quotation. 'It is hard to believe,' wrote Georges Lefebvre, 'that Bonaparte was unaware of Josephine's liaison with Barras, and that the influence she had retained did not serve him.'

On 2 March 1796, Bonaparte was appointed Commander-in-Chief to the Army of Italy in place of Schérer. On 9 March, he went through a civil marriage ceremony with Josephine de Beauharnais, leaving Paris two days later for his headquarters at Savona on the Genoa Riviera.

The Italian campaign determined the issue of the struggle between France and Austria. The plans, which had been drawn up in Year II by the Committee of Public Safety, involved first eliminating Piedmont and securing Lombardy, and then marching over the Alps on Vienna. Bonaparte opened operations with 38,000 men, 48,000 francs in gold, and 100,000 francs in bills of exchange, not all of which were accepted. He conducted operations with great rapidity.

In Piedmont, in less than two weeks, by engagements at Montenotte (12 April 1796), Millesimo and Mondovi (21 April), he split Beaulieu's 35,000 Austrians from Colli's 12,000 Piedmontese and forced the latter to fall back to cover Turin. The King of Sardinia signed the Armistice of Cherasco on 28 April; and by the Treaty of Paris, 15 May 1796, he ceded Savoy and the regions around Nice, Tonde and Beuil to France.

In Lombardy, Bonaparte pursued Beaulieu who had retreated to the north of the Po, behind the Ticino. Wheeling towards the south, Bonaparte crossed the Po at Piacenza, defeated the Austrians at the bridge of Lodi on the Adda (10 May), and entered Milan (15 May). The world was learning, as Stendhal was to write in the *Charterhouse of Parma*, 'that after so many centuries, Caesar and Alexander had a successor'. Bonaparte then, on 30 May, crossed the Mincio and set about besieging Mantua. The Dukes of Parma and Modena signed an armistice with the French, Bologna surrendered and on 23 June the Papacy came to terms. The conquered states were subjected to heavy war-indemnities, which caused part of the local populations to rebel against the occupying forces. Only the Italian Jacobins, who supported a unitary republic, came out for France. The Directory had only wished to secure bargaining-counters in order to strengthen its negotiating position. In the meanwhile, their policy was to exploit the occupied countries: Bonaparte is alleged to have milked Italy of 50 million *livres*, 10 millions of which reached the Directory. The Austrians were not yet ready to come to terms. They still held Mantua, the key to the highway over the Alps. On four separate occasions, Austrian armies came down from the Alps and attempted to raise the siege of the city. Wurmser's army was defeated at Castiglione on 5 August and at Bassano on 8 September 1796, and Alvinczy's army in turn was thrown back after heavy fighting round Arcole from 14 to 17 September, and then was thrashed at Rivoli on 14 January 1797. On 2 February 1797, Mantua fell. The road to Vienna lay open.

The German campaign, meanwhile, had not produced the successes which the Directory expected. The aim of Jourdan's and Moreau's armies, to whom the key role had been allotted, was to reach Vienna along the Danube valley. On 31 May 1796, Jourdan had crossed the Rhine, but had been subsequently thrown back by the Archduke Charles. However, when Wurmser, who had been containing Moreau, was sent to Italy following Bonaparte's victories, the French resumed the offensive against the Archduke. On 24 June, Moreau crossed the Rhine and reached Munich, while Jourdan seized Cologne, then Frankfurt, advancing in August to the Bohemian border. The French armies did not join up together, however, and Archduke Charles took advantage of this, attacking them separately, and after defeating Jourdan twice in the Main valley, forced him back across the Rhine in late September 1796. Moreau was now in an exposed position, and was therefore obliged to fall back. With the Archduke endeavouring to cut off his line of retreat, Moreau entered the gorges of the Black Forest and on 26 October 1796 recrossed the Rhine at Huningue. During the winter, the French lost the Kehl and Huningue bridgeheads.

At about the same time, the Irish expedition under Hoche's command failed. The French fleet had set sail in December 1796, but had been broken up by a storm. In January 1797, the Directory decreed that English merchandise to be found anywhere on French soil was to be seized. England's economic position was worsening, and inclining her increasingly towards negotiations. Indeed by that time, diplomatic preliminaries had already taken place at Lille, with Malmesbury acting as the English representative, from October to December 1796; negotiations had broken down, however, over the Belgian question.

On the eve of the 1797 campaign, therefore, the Army of Italy remained the Directory's main hope. Bonaparte was completing his pacification of the conquered territories. He had completely gone against the government's orders by organizing, on 15 October 1796, a 'Cispadane Republic', comprising the lands of Modena and the Legations which had been taken from the Pope. On 19 February 1797, he signed the Treaty of Tolentino with the Pope. Ignoring instructions from the Directory to destroy the temporal power of the Pope, Bonaparte went no further than exacting a few million *livres*, agreeing on the cession to France of Avignon and the Comtat-Venaissin and on the relinquishing of the Legations. Increasingly, Bonaparte's policies were becoming his own.

On 20 March 1797, the offensive was resumed against the Austrians, commanded now by Archduke Charles, and with substantial reinforcements. Bonaparte forced a passage over the Tagliamento, then reached the Tarvis pass. Masséna, in the van of the armies, reached the Semmering.

At the same time, the Sambre-et-Meuse Army under Hoche crossed the Rhine on 16 April 1797 and won a victory at Neuwied, near Cologne, on 18 April. Moreau, too, was getting under way. That very day, however, Bonaparte had signed both armistice and peace preliminaries with the Austrians at Leoben in Styria. The Italian victor was evidently so attached to his conquest that he feared being forestalled in his role as peace-maker.

The Leoben Peace Preliminaries enshrined the triumph of Bonaparte's Italian policies. The question of the natural frontier on the Rhine remained unanswered, however. It had only been the pressure of internal events which had led the Directory to acquiesce in the individual peace-making of one of their generals.

3. FRUCTIDOR AND CAMPOFORMIO (1797)

The internal situation following the royalist victory in the Germinal elections of Year V and the apathy of public opinion threw the Directory – whose very nature precluded its calling on the people to save the Republic – at the mercy of the generals. The orientation of foreign policy necessarily depended on the solution to be found to the internal crisis. The realization of this by the Coalition powers helps to explain the length to which the negotiations begun at Udine after the Leoben armistice, and those restarted at Lille by the English envoy Malmesbury, were drawn. England and Austria were hoping to obtain better terms if the royalist Right prevailed. This helped to cement solidarity between Bonaparte and the Directory. The former could not hope to see his Italian policies ratified by the royalist Councils, in which, on 5 Messidor (23 June 1797), he was violently attacked for his part in the Venice affair. As for the Directory, how could it withstand the demands of its saviour? In the event, the coup d'état of Fructidor and the Treaty of Campoformio were to be closely linked by this interplay of mutual influence and concession between Bonaparte and the Directory. The party who gained most, however, was Bonaparte.

The elections of Year V and the reaction

In Germinal Year V, elections were held in order to find replacements for the first third of the deputies in the Councils – including half the so-called 'perpetual' members – whose term of service had expired. Despite the brilliance of Bonaparte's Italian successes, from which the Directory had hoped to benefit, the influence of the royalists predominated. The elections passed off without a hitch. The Directorials were crushed in all but a dozen departments. Only eleven former deputies from the Convention were reelected, several of whom were royalists. The new third considerably strengthened the Right.

The reaction took shape immediately, with the Directory split over what to do about it. Reubell, supported by La Revellière, realized the danger: they wanted to bring the situation under control, if necessary by annulling the elections. Carnot, on the other hand, acquiesced in the results of the voting, and was firmly opposed to this course of action. Barras bided his time in his usual manner. The new Councils met for the first time on 1 Prairial (20 May 1797), when they designated Barbé-Marbois as President of the Ancients and Pichegru, the delegate for the Jura, as President of the Five-Hundred. After the drawing of lots had designated Letourneur as outgoing Director, the Councils, on the same day, elected in his place Barthélemy, the negotiator of the Treaty of Basle and a notorious monarchist. The Right wavered, however. Their endeavours to agree on a positive and concerted policy in their meetings in the Clichy Club were fruitless. The 'White Jacobins', who supported an immediate restoration of the monarchy, were only in a minority. The numerous constitutional monarchists were loath to resort to violence. The group nicknamed the 'Belly', also of royalist persuasion, planned to play a waiting game, bringing in routine reforms in the meantime. Pichegru, whom the White Jacobins were counting on to produce a coup d'état, showed himself incapable of decision.

Reactionary measures were passed in favour of the émigrés, to whom public office was thrown open by the repeal of the arrangements of the law of 3 Brumaire Year IV, and also to priests, the repressive laws of 1792 and 1793 against them being rescinded. A statement expressing allegiance to the laws was still required from members of clergy, however, the bulk of the laws against the émigrés stayed in force, and public office was again thrown open to amnestied terrorists. In the departments, the reaction was often excessively violent. Purchases of national lands were attacked, new branches of the Philanthropic Institute sprang up like wildfire, émigrés returned and outlawed priests circulated freely. The Directory had to send troops into Provence when violence broke out there. On 5 Thermidor (23 July 1797), the Directory, fearing to favour Jacobin influence, agreed to the law the Councils had passed suppressing the Constitutional Clubs in which the Jacobins had attempted to organize their resistance to the wave of reaction. The Right was emboldened by this Directorial passivity, and thereupon resolved to emasculate the Directory's influence by depriving it of all its financial powers. Yet though the Five-Hundred entrusted these powers, on 30 Prairial (18 June 1797), to the treasury, long renowned as a counter-revolutionary body, the Ancients refused to ratify the measure.

The conflict between the Directory and the Councils entered a crucial phase when Barras abandoned his stance of watchful caution to support Reubell and La Revellière against Carnot and Barthélemy. His choice became apparent over the change of ministers demanded by Carnot in order to please the Right. On 26 Messidor (14 July 1797), Merlin and Ramel, both of whom the royalists detested, were maintained in their posts; Talleyrand, proposed to Barras by Mme de Staël, was appointed Foreign Minister; and Hoche War Minister. The last appointment was particularly revealing, since for ten days previously the Sambre-et-Meuse Army under Hoche's command had been marching on Paris.

The coup d'état of 18 Fructidor (4 September 1797)

In the absence of any constitutional procedure on the matter, the crisis which the Germinal elections of Year V had provoked between the Directory and the Councils could only be resolved in one of two ways: either by having recourse to the people along the lines of Year II, or else by calling on the army, as on 13 Vendémiaire. La Revellière was firmly opposed to the former solution, which indeed was precluded by the very nature of the régime of notables. There remained the solution provided by the army. Bonaparte and Hoche were sounded out, and agreed to undertake the task. In Messidor, Bonaparte provided proof of Pichegru's treason, in a document discovered amongst the papers of the royalist agent, d'Antraigues. On 13 Messidor (1 July 1797), Hoche set his troops marching on Paris. The Directory thus had thrown itself at the mercy of the generals – in particular of Bonaparte, who was only lending his support to the government against the Councils in order to have his Leoben peace preliminaries and his Italian policies ratified.

The Councils realized the danger impending when, on 28 Messidor (16 July), they learnt of the ministerial reshuffle and the presence of troops within the 'constitutional precinct' around Paris, forbidden the army. They considered arraigning the Triumvirs, Barras, La Revellière and Reubell. However, Carnot, on learning of Pichegru's treason, refused to be party to a restoration. While, on 25 Thermidor (12 August 1797), the Councils authorized the formation of crack companies of the National Guard, thereby arming the bourgeoisie of the rich neighbourhoods, the Directory pushed ahead with its own preparations. Bonaparte had dispatched Augereau to take command of the Directory's forces and, under various pretexts, troop detachments entered Paris. 'The Directory will not treat with the enemies of the Republic,' La Revellière proclaimed to the envoys of the Cisalpine Republic on 10 Fructidor (27 August 1797). With the Right appearing even more determined to resort to force, the Triumvirs made the first move.

On 18 Fructidor Year V (4 September 1797), Paris was placed under a military occupation. Pichegru and a dozen deputies were arrested and imprisoned in the Temple gaol, along with Barthélemy. Carnot was able to flee. There was no resistance, and a decree stated that all those who wished to bring about the reestablishment of the monarchy or of the Constitution of 1793 would be shot on the spot. The Councils met on the night of 18–19 Fructidor (4–5 September) to vote the emergency legislation proposed by the Triumvirs. The elections were annulled in 49 of the departments; 177 deputies were removed, without provisions being made for their replacements; and 65 persons, including Carnot, Barthélemy and Pichegru, were sentenced to the 'dry guillotine' – deportation to Guiana. Some deputies, including Dupont de Nemours, resigned. The majority in the Councils was completely overthrown.

The repressive measures against the émigrés and priests were re-implemented: émigrés were allowed a fortnight to leave France, on pain of death; their relatives were once more excluded from holding public office, and even denied voting rights; those deported priests who had returned to France were forced into exile, on pain of deportation to Guiana; and all ministers of religion were compelled to swear the oath of hatred of the monarchy and the 1793 Constitution. The opposition press came in for some harsh treatment: forty-two newspapers in all were suppressed. To complement this battery of legislation, the Clubs were legalized and the Directory's powers were augmented: it now had the right to purge the administrative and judicial systems and also to proclaim a state of siege when it deemed necessary.

The coup d'état of 18 Fructidor struck a severe blow against the liberal republican system set up by the Constitution of Year III. The Right opposition had been decimated, but the humbled legislature was now embittered and on the look-out for a chance to take its revenge. Only the support of the generals and their troops had made the *journée* a success. The Directory was led to believe that the power of the army was in fact on the wane, for at that moment European peace was just being established. This was not, however, a 'natural frontiers' peace, but rather a peace established by the victor of the Italian campaign, whose already insatiable thirst for prestige increased proportionately.

The Treaty of Campoformio (18 October 1797)

The most notable feature of the Leoben peace preliminaries signed by Bonaparte on 18 April 1797 was its return to the diplomatic practices of the Ancien Régime. Whereas the Directory was planning to use Lombardy as a bargaining counter, in order to negotiate the acquisition of the left bank of the Rhine, Bonaparte merely exchanged Lombardy for the territory of the Venetian Republic. Austria thereby obtained access to the Adriatic, and though she ceded Belgium to France, the fate of the left bank of the Rhine remained undecided. The question was to be debated in a congress to be held in the near future, when peace would be concluded between France and the Empire. Although Leoben came close to completely destroying the Directory's Rhine policies, the Directors were compelled by France's internal situation to ratify the terms Bonaparte had negotiated. Only Reubell, whose 'natural frontiers' policies over the left bank of the Rhine had thus been sacrificed, voted against this ratification.

As soon as this was done, however, Bonaparte's Italian policies evolved even further. He now dictated his own terms to Italy. He formed a 'Cisalpine Republic' out of Lombardy, plus the Valtellina, part of the Venetian mainland and the Cispadane Republic; he provided the new state with a Constitution. At Genoa, the Italian Jacobins transformed the old republic into the 'Ligurian Republic'. On 2 May 1797, Bonaparte declared war on the Republic of Venice and on 12 May entered the city. Negotiations with a view to a definitive peace were opened at Udine with envoys from the Austrian government.

At the same time, England decided to resume negotiations with France. She had just undergone a serious banking and financial crisis. Ireland was up in arms. Mutinies were proliferating in the fleet in spring 1797. In July, Pitt sent Malmesbury to resume the diplomatic conversations broken off at Lille.

For the meanwhile, however, negotiations were inconclusive both at Lille and at Udine. Matters remained in a state of uncertainty so long as the internal crisis within France was not settled, for the

Coalition powers expected more advantageous conditions from a royalist victory. The coup d'état of 18 Fructidor in point of fact toughened the Directory's foreign policy, which Reubell took in hand once again. The Lille discussions broke down (July to September 1797): the Directory had demanded the restitution of French colonies and those of her allies, though had refused in return to give up her own continental conquests. The break finally came when England refused to release the Cape of Good Hope and Ceylon which she had acquired from Holland.

Negotiations had resumed at Udine between Bonaparte and Cobenzl, who had been sent as envoy by the Austrian Chancellor Thugut. On 18 October 1797, the Treaty of Campoformio was signed – actually at Passariano, where Bonaparte was living. Bonaparte deliberately ignored the Directory's instructions to cede the left bank of the Rhine and to reestablish the Republic of Venice, and instead allowed Austria to take Istria, Dalmatia and the mouth of the Cattaro, as well as Venice and the Venetian mainland up to the Adige. From the former Venetian territories, Bonaparte retained for France the Ionian Islands. Austria recognized the Cisalpine Republic 'as an independent power' and renounced all claim to Belgium. In secret articles, Austria 'gave her consent' to the annexation of the left bank of the Rhine up to its junction with the Nette: this comprised the Palatinate, the former electorate of Trier and Mainz, indeed everything but the Cologne region. Austria also undertook to use 'her good offices' at the forthcoming Congress at Rastatt between France and the Empire 'for the French Republic to obtain this same frontier'. Though disappointed, the Directory ratified the treaty. It is in fact difficult to imagine it being able to refuse to acquiesce. In the war-weary country at large, joy broke out on the announcement of the peace.

The revolutionary nation had thus repudiated its principles and set itself up as 'a broker in peoples'. France had abandoned the Prussian alliance for a precarious agreement with Austria who, though defeated, lost nothing in Germany, nor in Italy, where she merely exchanged Lombardy for Venetian territories. Bonaparte's 'Italian system', so foreign to the traditions and the wishes of the nation, put the Directory's 'Rhine system' into the shade. But already Bonaparte was carried away by new plans. During the Campoformio negotiations, he told Cobenzl, the Austrian plenipotentiary: 'The

French Republic considers the Mediterranean its own sea, and wishes to be dominant in it.' At the same time, he was urging the Directory to get hold of Malta: 'For France, this small island is priceless.'

War was a necessary, if latent, element in Bonaparte's Italian policy and in his Mediterranean schemes. The recourse to the army on 18 Fructidor had increased its role within the Republic. The policies of the Directory were increasingly subject to the ventures of the generals.

Chapter 3

The Second Directory:
the End of the
Bourgeois Republic (1797–1799)

After Fructidor and Campoformio, the Directory's policies were marked, in internal affairs, by an increasingly general recourse to authoritarian methods. The government gained thereby a certain effectiveness, and was able to implement important administrative reforms which paved the way for those of the Consular period. With the régime's social foundation still as narrowly Thermidorian as ever, political stabilization proved impossible. The system managed to keep going, so long as continental peace lasted – although even then only at the price of more attacks on the liberal workings of the Constitution of Year III. The formation of the Second Coalition and the resumption of the war precipitated the final crisis. The coup d'état of 18 Brumaire reconciled the restoration of state authority with the social predominance of the fraction of the bourgeoisie who were notables. But because the notables had been obliged to avail themselves of the help of the army in this *journée*, they thereby lost their political power.

1. REPRESSION AND REFORMS (1797–1798)

Although the organization of the government was modified after Fructidor, it was still marked by the same instability, attributable to both men and institutions. There was some change in governmental personnel. In the Directory, Carnot and Barthélemy were replaced by François de Neufchâteau, who was nothing but a good administrator, and Merlin de Douai, who was relatively influential politically. Of the ministers, only Ramel remained. With the exception of the Belgian Lambrecht, who replaced Merlin at the Ministry of Justice, the new ministers were not outstanding. As it turned out, the activity of the executive was still hamstrung by the liberal provisions of the Constitution of Year III which denied it any legal power over the Councils and the Treasury. There was an increasing demand for a strengthening of the executive. The problem remained intact, however, since procedure in cases of constitutional revision was extremely complicated and longwinded – under article 338 of the Constitution nine years were needed. To add to troubles, the annual elections could throw everything back into the melting-pot.

Emergency policies

Although it has been called the 'Directorial Terror', the emergency régime instituted after Fructidor was in fact only a pale reflection of that of Year II. For the Thermidorian bourgeoisie, there could be no question of an economic dictatorship along the lines laid down by the Committee of Public Safety. In any case, the Directory lacked the 'coercive force' which had been the distinguishing characteristic of the Revolutionary Government. Admittedly, the danger was not as great, since continental peace had been established and the internal counter-revolution had degenerated into brigandage. Military commissions, at Pont-Saint-Esprit, for example, at Carpentras and at Montauban, stamped out the resistance which followed 18 Fructidor. By a clause of the law of 30 Nivôse Year VI (18 January 1798), the death penalty was prescribed for criminal outrages committed by more than two persons. Repression came more to resemble a policing operation than a terroristic campaign: raids on homes, administrative internments, violation of the privacy of correspondence, restrictions on press freedom – not by reestablishing censorship but by banning a large number of newspapers (sixteen on 27 Frimaire Year VI – 17 December 1797, for example) – supervision of the theatres and purges of administrative personnel were all utilized. Priests and émigrés were the two main targets, although the repression merely entailed the strict enforcement of existing legislation rather than the introduction of any new measures.

In the case of the émigrés, it was enough merely to utilize the battery of existing legislation. This was accordingly re-implemented by the law of 19 Fructidor. In Year VI, the military commissions had 160 returned émigrés shot, some of whom admittedly, like Surville in the Ardèche, had taken up arms again. Some politicians would have acted in an even more extreme fashion. Sieyès, for example, who in this respect symbolizes very well the revolutionary bourgeoisie, as eager to destroy the aristocracy as to destroy the hopes of a return to democracy, proposed that all nobles should be banished. His proposal was not followed up, but it did inspire the law of 9 Frimaire Year VI (29 November 1797), reducing the nobles to the status of aliens:

> *Ci-devant* nobles may not exercise the rights of French citizens in primary, communal and electoral assemblies, nor may they be appointed to any public office without having satisfied the conditions and the prescribed period of residence required for the naturalization of foreigners under article 10 of the Constitution.

Although the regulations pertaining to the enforcement of this law were never considered, the law's intentions are nevertheless particularly revealing.

The legislation of 1792 and 1793 against priests was maintained, though the death penalty for deported priests who returned to France was tacitly replaced by the 'dry guillotine', deportation to Guiana. Some priests, however, who were on the list of émigrés were shot as émigrés. The Directory moreover was empowered to deport by individual decree any priest, even if he was acting within the letter of the law, who refused the oath swearing hatred of the monarchy, instituted on 19 Fructidor (5 September 1797). Between 1,700 and 1,800 priests seem to have fallen foul of these measures; 263 were actually deported to Guiana, while a thousand stayed imprisoned on the Ile de Ré or the Ile d'Oléron.

The religious policies of the Directory after 18 Fructidor were violently anti-clerical. Article 25 of the law of 19 Fructidor laid down that the law of 7 Vendémiaire Year IV (29 September 1795) on public worship and its supervision should be strictly enforced: thus any public ceremony or external symbol of worship remained prohibited. The law of 17 Thermidor Year VI (4 August 1798) prescribed the observance of the *décadi*, while that of 23 Fructidor (9 September 1798) obliged ordinary citizens as well as public officials to use the republican calendar, now to be known as the *annuaire de la République*, and which was described as a 'great and beautiful conception of the human mind'. The decree of 17 Pluviôse Year VI (5 February 1798) had placed private schools, which were for the most part Catholic, under the inspection of the municipalities 'with a view to establishing whether the *décadis* are observed, whether the republican festivals are kept and whether the name of citizen is honoured in them'. The Rights of Man were to provide, along with the Constitution, 'the basis of all rudimentary instruction'. The decadal festivals and the national festivals established by the Convention were celebrated in accordance with regulation. Some people even wanted to go further, and to provide the Republic with a civil religion to fight Catholicism; but the Directorial majority declined to espouse another experiment along the lines of the worship of the Supreme Being. La Revellière, however, protected Theophilanthropy, the cult of 'Adorateurs de Dieu et amis des hommes', created in January 1797 by the bookseller Chemin. The sect held 'the dogmas and the moral code of all nations on earth', and had as its objectives 'to attach, through religion, all men to their domestic and social duties'. Yet though the religion had a degree of success amongst the republican bourgeoisie, it never affected the people, and even the majority in the Directory accused La Revellière of rekindling fanaticism.

The Directory ultimately antagonized the bulk of believers, though it did, nevertheless, check the religious opposition to the new régime, in particular the opposition of the non-juring priests who had refused the oath of hatred for the monarchy. Emergency legislation had enabled it to hold back counter-revolution for a time. It now set about turning against the Jacobins, who had taken advantage of the extraordinary circumstances of the time.

22 Floréal Year VI (11 May 1798), and the anti-Jacobin repression

Very soon after 18 Fructidor, preparing for the Year VI elections became one of the Directory's major preoccupations. A great deal would be at stake, since with exclusions as well as the third retiring from office – and these included the so-called 'perpetual' members who were still sitting – there were in all 473 deputies to be replaced. The régime strengthened its position by the law of 12 Pluviôse Year VI (31 January 1798), which entrusted to the Councils then in office the job of verifying the powers of the newly elected members – which amounted to giving the Councils a carte blanche to purge the new deputies. It soon became apparent that the danger to the régime was coming less from the royalist opposition, cowed and disorganized by the Fructidorian repression, than from the left opposition.

Neo-Jacobin propaganda had expanded after 18 Fructidor, above all through the Constitutional Circles, which were now favoured by a great many commissioners and administrators appointed to replace the purged officials. The Directory recognized the danger the growth of Jacobinism presented and, in an effort to crush in advance any attempt at democracy, exploited the feeling of social fear against the neo-Jacobins, whom it dubbed 'terrorists'. On 9 Ventôse (27 February 1798) in the Constitutional Circle of the Palais-Egalité, known as the Club de Salm, Benjamin Constant came out with a speech which supported the government on four main points: 'The repugnance we owe terrorism, the dangers of arbitrary power, the contempt that royalism deserves and finally the need to prepare for elections which can strengthen the Republic.' By 'Republic', Constant meant the Republic of Year III based on property, which 'all the measures of the legislators must aim at maintaining, consolidating and surrounding with a sacred barrier'.

In its addresses on the elections to all Frenchmen (28 Pluviôse – 16 February 1798), to the primary assemblies (9 Ventôse – 27 February) and to the electors (4 Germinal – 24 March), the Directory employed the same set of arguments, denouncing the double danger, 'the two branches' of the opposition, and employing as slogan 'Against the Terror, against Reaction! No Royalty, no Dictatorship!' In this way, ignoring Barras's warnings against the grave consequences of a split among republicans, the Directory attempted to get rid of the opposition and to strengthen its own authority by bandying about denunciations of Jacobinism and extremism.

The distinguishing feature of the Year VI elections, which the government had painstakingly prepared by making a large number of administrative arrangements, was the great many secessions in the electoral assemblies. These were in fact instigated by Merlin, and allowed the Directory to validate those electoral assemblies which produced the deputies the most compliant with Directorial policies. Thus while the left-dominated electoral assembly in Paris was in session at the Oratory, the government encouraged the establishment of another assembly of 212 'seceders' out of 609 at the Institute. There was nothing about the new deputies which need cause the bourgeoisie any alarm. The Directory, however, was intent on having a docile majority. The supporters of the Directory in the Councils therefore threw their weight behind the 'seceders' and demanded their validation. On 8 Floréal (27 April 1798), Régnier told the Ancients, 'If you are to reassure France against her recently-conceived fear of seeing all the horrors of revolution repeated in her midst, then it is essential that you declare that you will only allow *bonnet rouge* royalists – who are just as dangerous as the white cockade ones – to enter this assembly over your dead bodies.' In much the same way, Chénier on 18 Floréal (7 May) attacked in the Five-Hundred 'the royalist faction and the anarchist faction'. The majority in the Five-Hundred took its cue from the Directory and, disregarding the protests of General Jourdan, accepted their list of deputies to be excluded. The Ancients acquiesced.

The law of 22 Floréal Year VI (11 May 1798), criticizing 'the conspiracy which has two branches', annulled the elections in eight departments where there had been no secession; declared valid those elected in 'seceded' assemblies in nineteen departments; and dismissed sixty elected judges and administrators. In all, 106 deputies were 'florealized'. In return, 191 government candidates entered the Councils: of these, 85 were commissioners and public officials nominated by the Directory and 106 judges and administrators who in theory had been elected, but many of whom in fact had been brought in by the government. The Directorial party now held a majority in the Councils. The Directory's hypocritical and violent policies at the elections had, however, discredited the régime a little more. The replacement of François de Neufchâteau on the Directory by Treilhard, 27 Floréal (16 May 1798), did nothing to boost the government's prestige. The new Director was a lawyer, a former deputy in both the Constituent Assembly and in the Convention, in which he had voted for the King's execution; a figure of little importance, he was a clumsy politician in addition. However, the executive was strengthened at least temporarily, and could pursue the work of reform it had begun following Fructidor.

The reforms of the Second Directory

For about a year, from Floréal Year VI to the Germinal elections of Year VII, from spring 1798 until spring 1799, the Directory, with the purged Councils now offering no concerted opposition, regained a certain equilibrium and energy. In this political atmosphere, the economic and financial reorganization of France was got under way. The durable reforms achieved, notably in the administrative field, in which the contributions of two ministers, Ramel at the Finance Ministry and François de Neufchâteau at the Ministry of the Interior, were especially valuable, paved the way for Bonaparte's reforms. The laws of Year VI and Year VII laid the foundations for the institutions established under the Consulate.

The government took in hand the problems of financial recovery and fiscal reform immediately after Fructidor. The 'bankruptcy of the two-thirds' or the 'Ramel liquidation' was organized: by the finance law of 9 Vendémiaire Year VI (30 September 1797) for the consolidated debt, and by the law of 24 Frimaire (14 December 1797) for the State's other financial obligations. A third was consolidated by being registered on the 'Grand Livre', or National Debt Register; payments outstanding were made not in currency but by means of bearer bonds called 'one-third consolidated bonds', which could only be used to pay taxes or else as the part of the price of national lands for which metal currency was normally only valid. This consolidated third was exempted from any taxation. The 'liquidated' two-thirds were reimbursed in bearer bonds issued by the national Treasury and which were allowed to be used for the remainder of the price of national lands. In this way, the budget was lightened by 160 million *livres*, representing the payment of the interest on the reimbursed two-thirds. This bankruptcy made the whole situation much healthier. The Consulate benefited from it and even initiated a further bankruptcy. Indeed by March 1801, the 'two-thirds bonds' were exchangeable against government annuities nearing 5 per cent interest at the rate of 0·25 per cent of their face value – that is, with a loss of 95 per cent on their nominal Year VI value.

The reorganization of the finances was conducive to balancing the budget, by ensuring more regular and more sizeable tax returns. The reform of the administration of direct taxes entailed the abandonment of the principles accepted in this sphere since 1789. The Constituent Assembly had entrusted the drawing up of direct tax lists and the levying of taxes entirely to the care of the elected authorities. The law of 22 Brumaire Year VI (12 November 1797), however, established in each department a Direct Tax Agency under the authority of the Ministry of Finances. These agencies were composed of commissioners appointed by the Directors who were to assess and levy taxes. This law prefigured Bonaparte's reorganization of the administration of direct taxes in Year VIII.

The whole tax system was recast. The law of 4 Frimaire Year VII (24 November 1798) created a new direct tax on windows and doors – a kind of general tax on revenue, calculated according to the outward appearance of people's homes. In autumn 1798, the existing direct taxes were reorganized: the *patente* in October, the land tax in November and the personal *mobilière* tax in December. Apprehensive beginnings were made too at reintroducing indirect taxes. Though the Ancients threw out the salt tax accepted by the Five-Hundred, they did agree to a slight increase in the tax on imported tobacco and to the institution of a road tax, called the *droit de passe*, and a 10 per cent tax on seats in public stage-coaches. The stamp tax was augmented, and applied to newspapers and posters. The urban tolls, or *octrois*, were re-established for Paris by the law of 27 Vendémiaire Year VII (18 October 1798), to ensure assistance was properly financed in the capital. The registration duty was reorganized by the law of 22 Frimaire Year VII (12 December 1798). These fiscal reforms proved effective, and their basic features have remained in force down to the present time.

The deficit remained, however. It was calculated that it stood at 250 million *livres* in Year VI; by Year VII, Ramel was reckoning it stood at 66 millions for the year in progress. The government was compelled to resort to the usual expedients: the sale of national lands, borrowing, the exploitation of occupied countries (the cost of the Egyptian expedition, for example, was partly covered by the Treasury of Berne). The Directory was still at the mercy of the financiers, the government-contractors and the sharks, who were as exacting as ever. Corruption was spreading, most notably around the war effort, where it was centred on Schérer, the Minister of War. The evil was deeply rooted, and not even Bonaparte's authoritarian régime was able to extirpate it entirely.

It was partly economic difficulties which spoiled the government's deserving efforts. Deflation made credit much dearer, and the drop in prices also inhibited economic recovery. There was still very little metal currency in circulation, and hoarding made it even rarer: in Year IX, under the Consulate, there was still only 1 billion *livres* in coin in circulation, whereas there had been $2\frac{1}{2}$ billions in 1789.

Credit, then, was expensive, the usual rate of interest being at least 10 per cent, and in the short term as much as 7 per cent per month. The network of banking institutions was still insufficient, despite the creation by Perregaux and Récamier in 1796 of a Current Accounts Bank, and in 1797 of a Trade Discount Bank, and despite the establishment of some banks in the departments – at Rouen, for example. More than anything else, these banks served as discount agencies for their shareholders.

The drop in prices springing from deflation was furthered by good harvests from 1796 to 1798. Agricultural prices were in general from a quarter to a third less than the 1790 levels, in what had then also been a good year. The problem of food supplies lost its acuteness, therefore, as the price of bread fell to 2 *sous* a pound. Bread prices at this level were conducive to peace between the classes. Discontent increased, however, among agricultural producers – the big landowners and big farmers – who were nearly all electors. Once again, the régime's popularity was affected.

Industry, as usual, felt the effects of the agricultural crisis. It was having difficulties in recovering from the consequences of the war, and was finding it hard to adjust to the extension of France's frontiers. Thus in Year VI, the Lille woolspinning employers had only 60 workers under them, as against 360 workers in 1788: they complained of competition from the occupied or newly-annexed lands, particularly the cloths of Verviers, Aix-la-Chapelle and Limburg. Low agricultural prices moreover lessened the purchasing power of the rural masses, and thus reduced the size of the market. The shortage of credit discouraged the spirit of enterprise. Finally, the poor state of the roads and the general insecurity of travelling impeded internal trade.

Foreign trade, too, was crippled. In 1797, the merchant fleet for trading abroad stood at only one-tenth of its size in 1789: trade with the West Indies had dried up; the Egyptian expedition caused the closure of the Levant. In spite of France's annexations, exports fell to about half their 1789 level. While English goods were flooding Germany, French industrialists, especially the cotton-masters, came out strongly against the creation of a home market encompassing the satellite countries. Fervent supporters of protectionism, French industrialists strongly urged the government to view the sister republics as colonies to be exploited. The customs tariff of 9 Floréal Year VII (28 April 1799) resumed and stepped up the stipulations of the 1791 tariff: import duties on manufacturd goods, on luxury goods and on goods produced in France; export duties on all raw materials. This tariff was to be the foundation of the Consulate's customs policy.

In such unpropitious circumstances, the Directory's economic achievement could hardly be wide-ranging. The multifarious activities of François de Neufchâteau at the Ministry of the Interior – the mainspring of the Directory's economic policy – were more exhortatory than coercive. Thus, although Neufchâteau was a supporter of the new agriculture, the abolition of *vaine pâture* and the redivision and reallocation of the commons, he was compelled to confine himself to increasing the number of circulars encouraging productivity. To provide industry with a stimulus, he arranged the first – highly successful – national exhibition at the Champ-de-Mars in Paris in autumn 1798. He organized a systematic population census, and a statistical inquiry into the state of agriculture, increased the number of central schools, and reorganized public assistance by creating an assistance board, the *bureau de bienfaisance*, in each commune. Yet the results of his endeavours were only slight. Industrial production was still at a lower level than in 1789, while technical progress, notably in the cotton industry, was still very slow in spreading, and the metal and woollen industries were at a standstill. Capitalist concentration was still basically commercial, not industrial: the big heads of firms like Boyer-Fonfrède, Richard and Lenoir, Ternaux, or the older-established Chaptal and Oberkampf were still capitalists on the old model, 'putting out' rather than concentrating production in factories, and supplementing their financial commitment in manufacturing by a large range of other commercial and banking activities. France was still rural, and the vast bulk of production was still agricultural. In spite of the proclamation of the freedom to enclose and freedom of cultivation, the old agriculture still persisted, new crops such as potatoes and fodder plants making only very slow progress.

To a great extent, the weakness of the economy under the Directory accounted for the political difficulties it experienced. Since a directed economy and a cutting back on profits along the lines of Year II was out of the question, the only alternative was to have the régime and the armies live off the conquered territories. When in Year VII defeats brought the armies back on to French soil, the Directory was obliged to increase the tax burden, and this had the effect of increasing its own unpopularity. Once more, the political problem came into the foreground.

2. THE SECOND DIRECTORY AND EUROPE (1797-1798)

After Campoformio, only England was still ranged against France. If the Directory were to push ahead with the struggle against England, it would have to ensure that the European peace which had just been achieved with such difficulty, was maintained. Instead, however, the Directory undertook a policy of expansion in Europe which very soon wrecked the likelihood of any permanent stabilization on the continent. Furthermore, it allowed itself to become involved in the Egyptian expedition, which spread the conflict into the Mediterranean. These adventurist policies compromised absolutely the endeavours at reform within France.

The struggle against England

On 5 Brumaire Year VI (26 October 1797), the Directory decided to form an Army of England under Bonaparte's command. The Directors set forth France's grievances against the English government in a proclamation of 1 Frimaire (21 November) which branded the Westminster cabinet as 'the most corrupt and the most corrupting of European governments'. They went on to stress the economic interests, especially maritime and colonial interests, at stake: 'This cabinet must necessarily desire war, since war enriches it.' The proclamation recalled the seizure of the French colonies and those of her allies. Guadeloupe had been reconquered in 1794 by Victor-Hugues, but Martinique, Tobago and Saint Lucia had all been lost, and although Toussaint L'Ouverture had expelled the English from Santo Domingo, the Directory's power there was purely nominal. Spanish Trinidad and Dutch Guiana were being occupied by the English, who had also installed themselves in Ceylon and the Cape of Good Hope. French colonial trade was in shreds, and merchant shipping annihilated by the British blockade, with the Republic's war-fleet standing by, powerless to help. The proclamation went on to attack perfidious Albion 'which, along with its treasures, amasses the tears and the blood of peoples and which grows fat on its spoils'. The Directory's political grievances were just as great: it made reference to the English gold which had financed the Coalition, Toulon, Quiberon and the Vendée. 'Let the Army of England now go and dictate peace terms in London,' it concluded. About 50,000 men were gathered at Brest for the expedition.

Despite the Directory's political grievances, it was in their economic rivalry that the struggle between England and France was grounded. The blockade, which till then had been conceived of along mercantilist lines and in a way which favoured the interests of the manufacturers, was more strictly enforced. Although the Convention had in theory prohibited English goods on 1 March 1793, the need to export and to procure raw materials for French industry had led to a great deal of flexibility in the enforcement of the legislation. Now, however, there developed a more belligerent conception of the blockade, under which it was seen as a means of reducing England to bankruptcy and forcing her to surrender by preventing her export any of her goods. A law of 10 Brumaire Year V (31 October 1796) decreed the seizure of any ship carrying English goods and the reinforcement of the prohibition on English goods, particularly manufactured textile goods and metal goods. Yet again, however, the government was obliged to take into account the interests of both French manufacturers and neutrals, and to relax the regulations. After 18 Fructidor, all such opportunism seemed to have been ruled out once and for all: the law of 29 Nivôse Year VI (18 January 1798) legalized the seizure of any ship which had undergone English inspection, or which was carrying English goods. Privateering increased, but neutrals abandoned French ports, relations with the United States became strained, and even French manufacturers who supported the prohibition on manufactured goods protested against the shortage of raw materials. Well-to-do consumers also complained of the disappearance of colonial foodstuffs.

Confronted with this threat from across the Channel, English resistance toughened. Fear of an invasion aroused national feeling. Pitt's government obtained supplementary financial resources by intensifying fiscal policy – in particular by establishing income-tax for 1799, at the rate of 10 per cent for all revenues over £200. Voluntary enlistments, prompted by a bounty system, began to increase in the subsequent military effort. The lack of a large enough fighting force – for military service was not obligatory in England – ruled out the possibility of a substantial expedition to the continent. Britain's fleet, which ensured control of the seas and the monopoly of commercial trade, and which was to enable her to prevent the French from landing in England, was the basis of her power. It smashed the Dutch fleet, defeated a Spanish naval squadron at Cape

Saint Vincent on 14 February 1797, and blockaded the port of Cadiz. Nelson's squadron entered the Mediterranean, preventing de Bruey's French squadron from leaving to rejoin the Army of England at Brest.

The English invasion plan was shelved, on the recommendation of Bonaparte's report in late February 1798. Utterly committed to his Eastern mirage, Bonaparte was already preparing for his Egyptian expedition, as the Directory was extending its sway in Western Europe. In their different ways, the policies of both general and government helped to knit together the Second Coalition against France.

The Great Nation and the sister republics

It was not long before the Directory's expansionist policies in the period following Campoformio alarmed the great powers, not least Austria. A great variety of ideological, political and economic factors explain this French expansion. Revolutionary fervour had been reawakened after 18 Fructidor, giving a new impetus to revolutionary propaganda. Once more it became a question of bearing liberty to those peoples subject to aristocracy's and despotism's yoke. The Great Nation came to surround itself with sister republics, satellite states which were both politically subjected to France and economically exploited by her. The struggle against England furthermore favoured expansionist policies, since it necessitated action to deprive England of her continental markets: in particular, controlling the ports and the main trading crossroads, so as to stamp out smuggling. Thus in 1798, the free city of Mulhouse was annexed, while Geneva became the local capital of the new department of the Léman.

The Batavian Republic was reorganized after 18 Fructidor, following a coup d'état on Fructidorian lines on 22 January 1798, which was contrived by Delacroix, France's representative at The Hague, Daendels, the Commander-in-Chief of the Batavian army, and Joubert, commander of the occupying forces. A unitary régime was set up, public officials being made to swear an oath of 'hatred for the Stadtholder, for federalism and for anarchy'. After 22 Floréal, however, the unitary democrats were denounced as anarchists, and the purged government and the local notables prevailed once more.

The Helvetian Republic replaced the old confederation of

independent cantons which had been dominated by bourgeois élites. Swiss patriots like Ochs from Basle and Laharpe from the Vaud were hoping simultaneously to terminate the oligarchical system and to create a unitary republic. Following intrigues in which Bonaparte was involved (he had annexed the Valtellina, and was wanting to ensure communications between the Cisalpine Republic and France through the Valais), the Vaud was occupied. During the night of 13–14 February 1798, Brune's troops marched on Berne and seized its Treasury. A Directorial Constitution was accepted by an assembly which met at Aarau, though the highland regions of Schwytz, Uri and Unterwald rebelled and had to be put down. To terminate resistance, the commissioner attached by the Directory to the Helvetian army, Rapinat, performed a coup d'état on his own authority on 16 June 1798. Ochs and Laharpe were elected on to a Helvetian Directory, and this led to a strengthening of the democrat party.

A treaty of alliance and a commercial agreement were forced on the Cisalpine Republic on 21 February 1798. The Republic remained burdened with an occupying force of 25,000 men, whom she paid for. The Directory had to intervene and to purge the Cisalpine Councils in order to obtain the ratification of the treaty. Its instructions to the minister Trouvé, who had been sent as plenipotentiary to Milan in June 1798, clearly reveal the state of subjection in which the French government intended to keep the sister republics. The Cisalpine Republic was to confine itself to 'serving the exclusive interests of the French Republic, and helping her to become the arbiter of all political disputes in the Italian peninsula; the Cisalpine Republic must become powerful enough to be useful to us, yet never so powerful as to become injurious towards us'. The authorities in the Cisalpine state were to be sustained in their 'feeling of weakness and inferiority'. The Directory was especially hostile towards the 'Jacobins', some of whom were leaders of the Cisalpine Republic, and who were partisans of Italian unity. The grounds for the Directory's hostility towards these 'Jacobins' was not opposition to republicanism, but rather the consideration that a divided Italy would suit French interests rather better than a united one.

The Roman Republic was established following a riot instigated on 28 December 1797 by Italian patriots. The riot had turned to the advantage of the patriots' opponents, who attacked the French, whom they held responsible, and even murdered General Duphot. Berthier, commander of the Army of Italy, marched on Rome, which the revolutionaries had christened the Roman Republic. The Pope was transferred to Sienna. A Civil Commission including Daunou and Monge forced through a directorial commission. When Masséna replaced Berthier, the newly-established Republic was given over to looting by government contractors and generals.

Piedmont managed to safeguard its independence in spite of an attempt at revolution in 1797, which was harshly repressed, and in spite of the machinations of the Cisalpine patriots. After 18 Fructidor, the King of Sardinia agreed to a treaty of alliance with France, and on 27 June 1798, the Directory's envoy, utilizing the disturbances started by revolutionaries within Turin as a pretext, forced him to accept a further agreement which allowed French troops to occupy the city.

The Congress of Rastatt, which the Campoformio Treaty had made provision for, in order to settle the fate of the left bank of the Rhine, had finally opened on 16 November 1797. French domination was secure and well-established in the area of Belgium which had formerly been Austrian, in the former bishopric of Liège and the annexed Dutch territories. Indeed, this latter area had already been divided into nine departments where French revolutionary laws now ran. In the Rhineland, the occupied territories had also by now been organized into four departments. Though willing to countenance this French expansion, the Austrian Chancellor Thugut did expect something in return. On 9 March 1798, the German Diet provisionally accepted the claim of Treilhard, the French envoy, for all the left bank of the Rhine, including the Cologne region. The Austrian plenipotentiary immediately demanded compensation, which Treilhard refused. In April, rioters in Vienna attacked the French embassy, where the tricolour had been hoisted. The break between the two states seemed imminent.

The *journée* of 22 Floréal apparently invalidated this impression. The Directory was now harassing the Left, and in the sister republics was breaking with the Jacobins. In particular in Italy, it made enemies of the Jacobins, and thus compromised French interests a little more. The anti-Jacobin campaign could not alone, however, bring about reconciliation with Austria. In fact, by denying Austria compensation in Italy, which the Austrians saw as their own preserve, the Directory was driving Austria ever closer to England, at the very moment, moreover, that the Egyptian expedition was winning the Republic even more enemies.

The Egyptian adventure (1798)

We may detect the origins of the Egyptian expedition, partly at least, in Bonaparte's 'Eastern dream', which his concern at Campoformio to ensure France possession of the Ionian Islands had attested. Doubtless, the Directory was not sorry to get off its hands on the eve of the Year VI elections a general with such enigmatic intentions and whose ambition it feared. Egypt, a nominal dependency of the Sultan, was not unknown territory for France: Marseille businessmen maintained long-standing commercial relations with it. As early as 1796, the French consul in Cairo, Magallon, had recommended its occupation, judging such an operation to be very easy. The idea cropped up of France compensating herself in Egypt for the loss of the West Indies. This theme was developed by Talleyrand in his speech to the Institute on 15 Messidor Year V (3 July 1797), entitled 'Essay on the advantages to be derived from new colonies in the present circumstances'. The nature of Talleyrand's involvement in the whole question seems very hazy. As a supporter of the idea of an agreement with England, it could not escape him that the conquest of Egypt would make England apprehensive for the security of the route to the Indies, and would also set Turkey against France. It may have been that Talleyrand merely wished to add to the military glory of his friend Bonaparte; or else 'to help his English friends', as it was put in a letter from his mistress Madame Grant, by diverting the threat presented by the Army of England towards an objective rather further afield. By 9 Thermidor Year V (16 August 1797), Bonaparte was already speaking of the useful purpose to be served by occupying Egypt: 'The time is not far off when we shall feel that, if we are really to defeat England, we must secure Egypt.' On 5 Ventôse Year VI (23 February 1798), he communicated to Barras a plan for the occupation, which the Directory approved on 15 Ventôse.

Preparations for the expedition were carried out extremely swiftly and in the greatest secrecy. Within two months, a squadron of 55 ships and a fleet of 280 transport vessels were amassed at Toulon. The expeditionary force numbered 54,000 men, of whom 38,000 were soldiers. Bonaparte also took with him a numerous staff and a commission of 187 scholars, writers and artists.

The Egyptian expeditionary force set sail on 30 Floréal Year VI

(19 May 1798). By 6 June, the fleet was at Malta, which fell without a shot being fired. Escaping from Nelson, the French managed to reach Alexandria, which they took by assault on 2 July. The army marched directly on Cairo. Egypt was theoretically ruled by beys, who were in fact under the sway of the Mamelukes, who exploited the country for their own profit. On 21 July, the Mameluke cavalry was smashed to pieces at the foot of the Pyramids against the French infantry, drawn up in squares. Bonaparte did not have the cavalry, however, to offer pursuit. On 23 July, he entered Cairo. On 1 August 1798, however, the English fleet under Nelson surprised Bruey's French fleet riding at anchor near Aboukir, and annihilated it, only two vessels escaping. At a single blow, England was mistress of the seas, and Bonaparte was imprisoned in his conquest.

Quite as much as Bonaparte's involvement in Italy, the Egyptian adventure marked a turning-point in the history of Revolutionary France. This expedition, which took the Republic's troops far from France when the struggle against England was still in progress and continental peace remained uncertain, was not consistent with the nation's interests. Till this time, Revolutionary France had been uninvolved in Eastern affairs. England, who since her occupation of the Cape of Good Hope in 1796 had been thinking that she controlled the route to the Indies, discovered the importance of the Suez route. Turkey, then Russia, became alarmed in turn. The alliance of these three powers ensued: this was the first step towards the formation of the Second Coalition.

The Second Coalition (1798–1799)

The formation of the Second Coalition (April–December 1798) was Europe's riposte to the invasionist policies of the Directory. For several months, England had worked at arousing a new enemy for France on the continent, without which England could not hope to deal her any really decisive blows. The Eastern and Italian Affairs gave England her chance.

The Egyptian affair drew Turkey and Russia closer to England. Turkey declared war on France on 9 September 1798. In Russia, the half-mad Paul I had succeeded Catherine II. Full of hatred for the revolution, he welcomed the pretender Louis XVIII and installed him at Mitau; more importantly, he resumed expansionist policies towards the Mediterranean. The struggle with France allowed him to come to an agreement with Turkey which, in a treaty, 23 December 1798, opened its ports and the Straits to Russia. A Russian fleet penetrated into the Mediterranean and seized the Ionian Islands. On 29 December, an alliance was signed between England, Naples and Russia; the latter undertook to intervene against France in Italy.

The Rome affair had restarted war in the Italian peninsula. Encouraged by Nelson, the sovereigns of Naples, Ferdinand III and in particular Marie-Caroline, who was firmly dedicated to fostering English influence, attacked the Roman Republic. On 26 November 1798, Neapolitan troops under the Austrian general Mack seized Rome. The Directory replied by first of all occupying Piedmont, whose king was allegedly an accomplice of the Austrians. Then Championnet, at the head of the French forces, took to the offensive, freed Rome and seized Naples on 23 January 1799. The King and the Queen crossed to Sicily in English vessels. Southern Italy was given over to looting. Championnet contravened his instructions from the Directory, creating a Parthenopean Republic, whereas the Directory had wanted to retain the territory and to use it as a bargaining counter in future negotiations. While Prussia maintained her neutrality, Austria, after initial hesitation, committed herself, just as the Russians were ready to intervene in the peninsula. The Austrians allowed the Russians safe-conduct through their territory. The Directory used this as a *casus belli* against Austria, declaring war on her on 22 Ventôse Year VII (12 March 1799), and immediately occupying Tuscany and transferring the Pope to Valence.

The Second Coalition reached its full complement when in October 1799 Gustav IV of Sweden adhered. No treaty existed, however, between Austria and England, and indeed, although the powers were united in their determination to force France back within her old frontiers, their understanding went very little further. English and Russian interests, for example, clashed in the Mediterranean, as did those of Austria and Russia in Italy. Once again, England financed the Coalition, though only this time by a supreme effort, and while workers' agitation was spreading (the Combinations Act forbidding strikes dates from 12 July 1799). The Russians put 80,000 men into the field, thereby securing the Coalition numerical superiority over France. The war spread gradually and became general in the spring of 1799.

The Rastatt outrage of 28 April 1798 emphasized the implacable character of the war which was about to recommence, a war between aristocratic Europe and the revolutionary nation. As they were leaving the Rastatt Congress on the night of 28 April, the three French plenipotentiaries were cut down by Austrian hussars, only one surviving. According to Sieyès, 'the tocsin for French extermination' was ringing in monarchical capitals in Europe. The Directory had little difficulty in arousing indignation. 'It is no longer solely the cause of Freedom that we must defend,' it proclaimed on 17 Floréal Year VII (6 May 1798), 'but that of humanity itself.' The war again assumed a revolutionary character.

3. THE FINAL REVOLUTIONARY CRISIS (1799)

The peace in Europe which had followed Campoformio had given the strengthened Directory a degree of stability. However, the resumption of the war and the failures of the campaign of spring 1799 brought the régime's equilibrium under severe pressure. The developments accompanying the death-throes of the Directory were to be the growth of Jacobinism, moderate reaction, and the final military *coup de force* of Brumaire Year VIII.

The army in Year VIII and the spring campaign (1799)

In Year VIII, the army experienced difficulties as great as those it had experienced in 1793, before the Committee of Public Safety had organized the war-effort. It consequently regained some of the popular complexion it was tending to lose. To solve the problem of diminishing manpower in the armies, the Directory had in fact returned to the principle of the *levée en masse*. The Jourdan Law of 19 Fructidor Year VI (5 September 1798) in effect instituted conscription: military service was obligatory for all men between the ages of twenty and twenty-five. Obligation did not necessarily entail service, however. The legislature acted as arbiter in the timing and the size of each batch: they could call up only enough to round out numbers, or else increase the army's strength. The law also regulated promotion democratically: 'No French citizen may be promoted to the rank of officer unless he has served three years as a soldier or as a non-commissioned officer except in the engineering corps and in the artillery and also for brilliant feats of arms on the field of battle.' On 3 Vendémiaire Year VII (24 September 1798), 200,000 conscripts were called up, and this was followed by successive call-ups until the law of 10 Messidor (28 June 1799), which placed all five contingents provided for by the Jourdan Law on active service in their entirety. Military substitutions, which had been permitted under the law of 28 Germinal Year VII (17 April 1799), were suppressed the following 14 Messidor (2 July).

That the enforcement of conscription did not proceed smoothly was partly due to the lack of properly-kept military registers, and partly due to desertions. The number of failures to report was huge. From the 200,000 men called up on 3 Vendémiaire, only 143,000 were found fit to serve, only 97,000 answered the call to colours, and only 74,000 ultimately joined their units. The army in Year VII no longer had numerical superiority over the enemy, unlike its counterpart of Year II. It proved, moreover, impossible to equip it. The 125 million *livres*' worth of national lands which were put up for sale to this purpose comprised only a belated and inadequate effort. The soldiers of Year VII, stationed in satellite states which had long since been drained of resources, experienced the same destitution as those of Year III. Conscripted recruits were 'amalgamated' with those troops who had been called up in 1793, and who had been in arms ever since, tending thereby to become professional soldiers. This continuation of the *amalgame* helped the army of Year VII to regain some of the popular impetus which had characterized the army of Year II.

The war in 1799 was basically a continental one. The English ruled the seas following Aboukir, and the attempted Irish expedition under General Humbert had proved shortlived (August 1798). On land, operations had begun slowly. The plan of campaign for spring 1799 envisaged three armies, each operating at reduced strength, holding Holland, the Rhine and Naples. The Danube Army under Jourdan, 45,000 strong, would march on Vienna via southern Germany. The Army of Italy under Schérer, and at the same strength, via Venetia and Carinthia. In the centre, the Army of Helvetia under Masséna ensured communications, threatened the Tyrol and was to be kept in reserve, to be deployed when necessary. The Austrians had adopted a similar set of arrangements: 75,000 men under Archduke Charles in Bavaria, 60,000 under Kray, and 20,000 in the Tyrol. The Directory looked to the Army of the Orient under Bonaparte to provide a diversion.

In Germany, the campaign started badly. Jourdan was defeated by the Archduke at Stokach on 25 March 1799, and retreated, along with Bernadotte's Rhine Army, which covered his left flank.

In Italy, Schérer attempted to force his way across the Adige at Verona, failed and retreated to the Adda where he handed over command to Moreau. At this moment, Suvarov's Russians took the field, forcing their way over the Adda, notably at Cassano, 27 April 1799, and obliging Moreau to evacuate Milan and Lombardy. Disappointed by the Directory's policies, the Italian patriots, the 'unitary Jacobins', sided with the Coalition powers and rebelled against the French. Moreau's troops regrouped at Alessandria and fell back to Genoa. The Army of Naples, however, in which Championnet had been succeeded by MacDonald, was laboriously making its way northwards. Suvarov turned against MacDonald's army, blocking its way and defeating it in a keenly contested battle lasting three days on the banks of the Trebbia (17–19 June 1799). He then retraced his steps towards Genoa.

In Switzerland, Masséna had at first occupied the Grisons and invaded the Vorarlberg. When the loss of both Germany and Italy exposed both his flanks, however, he in turn retreated. Attacked by Archduke Charles, he won the first battle of Zürich (4 June 1799), but abandoned the city, entrenching himself behind the Limmat, while General Lecourbe evacuated the Saint Gothard highway and the Reuss valley.

Though the natural frontiers were still intact, the Republic had retreated on all fronts. Splits in the Coalition now afforded the Directory some respite, however. The Austrian government resented Russia's presence in Italy, and Thugut was contemplating sending Suvarov into Switzerland, in order to give Austria a clear field in the peninsula. Even more significantly, the danger from abroad rekindled the will to fight in France and excited a final bout of revolutionary fervour.

The journée of 30 Prairial Year VII (18 June 1799)

The atmosphere in which the Year VII elections took place was unfavourable to the Directory, even before the military defeats had occurred. A general discontent was growing, which sprang from economic stagnation, an increase in the tax-burden and the introduction of conscription. The Belgian departments rebelled in November

1798, and Chouannerie restarted, even though the western departments had been specifically exempted from the new call-up. Once
again, in its circular of 23 Pluviôse (11 February 1799), the Directory denounced the double danger of royalism and anarchy:
'Frenchmen, you have staved off and defeated the powers of Europe.
The only task before you now is to defeat the internal enemies.'
François de Neufchâteau called the propertied classes to arms: 'Do
you want another *maximum* passed?' Of course in his circular of
14 Ventôse (4 March) he also denounced the royalist threat – 'Citizens, an end to hatred, to vengeance and above all to reaction' – but
his basic endeavour was to revive in the ranks of the bourgeoisie
the fear of a return to 'the frightful régime of 1793': 'Citizens of all
classes, you are joined together by a common interest to cry out
in unison, "An end to anarchy in France!"'

The Directory had recourse to its usual methods of bringing
pressure to bear on the elections: the sending out of special commissioners into the departments, dismissals of officials, the organization of secessionary assemblies, as for example in the Sarthe. The
current of opposition was so strong, however, that 121 of the 187
official government candidates were defeated none the less. This did
not overthrow the majority in the Councils, where despite the
strengthening of the Jacobin minority, the Thermidorian bourgeoisie still held sway. It was this bourgeoisie which, in the crisis
begun by the military defeats of spring 1799, was ultimately to have
the final word.

The fall of the Second Directory took place in a widely-acknow-
ledged atmosphere of disintegration. The armies were retreating on
all fronts, and were facing the most extreme shortages. Italy had been
lost. The royalists were taking up arms again. Financial exactions
were exasperating the propertied classes. As the discrediting of the
government became more widespread, chance came to the aid of the
opposition when, on 20 Floréal (9 May 1799), the lot for outgoing
Director fell to the most energetic of all five, Reubell. On 27
Floréal (16 May), the Ancients designated as his replacement Sieyes,
whose opposition to the Constitution of Year III was notorious.
Sieyès took office on 21 Prairial (9 June) and, supported by Barras,
who had realized the drift of affairs, encouraged the Councils to take
to the offensive against their Directorial colleagues. On 28 Prairial
(16 June), the Councils declared themselves *en permanence*. That
evening, they annulled Treilhard's election to the Directory as

contravening article 136 of the Constitution which specified a lapse of one year between a deputy leaving the legislature and being elected to the Directory. The following day, he was replaced by Gohier, a good republican and former Minister of Justice in Year II, but a second-rate politician.

On 30 Prairial Year VII (18 June 1799), the Councils resumed their offensive against the Directory. The attack was led by a former 'regicide' from the Convention, Bertrand du Calvados, who inveighed against the Directors: 'You have destroyed public feeling, muzzled liberty, persecuted republicans, smashed a free press, suffocated truth.' The Councils seemed to be aiming at exacting their revenge for the humiliation of Floréal, for Bertrand continued, 'The French people in Year VI had appointed to public office men worthy of its confidence; you dared to say that the elections were the product of an anarchical conspiracy and on those grounds you meddled most gravely with the representatives of the nation.' Boulay de la Meurthe continued the attack: 'Since 18 Fructidor, when the dictatorship was established, the legislature has been held in a state of continual abasement.' He was especially critical of Merlin, 'a man with little views, little passions, little vengeances and little decrees'; and also of La Revellière, who had been led by his fanaticism 'to create an indescribable religion, for whose establishment he sacrifices all accepted ideas and tramples under foot all the opinions prescribed by common sense'.

Called upon to hand in their resignation and abandoned by their colleagues, Merlin and La Revellière ultimately gave way and on 1–2 Messidor (19–20 June), Roger Ducos, a former 'regicide' in the Convention, and the little-known general Moulin, at that moment passing through Paris, were elected Directors.

A parliamentary *journée* rather than coup d'état, 30 Prairial Year VII was more than anything else the revenge taken on the executive by the Councils who had suffered 'florealization' at their hands the previous year. 'The Legislative Body,' Lucien Bonaparte told the Five-Hundred, 'has resumed the first place that it must hold in the state.'

The wishes of the Councils dictated who the new figures in the government should be. The ministers as well as the Directory underwent changes. General Bernadotte became War Minister, Cambacérès Minister of Justice, while Fouché was installed in the Police Ministry and Robert Lindet, the former member of the great

Committee of Public Safety, took over Finances. This latter nomination was particularly revealing: declared republicans were returning to power. It was at this moment that the victories of the Coalition imperilled the Republic.

The growth of neo-Jacobinism, the moderate reaction

A swing to the left and a national crisis thus coincided once again. Though united against the Fructidorians, the victors of Prairial were split, and for two months, neo-Jacobins held the upper hand over the Thermidorian bourgeoisie, and forced through their public safety policies. The bulk of these neo-Jacobins were former deputies in the Convention who had been defeated in the Year V elections by the royalists, who had been excluded in Floréal Year VI by the Fructidorians, and who thus returned quite naturally to the methods of Year II, which were again justified by the dangers threatening the nation. Press freedom was reestablished on 14 Thermidor (1 August 1799), and Jacobin newspapers reappeared. Clubs reopened and proliferated. The most important one was the Société des Amis de l'égalité et de la liberté, also called the Club du Manège, after the name of the room in the Tuileries where it met. The Club's first session was held on 18 Messidor (6 July), its first *régulateur* the hero of Varennes and Babeuf's comrade, Drouet. Numerous deputies attended the Club. The Jacobin minority gave the lead to the anxious majority in the Councils which, in order to face up to the situation, agreed to put everything into the war-effort, both by increasing manpower in the armies, and by raising extra financial resources, and even by countenancing methods which smacked of Year II.

Conscription was enforced in full. The law of 10 Messidor Year VII (28 June 1799), introduced by Jourdan, called up the full complement of potential recruits. On 14 Messidor (2 July), military substitution was suppressed: 'Those who have purchased replacement conscripts will be called up themselves if their replacement deserts, is cashiered or is himself conscripted.'

A forced loan of 100 million *livres* on well-to-do citizens had been provisionally adopted by the Councils on 10 Messidor, to cover the expenses arising from conscription. Terms and conditions of payment of the loan were fixed on 19 Thermidor (6 August 1799). It was applied, according to a sliding scale, on the revenue of all citizens paying more than 100 francs in *mobilière* taxation, or more than 300 francs land tax. Income and capital not affected by taxes (article 7 of the law specifically designated fortunes acquired by 'enterprises, contracting and speculation') were to be evaluated by a jury of citizens not subject to the tax.

The Law of Hostages, whose aim, according to a deputy in the Five-Hundred, was 'to check the course of the banditry and Chouannerie which are manifesting themselves in the departments of the Midi and the West', was passed on 24 Messidor (12 July). In a department which the legislature designated as 'notoriously in a condition of civil disturbance', the central administration of the department was empowered to take hostages from among the relatives of émigrés, from *ci-devant* nobles and from relatives of individuals 'notorious for participating in mobs or in murder gangs'. These persons would be considered 'personally responsible and liable for damages for murders and banditry committed inside the department out of hatred against the Republic'. If a public official, a soldier or a purchaser of national lands had been murdered, the Directory was to decree the deportation of four hostages. For each assassination, hostages were held jointly responsible and liable to pay in damages a fine of 5,000 francs plus indemnities of 6,000 francs for the victim's widow and 3,000 francs for each of his children. The Law of Hostages provoked opposition from all those who had some grievance against the Revolution, at the same time that the forced loan was throwing into opposition all those whom the Law of Hostages was aimed at protecting.

The anti-Jacobin reaction was not long in appearing. As early as 26 Messidor, the anniversary of the fall of the Bastille, Sieyès had recalled and inveighed against 'those disastrous times . . . in which all ideas were so topsy-turvy that those who were not officially in charge of anything were obstinately determined to take everything in hand'. Again, on 23 Thermidor, the anniversary of 10 August, he condemned 'that terror so justly abominated by Frenchmen. . . . Those who by their frenzied provocations dry up the sources of public wealth, kill credit, destroy trade and cripple all works, are not republicans at all!'

While conscription met with a universally hostile reception, the forced loan displeased above all the upper bourgeoisie, who organized passive resistance to it. Even before the law had been passed fixing the method of payment of the loan, the *Publiciste* noted, on 13 Thermidor (30 July), that 'as much pretence is employed these days to hide one's fortune as was formerly employed to display it or even to exaggerate it. This is the cause of the disappearance of luxury. It is unavoidable in the case of a very large number of persons, especially landed property owners. Others seek in this way to escape the enormous impositions universally feared. There are even some people who are going bankrupt in order to prove their distress more unequivocally.'

A press campaign was started, to demand that the government break with the *buveurs de sang*. The social fear of the propertied classes was reappearing. It was made more acute by the proposals of the Club du Manège, where on the anniversary of 14 July, for example, general Jourdan had proposed a toast 'to the resurrection of the pikes!' 'It is said that many people,' the *Moniteur* had written on 25 Messidor (13 July), 'were frightened by the speeches which were being delivered in this assembly, and began to shout "Down with the Jacobins" and to throw stones into the hall.'

There were an increasing number of brawls. Although the Jacobins still enjoyed the support of the old sans-culotte cadres – clerks, artisans, shopkeepers – they were unable to set the masses in motion again: since the sections had been suppressed, the masses had been completely disorganized, and had been virtually paralysed by the repression. Isolated and without any clear social programme, the Jacobins were powerless when confronted by a government which was firmly established, with the administration, the police and, since Fructidor, a garrison of 20,000 men as the props of its power.

The break between the Jacobins and the Directory came with the closure of the Club du Manège. The club had been criticized before the Ancients on 8 Thermidor (26 July) for contemplating 'the resurrection of the Terror and the exhuming of the proscription lists', and had been obliged to leave the Manège hall for the rue du Bac. Fouché, who had been appointed Police Minister on 11 Thermidor (29 July), lost no time in presenting a report to the Councils, 'on the need to protect the internal debates of political meetings by using the full measure of the Republic's strength to banish the Club du Manège from the State'. Though the Five-Hundred did not accept Fouché's report, his decision to close the Club on 26 Thermidor (13 August) did not provoke any reaction. The royalist threat and the military defeats allowed the Jacobins to keep going, however.

On 18 Fructidor (5 August), royalist insurrection broke out in the Haute-Garonne. Toulouse, which was in the hands of a Jacobin administration, was threatened for a moment, but held firm. The news reached Paris on 26 Thermidor (13 August). The Councils immediately authorized home raids for a month 'to arrest émigrés, royalist recruiting agents, cut-throats and brigands'. The rebels were defeated on 1 Fructidor (18 August) at Montréjeau. Disturbances recommenced in the West, however, during the summer.

A final Jacobin offensive took place over the military defeats. Joubert was defeated and killed in Italy on 28 Thermidor (15 August 1799). In Holland, the English landed a force of 25,000 Russians on the Helder on 10 Fructidor (27 August). As in 1793, the Republic's frontiers appeared to be threatened. On 27 Fructidor, General Jourdan proposed in the Five-Hundred the proclamation of '*la patrie en danger*'. Outlining the whole gamut of dangers with which he saw the country surrounded, Jourdan spoke of

Italy under the yoke, the barbarians of the North at the gates of Paris, Holland invaded, the fleets treacherously surrendered to the enemy, Helvetia laid waste, royalist gangs indulging in every type of excess in a great many departments, with republicans proscribed as 'terrorists' and 'jacobins'. One more setback, and the tocsin of royalty will ring out over the whole extent of French soil.

Jourdan's proposal gave rise to a furious debate, in which Lucien Bonaparte opposed him, contending that it was 'better to extend the constitutional powers of the Directory than to be exposed to being carried off by a revolutionary wave'.

Lucien Bonaparte was here posing the real problem confronting the politicians: whether, in order to cope with the danger, they should rely on the people as in Year II, or whether they should merely strengthen the executive. Daunou's speech in the debate was also to the point: he feared 'a return to the 1793 régime'. His point of view prevailed: Jourdan's proposal was rejected the following day by 245 votes to 171. On 2 Vendémiaire Year VIII (24 September 1799), Garau, from the Gironde, obtained a decree ordaining the death penalty for anyone who 'would propose or would accept peace terms which tend to impair the wholeness of the existing territory of the Republic'. The Jacobins' final victory had sounded: for by this time the war situation had been retrieved by decisive victories.

The summer campaign (*1799*)

The campaign began badly for France, but a recovery, facilitated by splits among the Coalition, soon came about. In Italy, Joubert took to the offensive without waiting for Championnet's troops, which were marching through Piedmont to join him. He was killed at the beginning of the battle of Novi, on 15 August 1799, and his troops were defeated by Suvarov's Russians. Italy was lost. The Austrian Chancellor, Thugut, was optimistic that Austria would be able to retain it, and started intriguing in order to get the Russians out of the peninsula.

In Switzerland, Masséna was faced by Archduke Charles's Austrians and Korsakov's Russian contingent, which held Zürich and the line of the Limmat. The Anglo-Russian landing in Holland gave Austria cause for concern, and the Austrian government ordered Archduke Charles to leave Switzerland and to proceed towards Mainz. On 11 September, Suvarov set off from Italy to relieve him in Switzerland. Before the two Russian armies could join together, the French defeated them separately. General Lecourbe seized Saint Gothard and the Reuss valley. While still containing Suvarov, Masséna attacked Korsakov, isolated and encircled at Zürich, and forced him back across the Rhine in the second, victorious battle of Zürich (25–27 September 1799). Suvarov, however, crossed the Saint Gothard and drove back Lecourbe's troops, though he soon came up against Mortier's contingent, supported by Masséna. He therefore withdrew in order to march against general Molitor, who was holding the Linth valley. Unable to force his way across the river, he retired to the Vorarlberg. Switzerland was once again in French power and Paul I, now totally mad, recalled his troops to Russia, 23 October.

The Anglo-Russian forces which had landed on 27 August in Holland had met with no success. The Duke of York took to the offensive, but was defeated by Brune's army at Bergen on 19 September 1799, and at Castricum on 6 October. On 18 October he signed the Alkmaar evacuation agreement.

By the beginning of autumn 1799, France's frontiers were still intact and the offensive of the Coalition powers had been smashed. Bonaparte and his Army of Egypt had had no hand in these successes. On the contrary, the Eastern diversion had completely miscarried.

The failure of the Egyptian expedition sprang from the naval defeat of Aboukir. After this, the French troops were in an impasse. Anticipating the Turkish attack, Bonaparte had marched on Syria in February 1799. Although he won the battle of Mont-Thabor, he failed to lift the siege of Acre, which the English kept supplied by sea. He was compelled to order a retreat to Egypt on 20 May. The march was hard, but nevertheless, in the battle of Aboukir, 25 July 1799, Bonaparte still managed to crush the Turkish army which the English had shipped from Rhodes. Yet though victorious, Bonaparte was still imprisoned in his conquest, with an army weakened by the climate and the war. Reckoning that he had lost this round, Bonaparte abandoned his command to Kléber and in August left Egypt secretly with two frigates. He escaped the English blockade and landed at Fréjus on 17 Vendémiaire Year VIII (9 October 1799).

Once the danger from abroad had been staved off, the moderate reaction began to prevail over neo-Jacobinism. On 2 Brumaire (24 October), the Ancients rejected Garau's proposal to institute the death penalty for those accepting proposals prejudicial to the integrality of French territory. Even more revealing of the trend of opinion was a further bout of challenging the forced loan: on 17 Brumaire, a little-known deputy in the Five-Hundred demanded the withdrawal of this 'graduated and arbitrary loan'. The coup d'état was finally to set the minds of the propertied classes at rest once and for all.

4. THE EIGHTEENTH BRUMAIRE YEAR VIII (9 NOVEMBER 1799)

After landing at Fréjus on 17 Vendémiaire (9 October), Bonaparte arrived in Paris on 22 Vendémiaire (14 October). The news caused a sensation. 'Bonaparte's landing in France,' wrote the *Messager des relations extérieures* on 23 Vendémiaire, 'is one of those events one hears recounted several times without believing it.' The *Moniteur* exclaimed on the same day: 'Everyone is intoxicated. Victory, which is Bonaparte's constant companion, has anticipated him this time, and he arrives in time to strike the final blows against the dying Coalition.'

Public opinion saw in Bonaparte the Campoformio peace-maker, the man who would once again impose peace on Europe. In actual fact, the invasion threat had been diverted, thanks to the victories in Holland and Switzerland; the year's campaign was at an end; and Bonaparte could not receive a high command before the following spring. Unwilling to allow the Directory to get the credit for reestablishing peace without his assistance, he made overtures to those who were thinking in terms of a coup d'état, of whom Sieyès was the key figure.

Social fear and revisionism

The constant dilemma of Directorial politics – the threat to governmental stability – and its social ramifications, had again come into the foreground. The danger had been averted, but an air of uncertainty and expectancy hung over everything. The foreign war was continuing and would resume in the spring. Civil war was restarting: on 22 Vendémiaire (14 October), the Chouans had seized Le Mans and then Nantes. Although they were at once beaten back, the alarm caused was revealing of the general political atmosphere. For in the spring of Year VII, elections would be held again, and if they produced a royalist or a Jacobin victory, the stability of the government could be brought into question again. The Constitution of Year III lay at the heart of the debate: not its property-franchise basis, but rather its liberalism, its balance of powers, and the annual renewal of one-third of the members of the Councils. The Directory had resolved the problem after Fructidor by setting up a disguised dictatorship. Since annual elections made everything uncertain, the aim now was to make them less frequent. This was what was called for by Daunou who, though one of the authors of the Constitution of Year III, was tired of the régime's incertitudes, and who found the prospect of either a restoration of the monarchy or democratization equally distasteful. The *Décade philosophique*, the newspaper of the 'ideologues', a group of thinkers centred on Daunou, expressed the same feelings. In the spring of Year V (1797), Benjamin Constant had published a work entitled *Des réactions politiques*, in which he called for 'the force and stability of government' which alone 'guarantee citizens the safety of their persons and the inviolability of their property'. Madame de Staël naturally shared these views. Finally Sieyès, whose cast of mind was thoroughly constitutional, declared for revision. The principle of national sovereignty remained sacrosanct. The Thermidorian bourgeoisie could not renounce this principle without denying its own raison d'être, and without playing into the hands of those who maintained that the government should be grounded in the principle of divine right. The point was, therefore, to reconcile the principle of national sovereignty with the requirements of a strong and stable executive power. Sieyès conceived of replacing election by the cooptation which characterized the Constitution of Year VIII. Indeed, the Thermidorians and the Directorials had already made hypocritical use of this method in the decree of the two-thirds and by the Fructidor and Floréal purges. The Constitution of Year VIII was to appear in many respects to be the culmination of the constitutional practice of the Directory.

The ease with which the Brumaire coup succeeded is very largely due to its social dimension: it would not have carried had it not satisfied the requirements of the dominant elements of the new society. The Thermidorians had consecrated, and the Directory safeguarded, the social preponderance and the political power of the conservative bourgeoisie. The recrudescence of Jacobinism in Year VII seemed to endanger the privileges of the propertied classes. Social fear reappeared, and provided revisionism with a powerful cohesive agent. The landowning peasantry and the commercial bourgeoisie were especially important elements in the new union of the propertied classes. Both the product of the Revolution, each in its own way favoured the establishment of calm and social stability.

The landowning peasantry wished to work in peace, without the social order constantly being disrupted by repeated bouts of brigandage. They were hostile to attempts to restore the monarchy, for this risked them losing the peaceful enjoyment of their property: feudal rights and the tithe would be reestablished and the whole question of the sale of national lands brought under review. This group was equally afraid of a popular upsurge, which could only, they maintained, entail anarchy and be a prelude to the *loi agraire*, the division of property. They were therefore ready to adhere to the régime which would reassure them against both these threats.

As for the commercial bourgeoisie, they considered that the expansion of their affairs was being inhibited by the régime's instability and by the prolongation of the war. Furthermore, the forced loan, which seemed to be moving in the direction of fiscal equality, was for them an abomination, a veritable *loi agraire*. This group hankered after a political system which would protect its interests, indefinitely guarantee its rights, and allow it to intensify its efforts to revive the economy. The commercial bourgeoisie and the landowning peasantry formed the social base for first the Consular and then the Imperial periods. The core of the notables was recruited from their ranks.

The revision of the Constitution of Year III, provided for under heading 13, was an extremely complicated process, which involved three successive votes in the Councils and the meeting of an 'Assembly of Revision', and which was stretched out over nine years. The alternative was a coup d'état, and Sieyès was resolved to use it. The army was again needed – as on 18 Fructidor – to force the hand of the majority in the Councils, with the difference this time that, whereas in Year VIII the majority was republican, in Year V it had been royalist. Sieyès had sounded out General Joubert to lead the coup, and he had accepted the offer, but was killed at Novi on 15 August 1799. Sieyès then approached Moreau, who was hesitant. When, just at that moment, Bonaparte landed, Moreau is alleged to have said to Sieyès, 'There's your man.' Indeed, everything marked Bonaparte out as a potential candidate for the job: his Jacobin past, which could be used as a smokescreen, his prestige, but also his ambition, his lack of scruples, and the dubious position in which he had placed himself by leaving his Egyptian command on his own initiative.

Preparations for the coup d'état were made swiftly. Talleyrand mediated between Bonaparte and Sieyès. Of the Directors, Barras's neutrality was won, and he condoned the whole business, while Roger Ducos followed Sieyès like his shadow. The President of the Ancients was won over. Lucien Bonaparte was voted to the Presidency of the Five-Hundred on 1 Brumaire (29 October). Funds were advanced, notably by army contractors, upset by the law of 7 Brumaire (29 October) which deprived them of rights of priority at Treasury cash-desks. The conspirators skilfully linked the idea of a general peace to that of a change in the Constitution. In order to win over the Councils and to coax the bourgeoisie into following their lead, they pandered to the social fear of the propertied classes, in whose ranks the spectre of egalitarian terrorism was again causing panic, as Madame de Staël attested.

We were very near the time [wrote the semi-official *Moniteur* on 19 Brumaire (10 November)] when it would no longer have been possible to salvage either liberty or property, or the Constitution, which is the safeguard of both.

The newspaper went on to recall 'that the spoliatory law on the forced loan has ruined our finances, that the Law on Hostages has produced civil war, that a portion of the revenue of Year VIII has been eaten up by requisitions and that all credit is at an end'. It was very apparent that the spectre of Year II was haunting the bourgeoisie: they intended to wipe it out once and for all.

The coup d'état

On 18 Brumaire (9 November 1799), the Council of Ancients was convoked at seven in the morning. Troops had been amassed in the Tuileries on the pretence of a military review. Speaking on behalf of the Commission of Inspectors of the hall of the Council – whose role at this juncture was decisive – a little-known deputy denounced a vague plot ('The conspirators . . . are only awaiting the signal to raise their daggers against the representatives of the nation'). The *Moniteur* the following day, either more informed or more inventive, alluded to the plans of the Jacobins 'to convert the two councils into a national Convention, to remove from it the deputies who displeased them and to entrust government to a committee of public safety'.

The Ancients voted for the transfer of the Councils to the château of Saint-Cloud, as they were empowered to do by article 102 of the Constitution of Year III. General Bonaparte was 'charged with the execution of the present decree', and the troops of Paris placed under his orders. This latter measure was illegal, since it lay within the sphere of competence of the Directory, not of the Ancients. The Directory was deprived thereby of all power – even its bodyguard passing under Bonaparte's command – and could only acquiesce. Barras resigned and withdrew to his estate at Grosbois. Moulin raged furiously, but to no purpose. He and Gohier were kept under close supervision by Moreau until they resigned. The meaning of the *journée* was made clear by the *Moniteur* the following day: 'There is talk of the repeal of the laws on the forced loan, and on hostages and of the closure of the émigré lists.'

The Councils' session began at Saint-Cloud at about one in the afternoon of 19 Brumaire (10 November 1799). Bonaparte had amassed from four to five thousand troops round the château. In the

Ancients, the deputies who had been absent the previous day demanded explanations, and challenged the very existence of a plot. At the beginning of the session of the Five-Hundred, where Lucien Bonaparte was president, the Left insisted that each deputy should individually and in turn renew his oath of fidelity to the Constitution. There was a real danger of the whole business becoming protracted. Bonaparte intervened.

In the Ancients, he vowed his dedication to the Republic, defended himself against the charge of wanting 'to establish a military government', and criticized the Council of Five-Hundred 'in which are sitting men who would be willing to restore the Convention, the revolutionary committees and the scaffolds'. He went on to threaten possible opponents with the intervention of his 'fine' companions in arms – 'whose bayonets I can see'. The Constitution 'thrice violated' no longer existed, he held, and 'there was no longer a Directory'. Finally, he made this promise: 'As soon as the dangers which have led to my having been entrusted with special powers are over, I shall abdicate these powers.'

Bonaparte entered the Council of the Five-Hundred encircled by grenadiers and general officers. The assembly was on its feet instantaneously: he had no right to enter the Council without being summoned. Some deputies took him by the scruff of the neck and manhandled him. Cries of 'Outlaw him!' and 'Down with the dictator!' were heard. Bonaparte was dragged free and taken outside by his grenadiers. The debate continued in a state of confusion. Lucien was in vain endeavouring to defend his brother when a squad of grenadiers arrived to take him outside, on Bonaparte's orders. The troops, especially the bodyguard of the Councils, were hesitant. Lucien harangued them from horseback, denouncing a minority of 'representatives of the dagger' who had attempted to assassinate their general and who were terrorizing the majority. He finally won them over and the soldiers advanced, a column led by Murat and Leclerc entering the Orangerie with drums beating, and dispersing the deputies, who left shouting 'Long live the Republic!'

The provisional Consulate was organized the same evening by the majority of the Ancients and the minority of the Five-Hundred. They decreed the end of the Directory, and deprived 62 deputies of their status as national representatives 'on account of the excesses and outrages they have continually committed'. An Executive

Consular Commission, comprising Sieyès, Roger Ducos and Bonaparte, 'Consuls of the French Republic', was instituted. The plenitude of Directorial power was vested in these three. The Councils
were replaced by two commissions, each of 25 members, whose task
was to vote laws presented by the Consuls and to prepare the revision
of the Constitution. The Constitution's objective was now, according to article 12:

To consecrate inviolably the sovereignty of the French people, the Republic one and indivisible, the representative system, the separation of powers,
liberty, equality, security and property.

At the end of the session, the Ancients annulled the measure which
had annoyed the contractors on the priority of payments by the
Treasury. The three provisional Consuls took the oath and returned
to Paris.

A placard posted up in Paris, referred to by the *Moniteur* of 24
Brumaire (14 November 1799), provides an accurate interpretation
of the aspirations of the bourgeoisie in the period directly following
the coup d'état:

France wants something great and long-lasting. Instability has been her
downfall, and she now invokes steadiness. She has no desire for a monarchy, which remains therefore proscribed; but she does want unity in the
action of the power executing laws. She wants a free and independent
legislature. . . . She wants her representatives to be peaceable conserva-
tives, not unruly innovators. Finally, she wants to enjoy the benefits
accruing from ten years of sacrifices.

The whole point, therefore, was to bring the revolutionary era to
a definitive close. Consolidation was to succeed upheavals, the social
primacy of the propertied classes was to be established once and for
all. In this, Brumaire is fully in line with 9 Thermidor and 'Eighty-
nine'. Yet though the bourgeoisie wanted to strengthen the executive and to reestablish unity in the government's workings, it did
not renounce thereby the exercise of freedom, provided this was
solely to its own advantage. In the event, its plans were thwarted.
The authoritarian régime that the Brumairians had wanted to install
switched dramatically to favour the increase of Bonaparte's personal
power. In a startling metamorphosis, the Republic of Notables
became a military dictatorship.

Conclusion

The Revolution and Contemporary France

Definitive stabilization, so vainly pursued till Brumaire, was now imminent, though the new reality was still far removed on many points from what the bourgeoisie of 'Eighty-nine' had wished for. Society was still in a state of flux. The new social hierarchy was not properly shored up. Despite the reforming endeavours of the Directory, institutions were still often ineffective, and administrative reorganization incomplete. The war, which was still in progress, could put everything back in the melting-pot. Nevertheless, the core of the new order was already plainly visible: despite the final fears of summer 1799, the social supremacy of the notables, grounded in property, was no longer contested. Socially speaking, the Revolution had come to an end as early as spring 1795, with the crushing of the Paris sans-culottes. From the double view of social continuity and institutional achievement, the Consular period comprised the necessary epilogue to the revolutionary drama.

Yet though unfinished, the work of the Revolution appears just as immense, and of incalculable importance in the destiny of France and the contemporary world. The way in which bourgeois society forced itself on Europe and the world owed everything, of course, to the triumph of the capitalist economy. National peculiarities, however, led to extreme diversity in the methods and manner of this conquest. Even before 1789, the English and American Revolutions had brought the Anglo-Saxon bourgeoisie to power. The influence of these precedents on the French case cannot be overestimated. The scale of the class struggle and the impact of the egalitarian efforts of Year II, however, bestow on the French Revolution an importance of quite another magnitude.

By destroying feudal structures and by proclaiming economic freedom, the Revolution paved the way for capitalism in France, and speeded up its evolution. The aristocracy's resistance and the civil and foreign wars forced the revolutionary bourgeoisie to carry the destruction of the old society to its conclusion. In order to win over the popular classes, it had to lay especial stress upon the principle of equality of rights, which it had only invoked in the first place in its struggle against the aristocracy. Consequently, the work of the French Revolution in fact presents, in its chronological sequence, important contradictory aspects, which increase both its remarkable character and its significance. The origins of bourgeois society and the bourgeois state are deeply rooted in the Revolution, yet during the same period the blueprint for a democratic state and an egalitarian society were drafted. The Revolution was still the revolution of bourgeois equality and national unity: but the régime of Year II attempted to transcend this formal equality, and to inform this unity with a social content which would truly integrate the popular classes into the nation. It was a grandiose attempt, whose contradictions doomed it to failure; but one nevertheless which startled the world, and whose echo is nowhere near dying out even today.

1. The New Society

If we try to draw up a balance-sheet of the French Revolution, bearing in mind the deep-seated unity of the social conflicts during the period 1789–99, and also the complexity of the old society and the importance of popular revolutionary currents, it soon becomes apparent that any facile attempt to impose a model falls far short of the reality. Carried through by the bourgeoisie, the Revolution destroyed the old system of production and the social relationships deriving from it, and in so doing destroyed the formerly dominant class, the landed aristocracy (though exactly to what extent is still an open question). The Revolution also overwhelmed, however, notably by inflation, those fractions of the bourgeoisie who, in differing capacities, had been integrated into Ancien Régime society. Thus, besides ensuring the triumph of the capitalist economy, by instituting economic freedom the Revolution also accelerated, though to different degrees, the decay of the social categories attached to the traditional system of production. In spite of this, capitalism was unable to assert itself unchallenged, in particular in the sphere of agricultural production.

1. THE DESTRUCTION OF THE FEUDAL ARISTOCRACY

The revolutionary bourgeoisie, assisted by the peasants and the sans-culottes, worked towards the destruction of the landed aristocracy and its privileges with a relentlessness which the aristocracy's resistance only intensified.

The aristocracy's landed foundations were destroyed by the suppression of feudal rights and tithes and by the sale of national lands.

Feudal rights provided incomes which varied greatly in size, but which were by no means negligible, as many noble families drew an important portion of their total revenues from this source. Rights over persons, which entailed peasant subjection, were abolished on the night of 4 August 1789, along with the tithes. Rights attaching to property were at first declared redeemable on 15 March 1790. On 18 June 1792, the Legislative Assembly suppressed redemption of *droits casuels* unless the original deed of contract was produced, and this suppression was extended to all rights on 25 August. Finally, the Convention abolished them all irremediably on 17 June 1793 and decreed the burning of feudal title-deeds.

The sale of national lands struck an equally telling blow against the aristocracy. Ecclesiastical land, called national lands *de première origine*, were placed at the nation's disposal on 2 November 1789. Exceptions to this law disappeared after 10 August 1792: the property of vestries were the first to be confiscated on 19 August 1792, and this was followed by the confiscation of the lands of the Order of Malta on 19 September 1792, of the colleges on 8 March 1793 and of charitable institutions on 24 Messidor Year II (12 July 1794). Emigrés' lands, called national lands *de seconde origine*, were put at the nation's disposal on 9 February 1792 by a decree which was finally ratified on 30 March. The decision to sell them was made on 17 July 1792.

The landed patrimony of the nobility was further reduced by the restitution of common land previously seized by seigneurs, and by the new law on inheritance. On 15 March 1790, the Constituent Assembly annulled the *triages* performed over the previous thirty years on common lands; on 28 August 1792, the Legislative Assembly recognized the communes as owners of the commons. The new inheritance law involved the breaking up of patrimonial lands. The decree of 15 March 1790 abolished 'primogeniture, preference for male offspring . . . and unequal divisions based on the standing of the persons concerned'. The decree of 8 April 1791 stipulated that successions *ab intestat* be divided equally. The Montagnard laws of 5 Brumaire and 17 Nivôse Year II (16 October 1793 and 6 January 1794) ratified this equal division: the testator could only make a bequest of one-tenth of his property if he had heirs in a direct line, one-sixth if he had heirs collaterally, and only to benefit non-heirs. On 4 June 1793, the Convention allowed natural offspring to share in the division of the property of their parents, and the law of 12 Brumaire Year II (2 November 1793) provided that their share be equal to that of legitimate offspring. These laws were backdated for all wills since 14 July 1789, though the Thermidorian Convention rescinded this retroactive effect.

Persons as well as property were affected. Quite apart from massacres and legal executions, the clergy and the nobility disappeared as orders, with the abolition of the division of Frenchmen into three orders on the night of 4 August 1789, an abolition ratified by the decree of 7 November 1789. With all distinctions between nobles and commoners suppressed, the aristocrat was reduced to the status of an ordinary citizen. On 19 June 1790, the Constituent Assembly abolished hereditary nobility, and noble titles and armorial bearings. The abolition of feudalism and the administrative and then judicial reforms deprived the seigneur of all his prerogatives over the peasants; he was reduced, in legal terms, to common-law status. Birth too was deprived of privilege: article 6 of the 1789 Declaration of Rights proclaimed that all citizens should be admissible to all dignities, positions and public offices, a provision that was extended to military ranks by the law of 28 February 1790. As the revolutionary crisis deepened, nobles were gradually excluded from public office, unless they had performed important services for the Revolution. The Committee of Public Safety, however, despite the popular outcry, never agreed to depriving them of their civil rights by a general law. The retention of this anti-aristocratic legislation by the Thermidorians and Directorials emphasizes again the degree to which, even after Thermidor, the direction of the class struggle remained unchanged. The law of 3 Brumaire Year IV (25 October 1795) prohibited the relatives of émigrés from acceding to public office. Although this measure was suppressed by the royalist majority of Year V, it was reimplemented after 18 Fructidor. Some people, following Sieyès's suggestion, went so far as to consider exiling all nobles who had held public office under the Ancien Régime, and reducing all others to the status of aliens. Though the law of 9 Frimaire Year VI (29 November 1797) only enshrined the second of these proposals, and though even this was never enforced, the intention to do so was just as significant.

The *noblesse de robe* was ruined not only by the attacks against aristocratic property, but even more perhaps by the suppression of the venality of offices, and the decision that reimbursement be at the official price and in devalued *assignats*. More often than not, these office-holders were removed by the administrative and judicial reforms, which were based on the principle of election, and they stayed without jobs.

We should not exaggerate however: the aristocracy was neither wholly nor irremediably stripped of its lands. Although all seigneurs lost by the suppression of feudalism and of seigneurial rights, only the émigrés had their lands confiscated. A great many nobles lived through the Revolution without coming to much harm and kept their property intact, though now admittedly it would be property of the bourgeois type, freed from feudalism. Fictitious divorces or repurchasing under an assumed name moreover allowed émigrés to keep hold of some territories or else to salvage them. In this way, a certain fraction of the old aristocracy remained: despite the loss of their titles, they preserved part of their traditional prestige and were in the nineteenth century to become fused with the upper bourgeoisie.

2. ECONOMIC FREEDOM AND THE FATE OF THE POPULAR CLASSES

The revolutionary bourgeoisie pursued the aim of destroying the old system of production and exchange, which was incompatible with the expansion of its capitalist businesses, with quite as much relentlessness as they had employed in destroying the aristocracy. True, the bourgeoisie had to make a pact with the sans-culottes, and agree to the renewal of checks on economic freedom, in the shape of price-fixing and trade controls. This was only an interlude, however, which the struggle against the aristocracy had justified. When, after 9 Thermidor, economic freedom was installed triumphantly on the ruins of the popular movement, the consequences were especially grave for the traditional popular classes.

The popular classes in the towns certainly benefited from the abolition of the indirect taxes, which under the Ancien Régime had raised the cost of living. This gain was largely nullified in the first place by the reintroduction of the urban tolls, or *octrois*; and secondly by inflation and price-rises – at least until the final years of the Directory which saw abundant harvests and a fall in prices. As for the artisans, although the suppression of corporations by the Allarde Law of 2 February 1791 might seem democratic to *compagnons* who were in a position to open a shop of their own, it was none the less prejudicial to the interests of the masters. Although the vast bulk of wage-earners experienced a certain rise in wages, their living standards were lowered by the persistence of unemployment, by the dismemberment of institutions of assistance and by their being forced to endure an inferior legal status, sanctioned above all by the property franchise and by the Le Chapelier Law.

Economic freedom thus meant that capitalism could expand: from this sprang a speeding up of the concentration of production. At the same time that the material conditions of social life were being transformed, therefore, the structure of the traditional popular classes was itself changing. Naturally, we must not exaggerate the progress made by capitalist production during the revolutionary period, during which time it was effectively shackled by the course of events – in particular the war – and was even then only confined to certain sectors, such as cotton-spinning. Nevertheless, the preconditions had now been assembled for the development of capitalism on a broad front, which would inevitably transform the bulk of the sans-culotterie into proletarians. The bourgeois revolution delivered up the popular classes defenceless to the new leaders of the economy: the Le Chapelier Law of 14 June 1791, prohibiting 'combinations' and strikes, proved an effective weapon with which to defend the development of industrial capitalism.

The economic evolution which the Revolution quickened led to differentiation among the san-culotterie. Some of the small and middling producers and merchants, who had formed the cadres of the popular movement in Year II, made successes of their businesses, and became industrial capitalists; others remained attached to the shop or to the artisanat; most, however, were gradually liquidated, and went to swell the ranks of the proletariat. Artisans and *compagnons* had a foreboding of what was in store for them – after all, for one artisan who raised himself to the level of an industrial capitalist, a great many more failed to do so. *Compagnons* realized that mechanization was increasing unemployment, artisans that capitalist concentration entailed the closure of their workshops and their own reduction to the level of wage-earners. Throughout the nineteenth century, artisans and shopkeepers clung desperately to their social and economic standing. It would be interesting to know, in this respect, the part played by the proletariat properly speaking in the *journées* of June 1848 and of the Commune of 1871, and the part played by the popular classes of the traditional kind. This information would enable us to gauge the disintegration of the latter group as industrial capitalism triumphed, and to emphasize at the same time one of the causes, and one of the enduring weaknesses as well, of the revolutionary attempts of the nineteenth century.

3. THE DISINTEGRATION OF THE UNITY OF THE PEASANTRY

The Revolution's agrarian reforms brought uneven benefits to the different social groups in the countryside, whose interests started to diverge as soon as the abolition of feudalism – which had cemented their unity in the early part of the Revolution – was achieved. The Revolution considerably strengthened the landowning peasantry. However, the dogged resistance of the small-holding or proletarian peasantry meant that it too did not emerge from the Revolution as defenceless as the popular classes in the towns. If the Revolution accelerated the dissolution of the rural community, it was unable to destroy it completely.

It was only the landowning peasantry which benefited from the abolition of the tithe and of feudal rights attaching to property, and from fiscal equality. Small farmers, sharecroppers and landless peasants only derived any benefit from the abolition of serfdom and rights over persons. The terms and conditions of the sale of national lands were loaded in such a manner as to favour those peasants who were already landholders; most notably, the big farmers in the areas of large-scale farming. Even during the period most favourable to the country people of the lower classes – the period of Montagnard legislation – sales by auction gave the landowning peasant the edge. The division of common lands provided for by the law of 10 June 1793 should have allowed the poor peasant to have access to private property, and thus to have an active interest in agrarian concentration. In fact, because the division was to include all domiciled members of the community of any age and of both sexes, and because this would entail the breaking up of the lands into tiny lots, most communities were firmly opposed to the measure: the plots seemed inadequate, and the traditional practice of grazing in common more advantageous. There were, as Georges Lefebvre noted, other cards which might have been played if the small peasantry's thirst for land was to have been satisfied: they were not played – indeed, they could not be, by a bourgeois revolution. It was the propertied classes, therefore, who obtained the vast bulk of the national lands. In the department of the Nord, the clergy's landed property, which altogether had amounted to 20 per cent in 1789, disappeared, and the nobility's share fell from 22 per cent in 1789 to 12 per cent in 1802 – an accurate gauge, this, of the downfall of the aristocracy. In the same period, bourgeois property in the department rose from 16 per cent to more than 28 per cent, and peasant property from 30 per cent to 42 per cent. These figures are especially and strikingly revealing when we consider the irresistible demographic pressure which was then evident in the countryside of the Nord.

The conception of property which came to be accepted was that of the landowning peasantry. In point of fact, this was identical to the bourgeoisie's conception. The attitude of the rural masses, though not hostile to the principle of individual property, was grounded in a belief in its being confined within the narrow limits set down by customary communal usages. In the eyes of the small peasantry, collective rights, common land and *seconde herbe*, gleaning rights and *droits d'usage* in the forests and on the commons were tantamount to the co-ownership of the land involved. The Constituent Assembly's proclamation of freedom of cultivation and of enclosure entailed the suppression of all regulation on these subjects. Theoretically, this led to the abolition of compulsory fallow and obligatory rotations; also, artificial meadows, even if not enclosed, were not included as part of the common land. All in all, the Revolution strengthened large-scale ownership and large-scale farming, both of which also benefited – apart from the *maximum* episode – from free trade. The peasants doubtless still approved of the Revolution for having rooted out the domination of the aristocracy from their villages. Despite appearances, the agrarian revolution had only moderate and, as Georges Lefebvre noted, 'conservative' effects. The bourgeoisie's conservative inclinations and the new order which had emerged from the Revolution were henceforth espoused by a powerful minority of peasant landowners.

Although the poor peasantry hardly improved its condition, it nevertheless managed to preserve most of its freedom of action. While it was unable, in large numbers, to gain access to property, the revolutionary assemblies did not dare to destroy the rural community irrevocably by abolishing joint landholding or collective practices. Enclosure was authorized, but not made obligatory. This settlement remained throughout the nineteenth century, and has not yet disappeared, since the law of 1892, which is still in force in France, places the decision to abandon common land in the hands of the village community. The Revolution, then, only effected a compromise in this sphere, whose full significance can be gauged if we compare the evolution of French agriculture with that of English agriculture. Because in France the maintenance of collective practices was left to the wishes of the peasants, the parcelling out of property and the continued subdivision of farming units provided a considerable check on the capitalist transformation of agriculture. The autonomy of the small countryside producers was thus allowed an added lease of life, and gave France's political history certain of its distinctive characteristics. Had enclosure and the reallocation of land been imposed in an authoritarian manner, as in England, capitalism would have triumphed as radically in the sphere of agriculture as in that of industry. The feudal aristocracy's dogged struggle against the Revolution, by long preventing a political compromise with the bourgeoisie, obliged the latter to deal sympathetically with the peasantry – including the poor peasantry, whose resistance to change made them even more formidable.

At this point, however, we must make certain qualifications: the same sort of qualifications in fact which apply to the social structure of the peasantry under the Ancien Régime. In the areas of large-scale farming, where the farmers of the middle and large types proved the active agents of the capitalist transformation of agriculture, the rural community disintegrated by coming to be devoid of any of its former content: the poor peasants were swiftly proletarianized and provided the labour-force needed by modern agriculture and large-scale industry. The development of areas of small-scale farming was slower. Here, the rural community was sapped from within by the antagonism between the landowning peasantry on the one hand and the poor peasantry, relentless in its defence of its *droits d'usage* in the woods and fields, on the other. This obscure and dogged struggle brought face to face two forms of the economy, one archaic, the other new and displaying the individualism of the capitalist producers. It was marked throughout the nineteenth century by agrarian disturbances of the traditional type, the last of which, from 1848 to 1851, were neither the least violent nor the least characteristic.

4. OLD AND NEW BOURGEOISIES

The bourgeoisie, which prepared and led the Revolution, drew the essential advantages from it, though there was a great deal of variety amongst the different categories within the class as to the exact nature of the effects of the Revolution on it. Certainly the class appeared to have been radically transformed, and its internal equilibrium modified: the traditional preponderance in its ranks of established fortunes gave way to that of businessmen and heads of enterprises, the leaders of production and exchange.

The Ancien Régime bourgeoisie (by which is meant the bourgeoisie integrated into the old social and economic system) to a great extent shared the fate of the aristocracy. Thus the bourgeois who had owned seigneuries and had 'lived nobly' off its various landed revenues saw its dues and feudal rights vanish, and also suffered from the fact that, until the law of 2 Thermidor Year III (20 July 1795) stipulated that half of all rents should be paid in grain, rents were paid in devalued *assignats*. The office-holding bourgeoisie was, along with the *noblesse de robe*, ruined by the suppression of venality. The bourgeoisie of the liberal professions was adversely affected by the abolition of the corporation of lawyers, and of the academies and universities on 8 August 1793, the big business bourgeoisie by the suppression of tax-farming. The Convention even, in fact, on 24 August 1794, abolished shareholding societies. The world of high finance suffered the harsh effects of the closure of the stock-exchange, of the disappearance of the Discount Bank (*caisse d'escompte*) and, in Year II, of price-fixing and trade controls – that is, of profit limitation. Revolutionary price-fixing and forced loans hit established fortunes hard. Finally, we should also bear in mind when calculating how much the Revolution struck against certain sectors of the bourgeoisie, the catastrophic repercussions of inflation. The traditional bourgeoisie placed its savings more in mortgage loans and bonds on the national debt than in commercial and industrial enterprises. In Year III, the collapse of the *assignat* prompted debtors to free themselves from their mortgage debts by not only paying off the interest due but also by restoring the capital sum in worthless paper currency. This obliged the introduction of the law of 23 Messidor Year III (10 July 1795) prohibiting repayment of mortgage debts contracted before 1 July 1792 and also the advance repayment of other debts. Cambon's manipulation of life annuities and perpetual revenues under the Convention, and the 'bankruptcy of the two-thirds' or 'Ramel liquidation' came as further blows. All these influences at work help to explain why an important fraction of the Ancien Régime bourgeoisie joined the counter-revolution, and also to explain the fact that, by virtue of this, it shared the aristocracy's fate. In the degree to which the bulk of its fortune lay in landed property – since the value in stocks and shares was only a relatively small fraction of inherited wealth – this bourgeoisie, if it had not emigrated, retained the basis of its fortunes and, once the turmoil was over, regained its sources of revenue unhindered by events. The primacy of this Ancien Régime bourgeoisie, however, in spite of the social standing that land bestowed, no longer went unchallenged.

Actually, a new bourgeoisie appeared in the centre of the stage: the heads of finance and the economy. Speculation, the sale of national lands, equipping, arming and provisioning the armies, exploiting the conquered territories – all provided businessmen with new opportunities to increase the number of their contracts and to further the evolution of capitalist concentration. The progress of capitalism was still of course slow, the size of enterprises remained often fairly small and commercial capital often preponderated. Yet some big concerns were appearing, especially in the textile industry: those of Richard-Lenoir at Paris, for example, as well as those of Bauwens at Passy, Lachauvetière at Bordeaux and Jeannettes at Amiens. Périer, called 'Milord' in Dauphiné, and Boyer-Fonfrède were great industrialists in their own right. The origins of these new, enormous fortunes were more bound up with speculation and army-contracts, however, than with industrial production. Many companies took advantage of the Directorial government's weakness to plunder the state: the Lanchère and Bodin companies, for example, which specialized in provisioning, the Felice company which specialized in clothing, and the Monneron company which specialized in transports. The bourgeoisie, therefore, was renovated by incorporating these *nouveaux riches*, of whom Ouvrard is the consummate example, and who often set the fashion for Directorial 'high society'. These men, the true adventurers of the new society, revitalized the ruling classes by their spirit of enterprise and their love of risks. They founded bourgeois families, from whose ranks – provided that they abandoned speculation and invested their capital in production – emerged the founders of industrial capitalism.

One rung further down the bourgeois ladder, many tradesmen and, to a lesser extent, artisans took advantage of the turn of events to increase the number of their undertakings and the size of their contracts, in short, to round off their fortunes and to emerge from the ranks of the people into the bourgeoisie. With these too, speculation often appears the essential factor in social promotion. The new ruling class soon recruited from this middle stratum officials for the public administrations, and also members of the liberal professions.

After ten years of turmoil, the different characteristics of the new society were still not immutably fixed. Its general outlines, however, were already clearly visible. The desire for order actuating the propertied classes – which sprang from their determination either to preserve what they had salvaged from their former wealth, or else to enjoy their new fortune in peace – was to facilitate social stabilization under the Consulate. The framework of the new society became settled during the Napoleonic period when the institutions which were to consecrate its supremacy were created, and when the fusion of the various elements of the new dominant class began. The rejuvenated bourgeoisie and that part of the aristocracy which had abandoned its attachment to the emigration worked hand in hand with the wealthy peasantry to produce an identification of the meanings of 'nation' and 'property'. Through this, one of the objectives which the men of 'Eighty-nine' had allotted the Revolution was finally attained.

5. THE IDEOLOGICAL CONFLICT:
PROGRESS AND TRADITION, REASON AND FEELING

The movement of ideas during the revolutionary period reflected the social and political conflict. The disintegration of traditional frameworks within society, the inability of many to adjust to the new order, the helter-skelter effect of men at the mercy of events, and the drift towards extremism bestowed a new vitality and prestige on the irrational. Since the Revolution appeared as the crowning achievement of the Age of Enlightenment, the counter-revolution fought its rationalism in the name of authority and tradition, and called up against it the obscure forces of feeling and instinct. The primacy of the intellect was challenged by the recourse to intuition. The anti-rationalist reaction spread to the sphere of letters and the arts. If, thanks to David, the classical aesthetic and the inspiration of the Ancients continued vigorously to dominate the plastic arts, the traditional literary genres came to be devoid of any real content. The classical disciplines did not stand up well to the impact of events, the emancipation of individuals and the exacerbation of passions. Intellectual life, like society, appeared to be seething with conflicts.

Despite everything, scientific research was still the domain *par excellence* of rationalism. In 1789, Lavoisier's *Traité de Chimie* had appeared; Laplace published his *Exposition du système du monde* in 1796; and Monge his *Traité de géométrie descriptive* in 1799: three great dates in the development and progress of the human mind. Lavoisier, who had analysed air and water and established general principles such as the conservation of matter, took stock of all the results formerly obtained in chemistry. Laplace, to explain the origin of the universe, suggested the hypothesis of the nebula whose progressive condensation had produced the stars and the planets. Monge, for his part, created a new branch of mathematics, descriptive geometry. Celebrated naturalists – Cuvier, Geoffroy Saint-Hilaire – were teaching at the Museum. At the end of the Revolution, in Year VIII, Cuvier published his *Leçons d'anatomie comparée*, a scientific synthesis which marked the end of an epoch, while Lamarck, previously a supporter of the idea of the permanence of species, conceived from 1794 to 1800 (although his *Philosophie Zoologique* only appeared in 1809) the great hypothesis of evolution.

The human sciences were dominated by the 'ideologues', who maintained the primacy of reason and experience. The group's storm-centres were, after 1795, the second class of the Institute, for 'Moral and Political Sciences', the great establishments of higher education set up by the Convention and, through their disciples, the central schools. Here and in their journal, the *Décade philosophique*, they exhibited their continued enmity towards tradition and the revival of religion.

Theology [wrote Destutt de Tracy in a book review of Dupuis's *L'Origine de tous les cultes*, which had appeared in Year III] is the philosophy of the world's childhood; it is time that it made way for the age of reason

Theology is a product of the imagination . . . whilst the latter type of philosophy is based on observation and experience.

'Ideology' thus has its niche in the history of philosophy between the Enlightenment and Positivism. In 1795 and 1796, Cabanis read to the Institute the first six of the twelve papers in his *Rapports du physique et du moral* (1802), in which he emerges as the founder of psychophysiology. He expressed a concern, moreover, to form moral sciences which would equal the physical sciences in certitude and which could provide a solid foundation for a morality independent of dogma. At the same time, Pinel the doctor at the Paris prison and hospital of La Salpêtrière, was creating the discipline of psychopathology: his *Traité médico-philosophique sur l'aliénation mentale ou la manie* was published in 1798. The spirit of the eighteenth century also informed a great number of works on the study of morals and the history of ideas. Following Voltaire's *Essai sur les mœurs et l'esprit des nations* (1756), Volney, who had made his name by his *Voyage en Egypte et en Syrie* (1787), published in 1791, while he was still a member of the Constituent Assembly, his great work *Les Ruines ou Méditations sur les révolutions des empires* in which he resumes all his generation's arguments against religion. Madame de Staël helped to widen the field of literary criticism by a work which introduces historical criticism into the study of literary works, her *La Littérature considérée dans ses rapports avec les institutions sociales* (1800), where she wrote, 'I have set myself the task of examining the influence of religion, morals and laws on literature.'

The century's philosophical testament was drawn up by Condorcet. Arrested and proscribed alongside the Girondins, he wrote in 1794 his *Esquisse d'un tableau historique des progrès de l'esprit humain*, which displays an indomitable certainty in unlimited progress and in human perfectibility. This unlimited progress, he maintained, was evident first in the field of science:

As we know proportionately more multiple connections between a larger number of objects, so we end up compressing them into simpler expressions and by presenting them in forms which allow a greater number of them to be apprehended.

The same unlimited progress was located too, he held, in the techniques associated with the sciences and finally in the moral sciences – since for Condorcet, the moral world was subject to knowable laws like the material world. The Convention showed its respect for rationalism in a decree of 2 October 1793, rendering the supreme homage to Descartes as a renovator of thought and method, admitting him to the Pantheon: 'René Descartes deserves the honours owed to great men.'

The progress made by the anti-rationalist reaction and by the counter-revolution was closely linked. Those who, on whatever grounds, had suffered at the hands of the Revolution, and from the dismemberment of the old society, soon came round to holding the century's ideology responsible for their misfortunes. This repudiation of the Enlightenment was evident among the émigrés after 1794 in the important work of the obscure abbé Sabatier de Castres, *Pensées et observations morales et politiques pour servir à la connaissance des vrais principes du gouvernement*, in which he maintained that 'the more peoples become enlightened, the more wretched they are'. Authority, tradition and revealed religion now came back into fashion, and were envisaged as either bulwarks of order or sanctuaries from it. The errors imputed to the Enlightenment and to the Revolution were alleged to arise from the false belief that the moving principles of social life were of human institution; whereas they were said to escape analysis and to transcend the puny power of reason.

If the movement remained weak in France itself, it made great advances in the circles around the different branches of the emigration. Some satisfied themselves with making capital out of events, utilizing irrational arguments. Thus the abbé Barruel, for example, who in his *Mémoires pour servir à l'histoire du jacobinisme*, which appeared in Hamburg from 1797 to 1799, reduced the Revolution to a dark masonic conspiracy:

Everything, down to the most horrendous and heinous crimes in this French Revolution, has been foreseen, contemplated, concocted, resolved upon, enacted. Everything has been the consequence of the deepest wickedness, since everything has been prepared and induced by men who alone have the thread of those conspiracies hatched in secret societies and who have been able to choose and to expedite commotions suitable for plots.

For others, however, responsibility for the catastrophe was due to fate or the 'force of circumstances'. In his *Essai historique, politique et moral sur les révolutions*, which appeared in London in 1799, Chateaubriand makes 'the fatality intrinsic in events', 'that necessity which is called the force of circumstances' intervene ceaselessly, and in the end affirms his inability to understand and to explain:

Despite countless efforts to penetrate the causes of the disturbances in states, one feels something escapes analysis: an indescribable something, hidden no one knows where; it is this indescribable something which appears to be the effective cause of all revolutions.

This same irrationalism is apparent in the writings of Mallet du Pan, a Genevan who became a naturalized Englishman, and who accounted for facts by 'the fatal flow of events', 'the imperative nature of circumstance, that is to say, that force independent of men and of governments'. The gap between the 'force of circumstance' and the 'finger of Providence' was soon crossed.

The first doctrinal foundation stone of the counter-revolution was laid by two works which appeared simultaneously in 1796: Viscount de Bonald's *Théorie du pouvoir politique et religieux dans la société civile*, and Joseph de Maistre's *Considérations sur la France*. Each work had its own specific characteristics.

In his *Considérations*, Joseph de Maistre deliberately resorts to providential explanations of events:

We are all attached to the throne of the Supreme Being by a limp chain, which holds us back without enslaving us. . . . In times of revolution, the chain attached to man is abruptly shortened, there is less play in it, and its guiding influence seems more of an illusion. . . . The French Revolution directs men more than men direct it. . . . Those men who established the Republic did so without wanting to and without knowing what they were doing: they were led into it by events and were the mere instruments of a force which knew more about it than they.

Providence 'punishes in order to regenerate', de Maistre continued. France had gone against her Christian calling and had thereby necessitated a regeneration that she was now experiencing in her deepest being. The counter-revolution would occur at a time foreseen by God. De Maistre's hidebound opinions in the *Considérations* presage the theory outlined in his *Soirées de Saint-Pétersbourg*, particularly in regard to the war, which is 'intrinsically divine because it is a law of the world'. In de Maistre, legitimacy had found its theoretician, and the pretender, Louis XVIII, accordingly directed to him a bounty of 50 *louis*.

De Bonald, in his *Théorie du pouvoir politique et religieux*, outlined a theory of the social organism which was both metaphysical and abstract:

Man can no more give religious or political society a constitution than he can give weight to mass or extent to matter.

Monarchy, the essential type of 'constituted society', was character-ized by the unity of power, by social distinctions and necessary hierarchies and by attachment to the Christian religion. The suc-cesses and the setbacks of the French monarchy had always depen-ded, he held, on its faithfulness to its immanent constitutive laws. Marked above all by a real effort at abstraction, the *Théorie du pouvoir* constitutes the first important attempt among the ranks of the emigration at doctrinal readjustment.

Published abroad, these works at first passed unnoticed in France, where the counter-revolution primarily capitalized on the persistence of irrational currents. The obscure forces of feeling and intuition, exalted by Rousseau, were seen as a remedy against the misfortunes of the times, as were the esoteric doctrines deriving from occultism and illuminism and even more so – despite its divisions – from traditional religion. Though the government and the republican bourgeoisie still opposed Catholicism, basing their hostility on their own social conservatism, and though religious practice appeared to be patently in decline among the masses, traditional religion none the less constituted for many people a refuge and a consolation, and for others a bastion and a safeguard. Both sets of attitudes facilitated Bonaparte's work of religious restoration.

The literary movement exhibits the same sorts of conflicts. The impact of the Revolution inspired new genres. Political passion was powerless to renovate the old classical ones. Speech was undergoing a profound transformation. Words became charged with a new emotive and affective force. Cherished words like 'nation', 'home-land', 'law' or 'Constitution', and execrated words such as 'tyranny' and 'aristocrat' seemed almost transfigured by an internal dynamic.

Apart from a few works inspired by topical events, the traditional genres, drama and poetry, dwindled perilously into ossified forms and rules and the outworn imitations of classical models.

We find only second-rate names in the field of poetry: abbé Delille (1758–1813), for example, and Ecouchard-Lebrun, called Lebrun-Pindare (1729–1807), whose *Ode au vaisseau 'Le Vengeur'* (1794) is still worth reading. Patriotic exaltation or political passion did inspire some more powerful and more rousing works. France was like a new divinity to whom were dedicated the verses of the *Chant de guerre de l'armée du Rhin* – the present French national anthem – by Rouget de Lisle (25 April 1792), and the *Chant du départ* by Marie-Joseph Chénier (14 July 1794). Liberty and patriotism fired the inspiration of André Chénier (1762–94), who in 1791 wrote a poem commemorating the Tennis Court Oath. André Chénier was soon overtaken by events, and was arrested as a suspect on 17 Ventôse Year II (7 March 1794). In prison, he composed *La jeune captive*, and, most important of all, his *Iambes*, poems whose form was inspired by models from Antiquity, but whose personal and emotional ardour presage Romantic lyricism.

The theatre too, to a certain extent, felt the impact of the period. Though still classical in form, it became first national, then republican. On 13 January 1791, the Constituent Assembly abolished royal censorship and all privilege in theatrical matters: 'Any citizen may establish a public theatre and stage plays of all types in it.' Nearly fifty theatres were opened in Paris alone. Actors, social pariahs under the Ancien Régime, were now 'citizen-players', and were often important contributors to the revolutionary movement. In 1793, the theatre became the school of citizenship. On 2 August of that year, the Convention decreed that there should be acted three times each week in those theatres designated by the municipality

the tragedies of *Brutus, William Tell* and other plays which recall the glorious events of the Revolution and the virtues of the defenders of liberty; one of these performances each week will be played at the Republic's expense. Any theatre in which plays are performed which tend to deprave public feeling and to rekindle the shameful superstition of royalty will be closed down.

On 20 Ventôse Year II (10 March 1794), the Théâtre Français became the 'Theatre of the People'. Certain plays were really very plainly inspired by events: thus Sylvain Maréchal's *Jugement dernier des rois* in 1793, in which all monarchs are deported to an island. The most prolific author was Marie-Joseph Chénier (1764–1811), who drew the subject-matter for his tragedies from antiquity (*Caius Gracchus* in 1792, *Timoleon* in 1794), and from French history (*Charles IX* in 1789, *Jean Calas* in 1791), and who enlivened them with revolutionary feeling and contemporary allusions. Nothing remains of this abundant and semi-improvised work, whose out-of-date form links it directly with a dead past.

New genres, directly linked with the political movement, made their appearance. As literary art placed itself at the service of political intervention, we must look for it in the newspapers or in the tribunes of the Assemblies and of the Clubs. It is noticeable once again that the new genres are of more relevance to history than to literature.

Political eloquence was, as Chateaubriand put it, 'the fruit of revolutions, in which it grows spontaneously and untended'. The rhetorical eloquence which was one of the Revolution's foremost literary genres, was of the type nurtured by the philosophy of the Enlightenment, often abstract and padded out with parallels from Antiquity, not without bombast and declamation, but often passionate and blazing with emotion as well. Until his death on 2 April 1791, Mirabeau dominated the Constituent Assembly by his rhetorical power, which was always controlled, and by his capacity to turn to good account his athletic bulkiness and his ugliness, which smacked of energy. His speech 'Sur la contribution du quart' and against bankruptcy (24 September 1789), his reply to his accusers (22 May 1790), remain justly famous. Vergniaud's eloquence was more elegant and fluent. The Girondin orator took pleasure in copious developments and sententiousness, resorting frequently to rhetoric's standbys, repetitions, allegories and Greco-Roman references. Danton, on the other hand, was above all an improviser, with little concern for artifice or composition. His manner of speaking was in some respects reminiscent of Mirabeau's – indeed, he was nicknamed the 'Riff-raff's Mirabeau'. Robespierre's eloquence, in contrast to Danton's (for he took great pains in preparing his speeches), bore evidence of the steadfastness of his principles and the blazing yet restrained fire which possessed him while he spoke. Saint-Just's rhetoric was tauter, his style more abrupt, his speeches abounding in aphorisms of exemplary striking force (*'Bronʒeʒ la liberté'*). Political eloquence became duller and more academic under the bourgeois republic, and in the end was altogether silent under the despotism of the Consulate.

Thanks to the freedom of the press and in spite of the restrictions which were set up in practice after 1792, political journalism made considerable progress after 1789. The predominantly literary periodicals of the Ancien Régime, such as the weekly *Gazette de France* and the monthly *Mercure*, were succeeded by a political press which proved unquestionably to be the true literary genre of the revolutionary period. Royalist newspapers did not last long: the *Journal politique national* in which in 1790 Rivarol contributed articles and the *Actes des Apôtres* until 1790, and abbé Royou's *L'Ami du Roi* until May 1792. As early as 1789, the patriot press was predominant, in both the political and the literary senses of the word. The most celebrated revolutionary newspapers were Elysée Loustalot's *Révolutions de Paris*, Marat's *Publiciste parisien*, which from its sixth number became *L'Ami du peuple*, and Camille Desmoulins's *Révolutions de France et de Brabant*. Mention ought to be made as well of Mirabeau's *Courrier de Provence* (1789–91), the *Chronique de Paris* (1789–93), in which Condorcet wrote, and the *Défenseur de la Constitution* which Robespierre brought out from May till August 1792. In Frimaire Year II, Camille Desmoulins launched his *Vieux Cordelier*, which ran to seven numbers. Apparent in this political press are many of the typical features of revolutionary eloquence: the passion for ideas, polemical vitality, a certain taste for rhetoric and frequent references to Ancient History – as in number three of the *Vieux Cordelier*, for example, which appeared as a paraphrase from Tacitus. The popular press was represented by Marat's newspaper and even more by the *Père Duchesne*, whose publication was started in November 1790. Its editor, Hébert, proved himself a good journalist, full of zest and imagination. He captured in his florid style the aspirations of the people, and was able to make himself their mouthpiece. After Thermidor, the popular press as a whole became anti-Jacobin and often royalist. Very little of the abundant supply of political broadsheets survives, though mention ought to be made of three of them: the *Décade philosophique, littéraire et politique*, founded in Floréal Year II, the *Gazette nationale* or *Moniteur universel* which Panckoucke started to bring out on 24 November 1789, and which in 1803 became the official government newspaper; and finally the *Journal des Débats et des Décrets*, whose long career started on 29 August 1789.

While literary production was undeniably inflected under the impact of the Revolution, the Revolution was also able to discover, in the field of arts, modes of expression commensurate with the greatness of the period as well as with the exigencies of an enlarged public. In painting, in music and in the splendid arrangement of the national festivals, it attained the highest peaks of art, where the enthusiasm exalted is no longer that of a minority of connoisseurs, but of a community thinking as one.

The accusation of vandalism has often been levelled against the Revolution. Though much destruction undoubtedly occurred, the revolutionary assemblies made constant endeavours to preserve the artistic heritage of the nation. Under the Constituent Assembly, the Commission of Monuments sent delegates all over France to search out and to classify all that merited conservation; under the Convention, the Committee of Public Instruction and the Temporary Commission of Arts performed the same role. On 26 May 1791, the Constituent Assembly had assigned to the Louvre the task of assembling all monuments from the arts and from the sciences, while on 27 Nivôse Year II (16 January 1794), the Convention entrusted the safekeeping of the museum to a Conservatory, divided into four sections (for painting, sculpture, architecture and antiquities). Alexandre Lenoir had assembled in the Petits-Augustins monastery a large number of works of art, notably the statues from the Abbey of Saint-Denis, which had been given over to destruction out of hatred for the monarchy. This was in fact the origin of the Museum of French Monuments set up on 15 Fructidor Year II (1 September 1794) by the Convention.

At the same time that the revolutionary assemblies were exhibiting a degree of sensitivity towards France's artistic heritage, artists were freeing themselves from many of the old constraints. In 1790, stimulated by David, they vigorously challenged the Academy's monopoly on the School of Rome and the Salon. In 1791, the latter was obliged to open its doors to all artists. On 8 August 1793, the Academy of Painting and Sculpture was suppressed, under the law suppressing universities and academies. The impact of the Revolution in the artistic sphere replenished the wells of inspiration of the artists:

It will perhaps seem strange to stern republicans [we read in the *Livret* of the Salon in 1793] to concern ourselves with the arts when all Europe is in league and laying siege to the land of freedom. ... We do not adopt the well-known adage, 'In armis silent artes', but will recall more readily Protogenus sketching a masterpiece in besieged Rhodes.

These few lines written at the height of the crisis, bear witness to the spirit which fired most artists during the revolutionary period: it was felt that art could not be separated from the general struggle for liberty. Paying homage to the Convention on 19 March 1793 by presenting to them his painting depicting the murder of Michel

Lepeletier for having voted for the King's execution, David declared:

Each one of us is accountable to our country for the talents we have received from nature. The form of these talents may differ, but their aim must be the same for all. The true patriot must avidly seize all means of enlightening his fellow-citizens, and constantly present before their eyes the sublime characteristics of heroism and of virtue. Citizens, heaven which divides its gifts among all its children wishes me to express my thought and my innermost being through the organ of my painting.

David (1748–1825) dominated revolutionary art both as a painter and as the organizer of republican festivals. Following the precepts of Winckelmann in his *History of Ancient Art* which had appeared in 1764 and which was translated into French three times between 1766 and 1793, David returned to models taken from the Ancient World, asserting the superiority of draughtsmanship and clarity of line over colour which, he held, appeals only to the sensibility. David broke, therefore, with the tradition of French art in the eighteenth century. His fame rested on a series of paintings in the style of the Ancients: 'The Oath of the Horatii' (1784), which was re-exhibited in the Salon in 1791 alongside his 'Death of Socrates' (1787); his 'Brutus' (1789); his 'Sabines' (1799); and his 'Leonidas', on which he worked from 1800 to 1804. He relinquished his classical models, however, for a short while, placing his art at the service of the Revolution: he formulated his plan for his painting of the Tennis Court Oath, which was exhibited in the Salon in 1791, organized arrangements for the national festivals, and painted 'Lepeletier, Martyr of Liberty' and 'Marat Assassinated'. In the latter, sitting sprawled backwards in his bath, covered by a sheet, Marat is dying, his breast pierced, his naked chest and bleeding wound fully exposed. His head, enveloped in a white madras cloth, lolls on one shoulder, and his mouth is formed in a heart-broken smile. The hand on the arm which hangs down touching the ground is still clutching the pen with which he has been writing, while the murder weapon lies on the ground nearby. This moving painting adorned the hall of the Convention and, while extolling civic virtue, reminded deputies of the need for public safety, so fraught with dangers. The unity which informs all David's paintings, from his paintings on the models from Antiquity to his revolutionary canvases, springs from his feeling for republican virtue and heroic tension.

Painting according to eighteenth-century canons continued regardless. Greuze (1725–1805), renowned for his sensibility, was still alive, as was Fragonard (1732–1806), whose style was less weighty, but who was an incomparable arist all the same; also alive was Hubert Robert (1733–1806), whose predilection for ruins marked him out already as a Romantic, and some of whose canvases convey an exact feeling for modern life; also, Prud'hon (1758–1823), enamoured of classical models quite as much as David, but in whose work a pre-romantic tonality is evident. Finally, in the field of sculpture, there was Houdon (1741–1828), whose fame rested on his statues modelled on the Ancients, and even more on his portraits.

The same duality was apparent in music. On the one hand, continuity with the eighteenth century was asserted in Grétry (1741–1813) and Dalayrac (1753–1809). On the other hand, the revolutionary impulse renovated sources and methods at the same time. Gossec (1733–1829) and Méhul (1763–1817) – as well as Grétry – composed the hymns sung at national festivals by huge choral masses, and which extolled patriotic feeling and republican civic spirit. The 'Chant du 14 juillet', the music for which was composed by Gossec for Marie-Joseph Chénier's 'Hymne pour la fête de la Fédération' remains one of the finest examples of this genre, while Méhul's music for Chénier's 'Chant du départ' was, along with the 'Marseillaise', the republicans' hymn, with which, under the Thermidorian reaction and the Directory, they countered the royalists' 'Réveil du peuple'. Gossec had been the first to draw up the idea of a National Institute of Music, which the Convention ultimately set up on 18 Brumaire Year II (8 November 1793). It was reorganized on 16 Thermidor Year III (3 August 1795) when it was given the title of 'Conservatory' and the task of 'performing and teaching music'. Its management was entrusted to five 'inspectors', Gossec, Grétry, Méhul, Lesueur and Cherubini. This list of names is evidence enough that, in this field as in all the others, the art of the eighteenth century and the new forms of expression coexisted, and divided the different genres between themselves.

Rupture and continuity, therefore, are as much features of intellectual and artistic life in these years as of society itself. Rationalism and tradition, intellect and feeling were brought face to face. The forms of classical art were still predominant. Already, however, Romanticism was feeling its way: Marie-Joseph Chénier translated

Ossian; and Madame de Staël asserted in 1800 her preference for the literature of the North, proclaiming: 'The peoples of the North are less occupied with pleasures than with sorrows, and their imagination is more fertile in them.' Beyond the misfortunes of the epoch, the myth of the 'good old days' was appearing with its processions of knights and troubadours. This was soon to be fortified by the development of a sentimental Catholicism, which Chateaubriand was able to cultivate. Through this renovation of thought and of feeling, the aristocracy and the emigration were searching, in a rather confused manner, for a means of adhering effectively to the new order. The same desire for social stabilization was haunting the new bourgeoisie. Little concerning itself with ideas, indifferent to principles, dreaming only of enjoyment or of making a career, this bourgeoisie clung above all to the maintenance of its new privileges, that is to say, the core of the changes brought about by the Revolution. The concern for social conservation was gaining the upper hand over the battle of ideas. Well-off bourgeoisie and a new and more sober aristocracy would readily join together to buttress the power which would guarantee their primacy, newly acquired in the case of the one, partly regained in the case of the other.

2. The Bourgeois State

The Revolution destroyed the Ancien Régime's absolutist State, which had been based on the theory of divine right and which had guaranteed the privileges of the aristocracy. In its place, it set a liberal and secular State, based on the principles of national sovereignty and civil equality. The application of these principles at elections, where ownership of property came to be a necessary requirement for voting, brought the new institutions into line with the social structure which had emerged from the Revolution. Thus the new State could only be a bourgeois one, which guaranteed the prerogatives of the new dominant class.

I. NATIONAL SOVEREIGNTY AND THE PROPERTY FRANCHISE

On the purely legal level, the destruction of the Ancien Régime state was accomplished on the night of 4 August 1789. Just as all citizens without distinction of birth were declared equal, so 'the peculiar privileges of provinces, principalities, regions, cantons, towns and communities of inhabitants' were abolished for ever. Venal offices were suppressed. The decree of 3 November 1789 placed the *parlements* and the councils of state in permanent recession. Everything which limited state power disappeared: privileges, intermediary bodies, particularisms, the vestiges of former autonomies. The new State, transformed in its very essence, emerged on the ruins of the old state apparatus.

The transformation of the State and the weakening of its powers was inherent in the principle of national sovereignty. The State was no longer the personal property of the monarch, but rather the emanation of the sovereign people. In much the same way as society, in conformity with the theory of natural law, was based on the free contract of its members, so the State was henceforward based on a contract between government and governed. The State was therefore envisaged as being at the service of its citizens, for whom – the second article of the 1789 Declaration of Rights asserted – it was to guarantee 'the conservation of the natural rights' of man. The 1791 Constitution subordinated the monarchy to the nation, the executive to the legislative power; it operated a strict separation of powers; and, by means of elections, it placed the state apparatus in the hands of citizens. The central administration was weakened by the new arrangement of public powers. On the local level, too, centralization yielded to autonomy: the law of 14 December 1789 on the formation of municipalities and the law of 22 December on the constitution of primary and administrative assemblies ushered in the most wide-reaching decentralization. The State was disarmed: the levying of taxes was outside its powers, as was the maintenance of order, which was entrusted to the municipalities. The upshot was a liberal state, but a bourgeois state none the less, for national sovereignty, which was limited to the ranks of the electors and the active citizens, fell under the sway of the notables, and the State thus became the bourgeoisie's private property. The aristocracy's resistance, and the civil and foreign wars put this new structure under severe pressure, however, and it did not survive the *journée* of 10 August 1792.

The strengthening of the power of the State came with the establishment and the stabilization of the Revolutionary Government. The elimination of the monarchy after 10 August 1792 allowed the reorganization of the executive on a new footing. The unrestricted implementation of the principle of national sovereignty and the introduction of universal suffrage expanded the State, so that it filled out to cover the contours of the whole nation, while at the same time the Terror removed hostile elements from the whole. On this new social foundation, the Jacobin state of Year II, though democratic, became authoritarian. It was out of sheer necessity that it did so: the public welfare demanded it. Its authoritarianism was further intensified by two features evident in the work of the men of 'Eighty-nine', but whose logical consequences were not fully elicited until 'Ninety-three', namely rationalism and individualism. In the name of rationalism, institutions were submitted to the rigorous line of reasoning according to which the State is the instrument of reason, before whose exigencies men and facts must bow. This led to the strengthening of the authority of the State. In the name of individualism, intermediary bodies, groups and communities were suppressed, the new State recognizing only single individuals, over whom it had a direct hold. Confronted, then, with a State with virtually unchecked powers, the citizen was defenceless as soon as the guarantee of his rights came to be missing and when the 'despotism of liberty' came to be installed. Robespierre elaborated this theme in his report 'On the principles of Revolutionary Government', on 5 Nivôse Year II (25 December 1793):

Constitutional government is mainly concerned with civil liberty, revolutionary government with public liberty. Under the constitutional régime, it is almost enough to protect individuals against abuses on the part of the public authority; under the revolutionary régime the public authority is itself obliged to defend itself against all the factions which attack it.

It was circumstance, then, which justified, in the Jacobins' eyes, the restoration of state authority and centralization. The law on the *maximum* (29 September 1793) bestowed on the State the direction of the economy. The decree of 14 Frimaire Year II (4 December 1793) placed constituted assemblies and bodies and public officials under the immediate inspection of the Committee of Public Safety and, for police matters, under the Committee of General Security. A double contradiction, however, was sapping the authoritarian Jacobin state from within. Control over the economy brought landowners and producers on the one hand, and wage-earners and consumers on the other into conflict. Secondly, centralization went against the natural bent of the sans-culottes for direct democracy. The dictatorship of the Committee of Public Safety submitted popular militants to a strict discipline, and crushed those of them who demurred. Because it was not rooted deeply in a social class foundation, as the liberal bourgeois state of 1791 had been, the Jacobin state of Year II had no visible means of support: after 9 Thermidor, the whole edifice crumbled.

The liberal bourgeois state was now restored. The economy was freed from state control. The Constitution of Year III returned to the liberal system of the Constituent Assembly, the property franchise removing the masses from power. The class consciousness of the notables emerged toughened from the democratic experiment of Year II. Although the Constitution of Year III reestablished the separation of powers and deprived the executive of all means of intervening in financial matters, it nevertheless strengthened the powers of the State and maintained a degree of centralization. Thus the Directory had responsibility for the internal and external security of the Republic, and had the armed forces at its disposal (article 144); it could issue subpoenas and arrest-warrants (article 145); it supervised and ensured the execution of laws in the administrations and in the legal system through commissioners whom it appointed itself (article 147). The administration was not wholly decentralized, since municipal administrations were subordinated to departmental administrations, and these were in turn subordinated to the ministers. The Directory's commissioners, whose powers were very extensive, and who were in direct correspondence with the Minister of the Interior, ensured the presence and the authority of the government at all levels. Other, even more typically centralizing features of the maintenance of state power in actual practice were the direct appointment of a great many members of the administrations and in the legal system, who were in theory elected; the widening of the Directory's powers to draft administrative decrees; the expansion of the police apparatus; and an increase in the arbitrary power of the police. The social basis of the State under the Directory still proved too narrow to permit effective government: firstly, because the mass of the population was still excluded by the property franchise; secondly because the aristocracy had not yet been won over to the Revolution; and thirdly, because a fraction of the bourgeoisie was still hostile to the Revolution. The resultant instability gave rise to violations of the Constitution, annulled elections (in Fructidor Year V and in Floréal Year VI) and, to a certain extent, resulted in the subordination of the legislature to the executive. In the sister republics too – in Holland, Switzerland and in Rome – executive power was strengthened. The yearly cycle of elections, though maintaining the system's liberal character, led to the paralysis of the executive, which was always at the mercy of a change in the majority. In 1799, the war abroad and the growth of Jacobinism justified, in the eyes of the bourgeoisie, the definitive strengthening of the executive power: hence the Brumaire coup d'état.

The Constitution of Year VIII replaced election by cooptation, reduced the legislature to a state of indefinite inferiority and concentrated executive power in the hands of the First Consul. The liberal state the men of 'Eighty-nine' had dreamed of was at an end. Yet though military dictatorship cheated the notables of political power, it nevertheless safeguarded their social preponderance. The new authoritarian State, which soon would broaden its social base so as to embrace the aristocracy who had come over to the Revolution, remained fundamentally bourgeois.

2. SECULARIZATION OF CHURCH AND STATE

Gradually, through the logic inherent in circumstances, the Revolution replaced the divine right state, based on the union of throne and altar, with a secular state distinct from the Church.

The old state of affairs, under which Catholicism had been the state religion, was first of all replaced by one in which it was merely the privileged form of public worship. Initially, the Constituent Assembly contented itself with ordinary toleration, which was proclaimed in article 10 of the Declaration of Rights. However, on 13 May 1790, the Assembly, considering that it 'neither has nor can have any power to exercise over consciences and over religious opinions', refused to maintain Catholicism as the state religion. The Civil Constitution of the Clergy which was ratified on 12 July 1790, nevertheless acknowledged Catholicism's claim to the monopoly of public worship. The registration of births, marriages and deaths, and teaching and assistance remained in the Church's hands. The schism which the Civil Constitution produced proved a potent agent of change: the struggle against non-juring priests and the progressively more widespread hostility for constitutional priests were increasingly injurious to the Church and indeed to religion itself.

Progress towards the secularization of the State speeded up after 10 August 1792. On 18 August, the Legislative Assembly, on the grounds that 'a truly free State cannot endure any corporation', suppressed religious congregations dedicated to teaching and to assistance: the property of hospitals and hospices, colleges and universities was put up for sale. Teaching and assistance were thus secularized. The same decree of 18 August prohibited the wearing of religious costume, except for priests actually performing their duties. On 26 August, non-juring priests were obliged to leave the country within a fortnight, on pain of deportation to Guiana. Especially important, too, was the secularization of the registration of births, marriages and deaths, a task which was now entrusted to the municipalities (20 September 1792). The same day, the Legislative Assembly instituted divorce, on the grounds that 'marriage is only a civil contract', and that 'the option of divorce ... is a consequence of individual liberty; an indissoluble undertaking would be tantamount to a loss of liberty'.

The separation of Church and State was a by-product of the vicissitudes of civil war and dechristianization. In the initial period after its establishment, the Convention displayed a conciliatory attitude towards the Constitutional Church, denying any intention, in its address of 30 November 1792, of depriving citizens of 'the ministers given them by the Civil Constitution' and, on 27 June 1793, proclaiming that ecclesiastical stipends should be part of the public debt. The Convention proved more severe than the Legislative Assembly, however, against non-juring priests, decreeing on 23 April 1793 their summary deportation to Guiana. As they came to be suspected of royalism and moderantism, the constitutional priests fell into disrepute. Gradually, hostile measures were passed. The problem of the marriage of priests came up in July 1793, and on 12 August the Convention annulled 'any dismissal of a member of clergy on the grounds of the marriage of individuals devoted to that particular religion'. This decree enabled married priests to resume or to continue their duties. The adoption of the revolutionary calendar, the institution of the *décadi* and, later, dechristianization, proved the decisive landmarks. Despite the solemn affirmation of the freedom of worship by the decree of 16 Frimaire Year II (6 December 1793), the churches remained closed. This *de facto* situation was sanctioned after 9 Thermidor, when at Cambon's proposal on the second *jour sans-culottide* Year II (18 September 1794), the Convention decreed that the Republic would no longer pay 'either the stipends or the expenses for any form of worship'. This was tantamount to the suppression of the Civil Constitution, and the separation of Church and State.

The manner in which Church and State were separated was regimented very exactly by the decree of 3 Ventôse Year III (21 February 1795): the Republic was not to provide salaries for the ministers of any form of worship; the law gave no official recognition to any minister; all public demonstrations or external symbols of worship were prohibited. On 11 Prairial (30 May 1795), the Convention authorized the free use of religious buildings which had not been alienated, though they were to be open concurrently to all forms of worship. The decree of 7 Vendémiaire Year IV (29 September 1795) codified all these measures and obliged all priests to swear the oath of 'submission and obedience to the laws of the Republic'. By the decree of 3 Brumaire Year IV (25 October 1795), the Convention maintained the laws of 1792 and 1793 against non-juring priests. The Directory subsequently ratified these laws once again in article 24 and the following articles in the law of 19 Fructidor Year V (5 September 1797). At the same time, the Directory implemented an aggresive secularizing policy, enforcing the use of the republican calendar in all acts of public life by its decree of 14 Germinal Year VI (3 April 1798), making each *décadi* a public holiday on 17 Thermidor (4 August 1798), and setting down regulations for its observance on 13 Fructidor (30 August 1798). By the end of the period under review, a fall was undeniably apparent in the influence and the prestige of the Catholic Church. This was shown by the distress and disorganization of the divided clergy, a drop in religious practice and by the progress unbelief was making amongst the popular classes. Church and Revolution, irreconcilable at the doctrinal level, remained enemies.

The need for social stabilization and the attachment of the majority of the nation to the traditional religion explain the rapidity with which religion was restored under the Consulate. Yet Bonaparte thought of religion as fundamentally a means of enforcing social submission, and of the Church as an instrument of government. Therefore, though he recognized Catholicism as the religion of the majority of Frenchmen, he denied it the status of a state religion, preferring instead, in the Organic Articles, to subordinate the Church strictly to the State. Thus, if the actual separation of Church and State remained submerged for a century, the State remained essentially secular none the less.

3. THE FUNCTIONS OF THE STATE

The Revolution completely recast the state apparatus, harmonizing the new administrative, judicial and financial institutions with the general principles of bourgeois society and of the liberal state.

The Constituent Assembly reestablished local administrative institutions along rational lines by applying the principle of national sovereignty to them. Thus, the administrators were elected, which entailed decentralization, the central power not being able to act dictatorially over the local authorities, which acted as the mouth-pieces of popular sovereignty. It also entailed a weakening of the administrative apparatus, since local authorities were to be both collegial and the product of elections. The frequency of elections, moreover, was conducive to instability. According to the 1791 Constitution, half the departmental and district administrations were renewable every two years, and the municipalities every year. The Year III Constitution provided for the annual renewal of one-fifth of the department administrations and half of the municipalities. In these circumstances, it proved difficult to train a competent administrative personnel. Members of departmental and district administrations were drawn from the bourgeoisie, while the municipalities were recruited more from the middle stratum of the artisanat, from shopkeepers and from among the liberal professions. In 1793, a strong tendency towards democratization was evident, at district level and especially in the municipalities, to which the sans-culotterie gained access. A shortage of competent personnel often made the formation of rural municipalities difficult, however, and this led, in the Constitution of Year III, to the creation of cantonal municipalities, formed of one municipal agent and an assistant to each commune. These too, however, had little success.

The tendency towards centralization was latent in the process of the rationalization of institutions. The development of this central-izing tendency was quickened, therefore, by the revolutionary crisis of 1793. The Revolutionary Government instituted permanently-sitting administrations and, through purges, in practice replaced election with appointment. The decree of 14 Frimaire Year II (4 December 1793) attached to municipalities and to district administrations 'national agents', who were to report back to the two Committees of government every ten days. This decree streng-thened and democratized the bureaucratic machine.

By returning to the property franchise, the Constitution of Year III restored the administrative monopoly of the bourgeoisie of notables. At the same time, the Constitution strengthened the State's battery of administrative weapons by providing for the appointment of commissioners representing the executive power, who were to be attached to the municipal and departmental administrations. The Directory made a real attempt to reorganize the administration in all spheres – as is witnessed for example by the often remarkable work of François de Neufchâteau at the Ministry of the Interior. It was partly on the foundation made by this reordering of institutions that Bonaparte's military dictatorship was built. The principle of election still remained, however, and with it instability and sometimes incompetence. Finally, in the law of 28 Pluviôse Year VIII (7 February 1800), Bonaparte suppressed the election, and instituted a cadre of authoritative public officials appointed by himself. In so doing, he stabilized the administrative machine, and increased the competence which it brought to bear in serving the authoritarian state.

Judicial institutions had been reorganized by the Constituent Assembly according to the same principles as administrative institutions. Elections did not involve the same difficulties in this sphere, however, since by the decree of 16 August 1790, judges were to be elected for a six-year term, were re-eligible for office, and could only be elected initially 'if they had practised publicly as a judge or lawyer and had been attached to a tribunal for five years'.

The Constitution of Year III reduced the term of office to five years. This in no way attenuated the tendency of the judicial reforms to strengthen the magistracy's stability and its competence. In the field of criminal procedure, the Constituent Assembly displayed a wide-ranging liberalism. The *parquet,* or public prosecutor, was abolished, and no new body was given the responsibility of endeavouring to track down crimes. Except for the initial stages of preliminary investigation, all legal proceedings were in public. The creation of two juries, one to decide if there was a case to answer, the other to decide on guilt, proved a safeguard for the defendant.

Judicial organization naturally experienced the same vagaries of fortune as the structure of the State, and evolved in the same direction as it. The Convention suppressed conditions of eligibility, making the age of twenty-five the only qualification, and thus making proceedings rather more straightforward on the whole. At the same time, the judicial power was brought under the executive. Indeed, the separation of the two powers disappeared in practice under the Revolutionary Government, which effected the concentration and the unity of powers. The legal system under the Terror was marked by both the creation of extraordinary tribunals, with expeditious procedure, and also by the suppression of safeguards for the protection of the individual. The judicial system under the Directory felt the repercussions of the system which had preceded it. The Constitution allowed the Directory the right to issue subpoenas and arrest-warrants; the idea of extraordinary jurisdictions was continued, in the shape of the military commissions which judged political opponents, whether Chouans or Jacobins.

Lastly, in the field of the codification of laws, the Revolution's work remained unfinished. The Revolution destroyed feudal and canon law, and also Roman law, with the aim in view of creating a uniform and national body of law. In August 1790, the Constituent Assembly decreed that there would be drawn up 'a general code of simple and clear laws, in keeping with the spirit of the Constitution'. On 25 September 1791 it ratified a Penal Code and on 28 September a Rural Code. In August 1793, at the very height of the crisis, the Convention debated the draft of a civil code put forward by Cambacérès on behalf of the Committee of Legislation. Though the revolutionary assemblies did not complete their plans, they nevertheless accomplished a considerable amount of work and, in the organic laws, laid down provisional foundations on essential questions: marriage and divorce, inheritances and the right to make a will, rural property and mortgages. In this sphere as in others, the Thermidorian and Directorial periods were marked by an undeniable regression compared with Montagnard legislation. The step backwards included, for example, the suppression of the retroactive effect of the law on inheritance.

All these reforms presaged the legal stabilization of the Consular period, which was to prove a reflection of the stabilization of society itself. The return to the appointment of judges and the gradual restoration of the public prosecutor strengthened state power.

The financial institutions established by the Constituent Assembly were characterized above all by fiscal equality and the institution of three main direct taxes, the land tax, the personal *mobilière* tax, and the tax on licences, the *patente*. The powers of the State were attenuated in this sphere by the suppression of indirect taxes, which thus deprived it of a consistent and important income, and by the disappearance of any bodies to organize the financial system, assessment and levying of taxes being entirely left to the municipalities. Here again, however, despite the temporary weakening in state power, the general trend was in the direction of increasing the powers of the State.

The fiscal system introduced by the Constituent Assembly was reshaped by the Convention which, on 12 March 1793, suppressed the *patente* and decided that industrial and commercial revenues should be included in the assessment of the *mobilière*. With civil war reducing in 1793 the amount of revenue procured by taxation, the Montagnard Convention had recourse to revolutionary price-fixing and the forced loan. This latter measure was decreed provisionally on 20 May 1793, and organized on 3 September; the loan was fixed at 1 billion *livres*, fell on citizens whose income exceeded 1,500 francs (1,000 francs for unmarried persons), and was calculated on a sliding scale. The Thermidorians returned to the system espoused by the Constituent Assembly: on 6 Fructidor Year IV (23 August 1796) they reestablished the *patente*. To combat the depreciation of the currency, the law of 2 Thermidor Year III (20 July 1795) decreed that half the land tax should be paid in *assignats* at their nominal value and half in grain at the 1790 prices. In Year VII, the whole fiscal system was recast by the Directorial Councils: the land tax by the law of 3 Frimaire (23 November 1798), which reestablished obligatory cash payment; the *mobilière* by the law of 3 Nivôse (23 December 1798), which greatly increased the scale of the imposition; the *patente* by the law of 1 Brumaire (22 October 1798), which modified the bases of the assessment for the tax; and a fourth direct tax was created by the law of 4 Frimaire (24 November 1798) on doors and windows. At the same time, registration duty (by the law of 22 Frimaire – 12 December 1798) and the stamp tax (by the law of 13 Brumaire – 3 November 1798) were reorganized. All this was to prove absolutely fundamental legislation which, in its essential components, remained in force for more than a century. The State's revenues did not cease to fall, however – which was in fact to the satisfaction of the propertied classes. The Councils stubbornly refused to reestablish indirect taxes, and merely contented themselves with a tax on tobacco, one on roads, called *droit de passe*, and also a tax on the price of seats in public stage-coaches.

The system of levying taxes established by the Constituent Assembly was to a large extent responsible for the smallness of the revenue from taxation, since the municipal authorities who were charged with the levying were not allowed to resort to constraint. The law of 22 Brumaire Year VI (12 November 1797) provided for the creation of a Direct Tax Agency in each department, comprising commissioners who would assist the municipal administrations in all 'work concerning the assessment and levying of taxes, and in all disputes arising therefrom'. The intention was not to create a specialized administration, but rather a simple supervisory agency.

Great progress, then, was made under the Directory in the work of strengthening the State's financial powers. Bonaparte satisfied himself on a large number of points with simply utilizing the instruments created by his predecessors. Having replaced the liberal state with an authoritarian one, he finished off the work of the Directory firstly by creating an effective financial system, subordinate solely to the central power, and secondly, shortly afterwards, by drafting a cadastral survey, which became the sole rational basis for land taxation. By setting the minds of the propertied classes at rest once and for all, he was able to restore state credit. The reestablishment under the Empire of indirect taxes, including the salt tax, terminated developments in this sphere, and underlined, incidentally, the power of the new authoritarian state.

3. National Unity and Equality of Rights

The French Revolution concentrated its full blast in certain words: 'nation' for example. When at Valmy the enemy cannon-fire threatened to unsettle the French lines, Kellermann cried out before the astonished Prussians, 'Long live the Nation!' The battle-cry reverberated and grew in conviction from rank to rank among the volunteers, the enemy wavered. 'This day and this place,' Goethe said, 'open a new era in the history of the world.'

In 1789 the word 'nation' had been injected with a new sense. It received an added dimension of meaning from the deeply-felt and enthusiastic impulses, the spontaneous collective emotions which revolutionary hope and faith inspired. Now, the nation was equivalent to the whole social organism. There were no more orders, no more classes: everything which was French helped to constitute the nation. This key word had resounded in the innermost being of the French collective spirit: it liberated latent forces, it raised men above themselves. Very swiftly, however, beneath the mask which this word came to wear, the reality of the new order asserted itself. 'Nation' became one of those 'word-illusions' that Ferdinand Brunot speaks of in his *Histoire de la langue française*. The social content of what in concrete terms the nation actually comprised varied according to the tempo of the Revolution. Though national unity made undeniable progress during the period, the inequality of rights between social groups introduced a fundamental contradiction within the new nation. Because it was interpreted on the basis of property and within the narrow framework of the property franchise, the 'nation' in fact excluded the popular masses.

I. THE PROGRESS OF UNIFICATION

The French nation took a decisive step in the direction of unity during the Revolution. The new institutions formed the framework of an administratively and economically unified State. At the same time, national consciousness was strengthened in the revolutionary struggles against the aristocracy and the Coalition.

The rationalization of institutions by the Constituent Assembly, the return to centralization by the Revolutionary Government and the administrative endeavours of the Directory rounded off the work of the Ancien Régime monarchy in destroying autonomies and particularisms and in setting up the battery of institutions appropriate to a unified State. At the same time, the gradually awakening consciousness of the nation as 'one and indivisible' was forged through the development of the network of societies affiliated to the Jacobin Club, by the anti-federalism and the congresses, or 'central meetings' of the popular societies in 1793.

New economic ties and relationships strengthened national unity. The end which had been put to the break up of estates under the feudal system, the abolition of tolls and internal customs dues (the so-called 'rolling back of customs barriers' throughout French territory), tended to unify the national market which was moreover shielded from foreign competition by a protectionist tariff. Free circulation within France awoke and consolidated the economic solidarity between the different regions, though only to the degree that the development of the means of communications made this possible. Economic unification required a uniform system of weights and measures. In May 1790, the Constituent Assembly created the Commission of Weights and Measures, and on 26 March 1791 agreed on the foundations of the new system, which was to be based 'on the length of the earth's meridian and on decimal division'. Delambre and Méchain in 1792 measured the length of the meridian between Dunkirk and Barcelona, while Hauy and Lavoisier determined the weight of a volume of water condensed at 0° and weighed in a vacuum. On 11 July 1792, the Commission settled on the nomenclature of the weights and measures which were orientated around two basic units, the metre and the gramme. The decisive decrees were passed on 1 August 1793 and 18 Germinal Year III (7 April 1795). Article 5 of the latter defined the metre as 'the unit of length equal to one ten-millionth part of the arc of the terrestrial meridian between the North Pole and the Equator', and the gramme as 'the absolute weight of a volume of pure water equal to the cube of the hundredth part of the metre, at the temperature of melting ice'.

The problem still remained of introducing the metric system into daily use. Delay followed delay before it was implemented. In the end, it was not until the Consular period that its enforcement was prescribed, starting on 1 Vendémiaire Year X (23 September 1801). In practice, however, the new units of length and of weight only replaced the Ancien Régime ones very slowly.

The national army, by reinforcing national consciousness, proved a potent factor in the process of unification. The Constituent Assembly had been reticent in this field, contenting itself with the abolition of the militia and on 28 February 1790 with the purchase of commissions, which henceforward were to be open to all. The decree of 9 March 1791 maintained the system of recruitment by voluntary enlistment. At the same time, however, the Constituent Assembly did legalize one product of the Revolution, the National Guard, though admittedly in the general principles set out in the law of 6 December 1790, maintained and clarified by the law of 19 September 1791, it restricted membership of the guard to active citizens. The disintegration of the line army and the threat of war at the time of the flight to Varennes decided the deputies into levying 100,000 volunteers from the National Guard, who were to be organized into battalions (21 June 1791). These volunteers were supplemented by the levies decreed by the Legislative Assembly. The fall of the King, the threat to the nation provided by the allies and the entry of the sans-culottes into the political arena supplied the decisive impetus towards the formation of a unitary army. In July 1792, passive citizens entered the battalions of the National Guard, which thus became truly national. On 24 February 1793, the Convention decreed a levy of 300,000 men, while on 21 February it had voted for the *amalgame* of regiments of the old line army with the volunteer battalions.

Actually, unification made only slow progress. The methods of enrolment were not decided upon until a decree of 19 Nivôse Year II (8 January 1794). Furthermore, despite the *levée en masse* introduced on 23 August 1793, not all Frenchmen were obliged to serve in the army. Notwithstanding the general character of the call-up, only bachelors and childless widowers between the ages of 18 and 25 had to serve. Moreover, the Convention did not enforce a further call-up the following year. Obligatory service thus remained the exception rather than the rule – a state of affairs made permanent by the

Jourdan Law on conscription, voted on 19 Fructidor Year VI (5 September 1798). This stated that

All Frenchmen are soldiers (article 1).
Military conscription includes all Frenchmen between their twentieth and twenty-sixth birthdays (article 15).

All conscripts did not serve, however, for the size of the contingent to be called up was decided by the legislature in a specific law. Moreover, the law of 28 Germinal Year VII (17 April 1799) introduced the principle of 'military replacements' which, though suppressed on 14 Messidor (2 July 1799), was reestablished by Bonaparte as a sop to the notables. In spite of these limitations, however, the army was truly unified and nationalized in this revolutionary period: first, by means of the *amalgame*, and secondly by means of the annual *levée en masse* – which is what conscription boiled down to if all the categories of potential recruits were called up, as was the case in Year VII and under the Empire. Naturally, the reaction after Thermidor transformed the army's corporate feeling of citizenship. Nevertheless, the principle behind the army was still the same, that is, the idea of the nation in arms; rapid promotion as a reward for bravery also continued to be the popular symbol of equality. By virtue of these two elements of continuity, the incomparable war-weapon inherited by Bonaparte remained one of the essential factors behind national unity.

The development of the French language followed much the same course. In 1789, most Frenchmen had only spoken dialects or *patois* which distanced them to a great extent from the main currents of intellectual and political life. The Constituent Assembly promoted local autonomy, safeguarding linguistic particularism by voting on 14 January 1790 that all of its decrees should be translated into all the dialects then in use in France. The Convention, on the other hand, having nationalized the war-effort, applied itself to making French the national language: the uniformity of the language was to help to weld the nation's unity. Great efforts were made in this direction in the clubs and popular societies, where expressing oneself in French came to be regarded as proof of patriotism. Under the Terror, dialects were treated as if they were the accomplices of the counter-revolution and the Coalition. To a certain extent, we are justified in talking of a 'linguistic terrorism' which was deployed against the dual enemy – as in the work of Saint-Just, for example, in Alsace, during his famous mission. On 8 Pluviôse Year II, Barère, speaking on behalf of the Committee of Public Safety, made a full-scale attack on the 'old idioms':

Federalism and superstition speak in *bas-breton*; the émigrés and hatred of the Republic speak in German. . . . The monarchy had its own reasons for resembling the Tower of Babel; in a democracy, however, to allow citizens to remain ignorant of the national language, and incapable thereby of supervising the exercise of power, is to betray France. The French language, which has had the honour of being utilized for the Declaration of the Rights of Man, must become the language of all Frenchmen. It is our duty to provide citizens with the instrument of public thinking, the most certain agent of revolution, that is, a common language.

Largely because of this speech, the Convention made French obligatory in all public and notarial documents and transactions, and decreed the appointment within ten days of schoolmasters in all those departments where the inhabitants spoke Breton, Basque, Italian and German. After Thermidor, there was a general return to tolerance: soon public acts were being translated once more into the local dialects. The same reaction is evident in the teaching of French: whereas the law of 27 Brumaire Year III (17 November 1794) on primary schools provided for the teaching of the 'rudiments of the French language', there was no provision in the law of 3 Brumaire Year IV (24 October 1795) for the teaching of French or even for teaching in French. The national language superseded Latin and came to hold sway unchallenged only in the central schools and in higher education. Thus in this sphere too, national unity was tinged with a degree of social discrimination.

It was thought that training in citizenship would, in the final analysis, quicken the process whereby Frenchmen would sense that they belonged to one nation. From this consideration sprang the attention that the revolutionary assemblies paid to education: the aim was to train citizens. Under the Constituent Assembly, curés read aloud the Assembly's decrees and proclamations from the pulpit. Reading and commenting on the Declaration of the Rights of Man and the Constitution were always prescribed by any plan which dealt with public education. The law of 29 Frimaire Year II (19 November 1793) stated that the rudimentary texts for study were 'the Rights of

Man, the Constitution and the depiction of heroic or of virtuous actions'. The Thermidorian laws on primary schools stipulate the same syllabus for all – the Rights of Man and the Constitution, of course – plus instruction in 'the elements of republican morality'.

The great national festivals were fully commensurate with this objective. If the first festival chronologically was the Fête de la Fédération (14 July 1790), the festival of 11 July 1791, in honour of the translation of Voltaire's ashes to the Pantheon, really constituted the first philosophical festival: it was carried out in accordance with an idea of David's, in the manner of the funeral pomp of the Ancient World. For each great event after this, there was pageantry and display. The painter David and the composers Gossec and Méhul often lent the glamour of their art to these occasions. Among the most notable were the Festival of Liberty (15 April 1792), the Festivals of the Unity and Indivisibility of the Republic (10 August 1793) and the Festival of the Supreme Being (18 Floréal Year II – 8 June 1794). The decree of 18 Floréal Year II (7 May 1794) which installed the religion of the Supreme Being, established decadal festivals and great national festivals to celebrate either the glorious events of the Revolution or else 'the virtues which are most dear and most useful to man'. The decree of 3 Brumaire Year III (24 October 1795) anticipated seven great national festivals. The Constitution of Year III stressed that the aim of these in theory was 'to sustain fraternity between citizens and to attach them to the Constitution, to their country and to the laws'. Under the Directory, the festivals to commemorate the Peace of Campoformio, and in honour of Hoche and of Jean-Jacques Rousseau were especially splendid; on 27 July 1798, Liberty and the Arts were extolled in an imposing procession.

The development of the great civic festivals emphasizes, however, the considerable limitations on the progress of the feeling of nationhood during the Revolution. Their apogee had been reached in Year II. Then they had their full significance as expressions of nationhood: the people were not only present, they also participated, as essential ingredients in the occasion, which honoured their role in the nation. David, the creator of the new art of arranging these festivals, drew upon everything that the plastic arts – painting and sculpture – could offer; music played an essential part, in the presence of imposing choral and instrumental masses; the arts of costume and scenery also had a contribution to make; finally, for the arrangement of the processions, David availed himself of everything at his disposal. The national festivals bore to its highest pitch the enthusiasm of all Frenchmen, who joined in communion in the same patriotic faith and the same feeling of dedication to the Republic. Once the reaction had set in, however, the great festivals soon became empty of any social and political content. The people, formerly actors in the great occasion, were gradually reduced to walk-on parts, and then to the status of spectators. The demonstrations lost their truly national character. Shortly after, military reviews and 'official' rejoicings replaced 'national' festivals. With the people now shut out from political life, unity was only a show, which hid the underlying inequality of rights.

2. EQUALITY OF RIGHTS AND SOCIAL REALITIES

The equality of rights proclaimed by the first article of the 1789 Declaration of the Rights of Man and the principle of national sovereignty asserted in article 3 comprised in theory potent factors in the development of national unity. The theoretical proclamation of equality was, together with the suppression of the privileges of individuals and of the corporate bodies on which the Ancien Régime's social hierarchy was based and the individualist conception of social relationships which held sway in the Constituent Assembly, to shape the foundations of an egalitarian society and of a unified nation. However, by designating the right of property as a natural right, and by making economic freedom the very linchpin of the new organization of society, the bourgeoisie's representatives in the Constituent Assembly set at the heart of the new society a contradiction which they were unable to overcome. Contradictory in much the same way was the contiguity in the Assembly's political work of the principle of national sovereignty and the property franchise. The principle of the equality of rights had only been advanced by the bourgeoisie in 1789 so as to carry the assault against aristocratic privilege; they only contemplated a theoretical equality in the eyes of the law to govern their dealings with the popular classes. There was no talk of social democracy; indeed, even political democracy was rejected. The legal nation was narrowly circumscribed within the boundaries of the property-franchise bourgeoisie.

The popular masses had a much more concrete idea of what

equality of rights meant, taking at face-value what for the bourgeoisie was only a theoretical formula. For the people, the point was to give a real content to the Great Hope of 1789. From equality of rights, the militants of the popular movement inferred the right to existence. This recognition and their subsequent organization allowed the popular classes to become integrated as equal partners in the nation. The problem of food-supplies was an especially important precipitatory factor in this realization: economic freedom and free profit, which property rights implied, seemed to contradict the principle of the equality of rights and also the creation of a unified nation. Circumstances thrust this problem into the foreground and forced the bourgeoisie to make concessions.

The Revolution of 10 August 1792, by prompting the introduction of universal suffrage and of the arming of passive citizens, integrated the people into the nation and marked the advent of political democracy. At the same time, the exigencies of the struggle against the Coalition and the counter-revolution emphasized the social character of the new nation. Though the Declaration of Rights of 24 June 1794 restated the bourgeois definition of the right of property (article 16), it nevertheless asserted in its first article that

the aim of society is the common happiness. Government is instituted to guarantee man the enjoyment of his natural and imprescriptible rights.

The right to assistance and to education were also recognized (articles 21, 22). In the course of the social and political struggles of the summer of 1793, the leaders of the popular movement went even further: by making the rights of property inferior to the right to assistance, they laid the theoretical foundations for a unitary nation extended to include the popular classes. Soon, they were quite naturally inferring from the right to existence the *égalité des iouissances*.

It is not sufficient that the French Republic be based on equality [Félix Lepeletier proclaimed to the Convention on 20 August 1793, on behalf of the commissioners of the primary assemblies]. It is also essential that laws and morals tend, in happy harmony, towards the disappearance of *inégalité des jouissances*.

From this theoretical starting-point arose the tenacious popular demands of Year II for the limitation of property rights and for the organization of the right to work .the right to assistance and the right to education.

The attempt to institute a social democracy which had marked the egalitarian republic of Year II was not viable. Grounded in private property, the principle of which was never challenged, the system of the directed economy, characterized above all by profit-limitation, tried to reconcile the interests of the propertied classes and those who did not possess property, of producers and consumers, of employers and wage-earners. The antagonism was not merely between supporters of economic freedom and supporters of economic controls. At the very heart of the sans-culotterie itself, the principle of private property, to which artisans and shopkeepers clung, and to which *compagnons* aspired, came into conflict not only with the price-fixing and trade-controls which they were demanding but also with their conception of limited property, based on personal labour. These multiple contradictions inevitably brought about the fall of the social system of Year II and of the Revolutionary Government. The nation, which for a short time had been extended to include the masses, came to be restricted once again to the propertied classes. Once again as well, once social and political democracy had been firmly set aside, the framework for the new republic was the property franchise.

The contradiction between the equality of rights and economic freedom, which rendered illusory any attempt at social democracy or at the *égalité des jouissances* vainly demanded by the sans-culottes, was dissolved by the theoreticians of the Conspiracy of Equals, Babeuf and Buonarroti. They made a decisive break with the past by levelling their criticisms against the private appropriation of the means of production. The 'Plebeians' Manifesto' of 9 Frimaire Year IV (30 November 1795) repudiated the *loi agraire* for its necessarily ephemeral character, urged the suppression of inheritance and expressly stipulated the abolition of the ownership of land. The community of goods and of labour would allow the *égalité des jouissances* to be attained, since it implied a real equality of rights and a national unity which was not merely formal. This fertile direction of thought set the trend for later socialist theoreticians.

The Thermidorian bourgeoisie had, in its fear, rejected not merely any idea of social democracy, but also any trace of political equality. The Constitution of Year III returned to the property franchise; the Declaration of Rights took pains to stress that 'equality resides in the fact that the law is the same for all men, whether in protecting or in punishing' (article 3). In other words, for the Thermidorians, the only kind of equality was civil equality. By their ideas in this sphere, the link was effected with the tradition of 'Eighty-nine', and the framework of a nation of notables, that is, of well-to-do property owners, took shape. The danger from abroad in June and July 1799 brought the fragile equilibrium of the bourgeois nation into question again. There was now no chance, however, of the masses putting the social and political preponderance of the bourgeoisie in the balance once again. The reaction soon made its appearance. It is as part of the reaction, in fact, that the coup d'état of 18 Brumaire must be understood: by it, the nation preserved the boundaries assigned it by the notables in Year III; equality remained only a formal prescription; and national unity was less expressive of the social content of the nation than of a purely institutional framework.

3. SOCIAL RIGHTS: ASSISTANCE AND EDUCATION

The sans-culottes viewed the equality of rights as an attempt to efface inequality in general living conditions. Their general demand, the point of which was to ensure each citizen his livelihood, included the right to assistance. The idea behind their claim to education, on the other hand, was that the sans-culottes would climb to the level of the *hommes à talent*, and thus be in a position to control their destinies. The bourgeois revolution, however, disappointed these two aspirations.

Following the confiscation of clerical property, assistance, which had been in the hands of the Church under the Ancien Régime, was secularized and recognized as a state service. In 1790, the Constituent Assembly set up a Committee of Mendicity, which implemented the general principle according to which society had a duty to assist those of its members who were in distress, and that the responsibility and the expenses arising for this fell to the State. The first sub-heading of the 1791 Constitution ('Fundamental provisions guaranteed by the Constitution') envisaged the creation of 'a general establishment for public relief, to raise foundlings, to comfort sick paupers and to provide work for those able-bodied paupers who have not been able to procure work'.

Actually, the Constituent Assembly was not up to the task of effecting overall reform in this sphere, preferring instead to leave

The Revolution and Contemporary France 599

matters in their existing state and to exclude the property of hospital foundations from the sale of national lands. When hospital revenues shrank after the suppression of tithes and of feudal rights, the Assembly endeavoured to compensate the hospitals for their loss by government subsidies. The only two fundamental measures it passed in this sphere were the decrees of 30 May and 31 August 1790 relating to the establishment of charity workshops. The Legislative Assembly, under which the Committee of Mendicity gave way to the the Committee for Public Assistance, considerably worsened the situation by suppressing, on 19 August 1792, all religious charitable institutions. In practice, then, the old hospital system was destroyed without anything having been built to replace it.

The Convention gave a new boost to legislation on assistance, without however being able to put the laws it passed into effect. On 19 March 1793, the decree on the bases of the general organization of public relief stated:

1. That each man has the right to his livelihood, by work if he is ablebodied, by free assistance if he is not in a condition to work.
2. That the business of providing for the livelihood of paupers is a national debt.

In article 21 of the Declaration of Rights, 24 June 1793, the same principles are recapitulated:

Public relief is a sacred debt. Society owes its unfortunate citizens their livelihood either by procuring them work, or else by providing the means of existence for those not in a condition to work.

Accordingly, the law of 28 June–8 July 1793 extended relief to pauper children and foundlings, to the aged and to indigents. The law of 15 October 1793, 'to extinguish mendicity', provided for 'relief work', but also for 'houses of repression' for vagabonds. These measures were in fact tantamount to the re-adoption of the charitable methods of the Ancien Régime, that is, the 'confinement of paupers' and charity workshops. Financial difficulties, however, acted as a considerable inhibiting force on the reforming endeavours of the government and the municipalities. This led to incessant demands from the organizations of the popular movement throughout the winter of Year II. The decree of 22 Floréal Year II (11 May 1794) finally provided for the opening of a 'Register of National

Beneficence', and outlined the social security system which the sans-culottes had confusedly been demanding. The law only applied to the countryside, however. Under it, relief was to be afforded to a limited number of peasants and artisans in each department who were either sick or over sixty years old, and also to mothers and widows burdened with children. After the suppression of the Ministries, a Commission for Public Assistance was organized. A veritable Ministry of Assistance, the new commission was put in charge of ensuring the distribution of relief to hospitals, including military hospitals. Lastly, assistance was nationalized by the law of 23 Messidor Year II (10 July 1794) which declared 'the assets and the liabilities of hospitals and of other establishments of beneficence' national property. Just then, however, Thermidor occurred. From this Montagnard legislation there was to survive nothing but a great popular hope, which had not been fulfilled.

The Thermidorian and Directorial bourgeoisie, more in a spirit of realism than out of self-interest, steered clear of both the theoretical pronouncements of the Constituent Assembly and the vast projects of the Convention, and confined itself to measures of a more practical nature. The Thermidorians restored all hospital property which had not yet been sold. The Directory, gauging the nationalization of assistance to be unfeasible, municipalized it. The law of 16 Vendémiaire Year V (7 October 1796) entrusted the municipalities with the close supervision of hospitals and hospices, whose financial administration was to be assured by an 'administrative commission' appointed and supervised by the municipality. The municipalities were also empowered by this law to recover the parts of the hospital patrimony which had been confiscated and sold. In spite of the considerable work of these administrative commissions, the financial situation of the hospital establishments remained often disastrously bad. The law of 7 Frimaire Year V (27 November 1796) setting up *bureaux de bienfaisance* – local assistance boards – also entrusted the municipalities with responsibility for indigents. The *droit des pauvres* – a levy on theatres at the rate of 2 *sous* per franc – ensured that the new service was properly financed. Beggars were to be interned. Lastly, by the laws of 27 Frimaire and 30 Ventôse Year V (17 December 1796 and 20 March 1797), foundlings were put within the care of hospitals and hospices; the State was to undertake expenses for this service. The hospitals and hospices were to farm out the foundlings to nurses in the countryside, although they were still under the supervision of the administrative commissions.

Assistance, then, emerged secularized from the Revolution. In comparison with the ambitions of the Constituent Assembly and the great laws of the Montagnard Convention, the work of the Directory comprises, in the sphere of general principles at least, a clear regression. This does, however, bear witness to the Directory's real concern to set things in order and to adjust practically to contingencies. Within these limits, the Directory's work was effective and durable. Nevertheless, smacking as it did of the traditional conception of charity, and set within the Directory's general reorganization of institutions, this bourgeois legislation was far from answering the wishes of the popular masses; far from finding a remedy for the *inégalité des jouissances* which would have allowed the masses to join in the nation in social terms.

Although educational reform was a constant preoccupation of the revolutionary assemblies, the reorganization of education in the revolutionary period was to provide just as much disappointment for the masses as the reorganization of assistance had done.

The Constituent Assembly soon made clear its intention of bestowing on the country a new system of education: amongst the 'fundamental provisions guaranteed by the Constitution', it placed the principle of 'public education for all citizens, which should be free in respect to that teaching which is indispensable for all'. In actual fact, the Assembly contented itself with ensuring that the teaching establishments then in existence continued to function, by adjourning the sale of lands belonging to them (28 October 1790), and by granting the colleges subsidies from public funds. It was not until 10 September 1791 that the Assembly gave a hearing to Talleyrand's report on education, and even then it did not go on to debate it. The Legislative Assembly seemed more concerned to produce something definite, setting up a Committee of Public Instruction. The main achievement of this body was the drafting of a project on the 'General Organization of Public Instruction' which, on 20 and 21 April 1792, was read to the Assembly by Condorcet. This plan, the most important of those presented to the revolutionary assemblies, bears the imprint of its age, both by its breadth of vision and by its ingrained optimism. It proposed to develop all talents and all abilities through education and 'thereby to establish between citizens an actual equality' which would help to erase inequality which sprang from the property franchise. Thus the Revolution would contribute towards

the general and gradual perfection of the human species, the ultimate end towards which every social institution must be directed.

The Legislative Assembly, however, did not have enough time even to begin to debate Condorcet's plan.

The Montagnard Convention ranked education among the rights of man:

'Education is the requirement of us all,' article 22 of the Declaration of 24 June 1793 maintained: 'Society must favour with all its might the progress of public reason, and must place instruction within the grasp of all citizens.' On 13 July 1793, Robespierre read to the Convention Lepeletier de Saint-Fargeau's 'Plan for national education', a text which was deeply influenced by Rousseau, and which proposed the institution of a state monopoly of education. However, popular militants were demanding – notably in their addresses in favour of accepting the Constitution in July 1793 – a system of education which would give children both a civic and a technical training. They had to wait for this until the decree of 29 Frimaire Year II (19 December 1793) on primary schools, which instituted a system of education based on non-payment, compulsory attendance, and state supervision – though private individuals were allowed to open their own schools. The system was decentralized, and fairly well in harmony with what the people wanted. It still remained to implement this system. In practice, the attention of the Revolutionary Government was so monopolized by the conduct of the war that it neglected this task. The disappointment of the sansculotterie was made greater because they had hoped for a great deal from education, seeing it as a means of consolidating the régime and achieving equality of rights.

Although the Thermidorian bourgeoisie at first maintained the work of the Montagnards, it inflected its policies in the direction of its class interests, gradually abandoning the principles of free and compulsory schooling. On 10 Vendémiaire Year III (1 October 1794), the Convention decreed the opening of a teachers' training college, which was to produce within four months 1,300 teachers from youths designated by the districts for their civic qualities, and who would in turn train teachers. Primary schools were instituted by the decree of 27 Brumaire Year III (17 November 1794), at the rate of one school per thousand inhabitants. The decree did not, however, insist that the schooling should be compulsory. The teaching in these schools was centred on republican morality, which was rigidly demarcated from revealed religion. Teachers were to be chosen for them by a committee appointed by the district administration and were to be paid by the State. The right of all citizens was recognized 'to open private and free schools, under the supervision of the constituted authorities'.

In secondary education, the aim was to train the cadres of the new society and the new State. The Thermidorian bourgeoisie viewed this branch of education as much more important. On the recommendations contained in Lakanal's report, the decree of 7 Ventôse Year III (25 February 1795) set up a central school in each department 'to teach sciences, humanities and the arts'. The pupils followed three courses of study: between the ages of twelve and fourteen, they were taught modern and ancient languages, natural history and design; from fourteen to sixteen, mathematics, physics and chemistry; and from sixteen to eighteen, general grammar, belles-lettres, history and legislation. Teaching was thus modernized by the priority now accorded sciences and French language and literature, while research and popularization were combined in an unusual manner. Teachers formerly chosen by a selection committee were appointed by the departmental administrators. While the syllabus and methods of the central schools were fully in keeping with the ideological movement of the Age of Enlightenment, the conservative reaction was apparent in the absence of free schooling, though this was admittedly diluted by the granting of scholarships to *élèves de la patrie*.

Higher education occupied the attention of the Thermidorians for much the same reasons. The old universities and academies had been suppressed. On 14 June 1793, the Montagnards had transformed the Jardin du Roi into a new body, the Museum, whose aim was 'publicly to teach natural history in all its aspects, and applied in particular to the advancement of agriculture, commerce and the arts'. On 7 Vendémiaire Year III (28 September 1794), the Convention set up the Central School for Public Works, which one year later became the Ecole Polytechnique. On 19 Vendémiaire (10 October 1794), on the recommendation of Grégoire's report, the Conservatory of Arts and Crafts was consecrated to applied science:

this was to preserve machines and models and also to function as a teaching institution, concerning itself with 'the use of machines and tools useful to the arts and professions'. The decree of 14 Frimaire Year III (4 December 1794) created three medical schools, in Paris, Strasbourg and Montpellier. The School of Oriental Languages and the Bureau des Longitudes or Central Astronomical Office, were founded on 10 Germinal (30 March) and 7 Messidor Year III (25 June 1795) respectively. To crown the whole edifice, the Convention organized the National Institute of the Arts and Sciences by a decree of 3 Brumaire Year IV (25 October 1795). Divided into three classes – for the physical sciences and mathematics, for the moral and political sciences, and for literature and the fine arts – the Institute had as its aim 'the perfection of the arts and sciences by uninterrupted research, by the publication of discoveries and by correspondence with learned and foreign societies'. It was both to illustrate and to demonstrate the unity and solidarity of the sciences. 'The happy results,' Daunou had declared when he introduced the law setting up the institution, 'of a system which has to keep sciences and arts in perpetual dialogue and submit them to the normally reciprocal reaction of progress and utility, are incalculable.'

The great law of 3 Brumaire Year IV (25 October 1795) on the organization of public education integrated these differing institutions into a vast ensemble, in which were set primary schools, central schools, the specialized schools and the National Institute. Reaction soon made its mark, however: schooling became no longer compulsory; free education disappeared; the State restricted itself to providing accommodation for teachers, who were remunerated by their pupils. This was the state of affairs when the Directory came to office. On the one hand, the Directory endeavoured to develop the central schools, which were really successful from 1796 till 1802, when they were suppressed in their prime by Bonaparte. On the other hand, because there was not enough money to create primary schools everywhere, or to educate the necessary teachers, private, religiously orientated teaching sprang up, though it was subject to municipal supervision. According to the decree of the Directory dated 17 Pluviôse Year VI (5 February 1798), 'this supervision is becoming more necessary than ever in order to check the progress of the baleful principles with which a host of private teachers are trying to instil their pupils'.

The work of the Revolution in the educational sphere might

seem, at the end of the period, considerable; it was nevertheless incomplete. The monopoly of the Church had been destroyed. Education had been secularized and modernized. Yet in social terms, education remained the privilege of a minority. In Ventôse Year II, the Sans-Culottes section in Paris had demanded the urgent organization of primary education 'in such a way that each individual acquires the talents and virtues necessary in order to enjoy his natural rights in all thoroughness'. There is a clear parallel here with Condorcet's great idea of realizing through education an actual equality, and thus 'to make real the political equality recognized by the law'. After ten years of revolution, this objective was still far from attainment.

4. THE WINNING OVER OF THE ARISTOCRACY TO THE PROPERTY-OWNING NATION

On the eve of Brumaire, the integration of the propertied classes – both bourgeoisie and *ci-devant* aristocrats – within the framework of the property franchise was gradually bringing about the stabilization of France's social system. Civil war and the Terror had tended temporarily to cut off from national unity the sizeable minorities of émigrés and non-juring priests. Their reintegration within the nation was presaged towards the end of the Directorial period.

A gradual change in the sensibilities of many aristocrats while they were absent from France was conducive to their changing sides, and coming over to the new nation. Having left France out of attachment to traditional values, on a point of honour or by class egotism, having for long pronounced the words *nation* and *patrie* with contempt, the émigrés were reduced by the hardships of exile to relearning France, to becoming attached to a new homeland seen in terms of the new values. The longer their exile was prolonged, the more the aristocracy's memories and regrets crystallized round their native land. Now that they had lost their lands in the confiscations, the émigrés discovered their sentimental value. The point of honour and dedication to the person of the King gave way to nostalgia, to tender and melancholy memories which went back to childhood. Abandoning their erstwhile cosmopolitanism, the émigrés gained a deeply-felt sense of the absence of their country. This blossomed out as a new literary theme in the *Tristes* and *Regrets* which proliferated among them, and which acted as a prelude to Chateaubriand's 'sweet remembering':

To depict that languidness of soul that one experiences outside one's homeland [Chateaubriand was to write in his *Génie du Christianisme*], people say: this man is homesick. It is truly a sickness, and one which can only be cured by one's return.

At the same time that the new current of feeling was spreading amongst the émigrés, the new settlement of the landed property situation was paving the way for the return of the aristocracy to the political fold. For the former deputy in the Constituent Assembly, Mounier, property was to be the fulcrum of the new order. In 1795, he had observed that 'most Frenchmen are now yearning for order, calm, personal safety and respect for property'. In a letter dated 4 March 1798, he wrote 'I see but one means of salvation remaining: to seek a support in property.' Mounier thus understood that the changed situation of property had led to a new stability, around which it was essential for the aristocracy to rally. In the *Mercure britannique* of 25 January 1799, Mallet du Pan predicated as the essential condition for the aristocracy to rally to the new order 'the adoption of theoretical formulas which protect individual liberty and the freedom of property'.

After ten years of revolution, aristocratic emigration and property-owning bourgeoisie therefore met up again in an alliance. Despite all that could oppose them, the two groups had now come to an understanding, tacitly grounded in their adherence to their native soil and to landed property. They repudiated any alliance with those who did not own property and who were therefore unable to focus their patriotism on a conception of property: they both agreed on identifying the French nation with the actual soil of France. The changes the Revolution had wrought in landed property had in fact attached the property-owning classes more closely to the land. The abolition of feudal rights and of ecclesiastical tithes, and the acquisition of national lands had robbed the peasant landholders of any revolutionary zeal, had dug a ditch between them and the rural masses and had strengthened their conservative solidarity with the urban bourgeoisie. In 1789 the 'nation' had been an abstract idea, richer in hopes than in reality. Now, the new attachment to the soil which the Revolution had brought about had made the 'nation' – for the bourgeoisie and the well-off peasantry at least – a concrete idea, a tangible form: the nation now meant the land possessed in its plenitude. Patriotism, devoid of its political and social spirit of 'Eighty-nine', had been made flesh in the shape of landed property. By a spiritual journey that was quite different – by returning, in fact, to the values of instinct and feeling, which overcame their traditional prejudices – the émigrés also concretized the idea of the nation, making it equivalent to the land. This prepared the aristocracy to come over to the nation of landowners.

Bonaparte's contributions in this field were fully in keeping with the aspirations of both groups. He helped to stabilize society by integrating the returned émigrés into the new social hierarchy grounded in property; while he strengthened the principle of authority, he adjusted them to the new order which had initially been built against them. As he threw the frontiers wide open to the émigrés by his senatus-consultum of 6 Floréal Year X (26 April 1802), Bonaparte proclaimed his wish 'to cement peace inside France by every means which can rally Frenchmen and quieten dissension within families'. Nothing was as capable of bringing harmony to families and of rallying bourgeois and aristocratic France under the same banner as property. The integration of the repentant aristocracy into the bourgeois nation started the process of the fusion of elements of the new ruling class. In this way, one of the principal goals of the revolutionaries of 'Eighty-nine' was achieved.

The Revolutionary Heritage

The coup of 18 Brumaire is best understood in the light of this integration of bourgeois and aristocratic France within a 'nation' conceived of along property-owning lines; it is this which confers all its historical importance on the *journée*. The reign of the notables was beginning: it would be a long time before it was challenged. *Nation* and *patrie* had seemed at the dawn, in 1789, to be ideas all the more revolutionary for seeming to contain all possibilities. By 1799, however, the words had become contracted and weighted: they were now only meaningful within the context of property. The structure of the State had been transformed at the same time as the structure of society. Bonaparte followed up the work of the Directory, perfecting institutions and strengthening the authority of the State. He did not, however, change the nature of the State. The notables considered that the State had been constituted as the bulwark of their prerogatives, which enabled their law to be respected and their social order to be maintained. In this at least, 18 Brumaire set the minds of the notables at rest once and for all, even though it is true that progress in this direction had been evident since 9 Thermidor and the *journées* of Prairial.

Admittedly, Bonaparte foiled the calculations of the Brumairians by taking away their freedoms – even their bourgeois freedoms – and establishing his own personal power. Yet it is easy to exaggerate. Despite the forcefulness of Bonaparte's personality, continuity in this sphere was only broken in appearance: the roots of his power went far into the period when the Revolution had been launched into war. Robespierre had foreseen this development in January 1792. Because civil and foreign war was persisting, and because the bourgeoisie's fear of social democracy excluded the possibility of seeking popular support, ineluctable necessity led the Property-owners' Republic, beneath its liberal façade, gradually to strengthen the powers of the executive. The Directory relentlessly applied itself to this policy and, while undertaking real reforms and a real attempt at social stabilization, did not think twice about violating the Constitution, utilized methods of hypocritical violence, and had recourse to ill-concealed cooptation in order to rectify the results of elections. Bonaparte's domineering personality concentrated power in order to inject into it the required dose of effectiveness. In so doing, he was merely speeding up a development which it was not within his power to stop. The legendary glamour of the Consulate cannot totally mask the importance of the work of the Directory and the extent to which the two periods are interdependent.

Though Bonaparte was soon to assert that the Revolution was finished – so that he would receive the credit himself for stabilizing the State and society – it had really been finished since the spring of 1795 and the dramatic *journées* of Prairial. Since then, the bourgeoisie, under various designations, had been searching for its point of balance. Whether this bourgeoisie was Thermidorian, Directorial or Brumairian, its aim was always to consecrate once and for all its social and political conquests. Bonaparte provided the answer for the wishes of the notables, setting their minds at rest against both a return to the democratic régime of Year II and a restoration of the Ancien Régime. By reconciling the aristocracy with the bourgeois order, the Church with the new State, he kept the promises of 'Eighty-nine'.

Ten years of the vicissitudes of revolution had utterly transformed the nature of French society. It now corresponded in all essentials with the views of the bourgeoisie and the propertied classes. The privileges and the preponderance of the aristocracy of the Ancien Régime had been destroyed, the last vestiges of feudality had been abolished. By making a *tabula rasa* of all feudal survivals, by freeing the peasantry from seigneurial rights and ecclesiastical tithes and to a certain extent also from community constraints, by destroying corporate monopolies and by unifying the national market, the Revolution speeded up evolution and marked a decisive stage in the transition from 'feudalism' to capitalism. Moreover, by destroying provincial particularisms and local privileges and by spiking the guns of the Ancien Régime State, it made possible the establishment of a modern state which corresponded to the bourgeoisie's social and economic interests. This latter work was undertaken in the period ranging from the Directory to the Empire.

.   .   .

The French Revolution was perhaps the most striking of all bourgeois revolutions, overshadowing, by the dramatic character of its class struggles, the revolutions which had preceded it. If we adopt the terminology of Jaurès in his *Histoire socialiste*, the French Revolution seems 'bourgeois in a wide sense, and democratic', as opposed to the Revolutions of the United States and England which had been merely 'bourgeois in a narrow sense and conservative'. The French Revolution owed much of its radical nature to the stubbornness of the aristocracy, which made any political compromise on Anglo-Saxon lines impossible, and which obliged the bourgeoisie to aim, no less relentlessly, at the total destruction of the old order – a task it could only perform with popular support. Marx spoke of the 'terrible hammer-blows' of the Terror and of the 'giant's broom' of the French Revolution. The social and political agent of this radical change was the Jacobin dictatorship of petty bourgeois and middle bourgeois elements, supported by the popular and rural masses – social categories whose ideal was of a democracy of autonomous small producers, peasants and independent artisans, who would work and exchange freely.

The attempted social democracy of Year II despite its ultimate failure was very important as an example. The men of 'Ninety-three', above all the Robespierrists, tried to overcome the basic contradiction between the exigencies of the equality of rights proclaimed in theory and the actual consequences of economic freedom, so as to produce *égalité des jouissances* within the framework of a social and democratic republic. This imposing attempt, dramatic even in its powerlessness to succeed, allows us to gauge the irreducible antagonism between the aspirations of a social group and the objective state of historical necessity. The question was: how to assert the imprescriptible character of property rights, and thus recognize the exigencies of private interests and the pursuit of free profits, and yet in the same breath express the desire to nullify the effect of these rights on certain social groups, and build an egalitarian society?

This 'Convention-conducted revolution' seems without question to have been, as Ernest Labrousse has put it, 'a period of anticipations'. The attempt at social democracy in Year II nurtured the social thinking of the nineteenth century; recollection of it weighed heavily on political struggles. The outlines of the Montagnard ideal had only gradually become visible; especially in regard to public education, whose accessibility to all was viewed as an essential pre-condition of social democracy. At the same time, however, as economic freedom and capitalist concentration increased social differentiation and intensified antagonisms, the *égalité des jouis-sances* became further and further out of reach. Clutching grimly on to their status, the artisan and shopkeeper descendants of the sans-culottes of 'Ninety-three', still attached to small property based on personal labour, oscillated between utopia and revolt. The same contradictions and the same impotence always inhibited their attempts at social democracy, as the tragedy of June 1848 bore witness. Year II, when Saint-Just could proclaim on the one hand 'Neither rich nor poor are necessary' (in the fourth fragment of his *Institutions républicaines*) and yet on the other hand note (on his agenda-paper): 'Not to allow the division of property' – did not this chimerical Year II smack of the world of utopias? . . . The egalitarian republic remained an anticipation, Icaria never reached but always sought.

The contradictions of social democracy had already been sur-mounted at the time of the Revolution, however – by Babeuf. He had held that the 'community of goods and of labour' was alone capable of ensuring the *égalité des jouissances* and of actually imple-menting the 'common happiness'. The abolition of private property and the collectivization of the means of production thus appeared for Babeuf, though only in a very confused fashion, as the necessary conditions for a real social democracy. Babouvist ideology, the first blueprint of the revolutionary ideology of the new society born of the Revolution itself, was an evident mutation of the ideology of Year II. This new ideology, which marks the beginnings of socialist thought and action, was transmitted by Buonarroti to the generation of 1830. Thus were born of the French Revolution ideas which led, in Marx's words, 'beyond the ideas of the old state of affairs' – con-ceptions, in sum, of a new social order which would not be the bourgeois order.

From this time on, the French Revolution is situated at the very heart of the history of the contemporary world, at the crossroads between the different social and political currents which have divided nations and which still divide them. Through the recollec-tion of struggles for freedom and for independence, as well as by its dream of fraternal equality, the Revolution, child of enthusiasm, still excites men and women, or else arouses their hatred. Child of the Enlightenment, the Revolution also focuses its attacks on privilege and tradition, or else inspires the intellect by the enormous efforts it made to organize society on rational foundations. Still admired and still feared, the Revolution lives on in our minds.

Recommended Further Reading

[For a full bibliography adapted to English usage, the reader is referred to George Lefebvre, *The French Revolution*, vol. 2 (London and New York, 1964), pp. 363–95. The short list that follows is provided only as a preliminary pointer to the abundant literature on the Revolution.]

The following general works should be consulted for the period as a whole: *Histoire générale*, edited by Ernest Lavisse and A. Rambaud (Paris, 1896) (vol. VII for the eighteenth century); *The New Cambridge Modern History*, vol. VIII, *The American and French Revolutions, 1763–1793*, edited by A. Goodwin (Cambridge, 1965) and vol. IX, *War and Peace in an Age of Upheaval, 1793–1830*, edited by C. W. Crawley (Cambridge, 1965); R. R. Palmer, *A History of the Modern World* (New York, 1950); *Le XVIII siècle. Révolution intellectuelle, technique et politique, 1715–1815*, edited by R. Mousnier and E. Labrousse with the collaboration of M. Bouloiseau (Paris, 1953); R. R. Palmer, *The Age of the Democratic Revolution. A Political History of Europe and America, 1760–1800*, vol. I, *The Challenge* (Princeton, 1959); and George Rudé, *Europe in the Eighteenth Century. Aristocracy and the Bourgeois Challenge* (London, 1972).

The classic histories of the French Revolution are those of Adolphe Thiers (Paris, 1823–27; English translation, London, 1838), François Mignet (Paris, 1824; English translation, London, 1826), Jules Michelet (Paris, 1847–53; English translation, London, 1847), and Louis Blanc (Paris, 1847–62; no English translation). Of these Michelet's is outstanding for its literary qualities. The works of Thomas Carlyle, *The French Revolution* (London, 1837), Edgar Quinet, *La Révolution* (Paris, 1865), and Hippolyte Taine, *Les origines de la France contemporaine* (Paris, 1876–93; English translation, London, 1876–85) are not historical accounts; the first is a series of *tableaux*, the others doctrinal rather than historical. A. de Tocqueville, *L'Ancien Régime et la Révolution* (Paris, 1856; new edition with a preface by George Lefebvre, Paris, 1952; English translation, New York, 1955) is important for its deep understanding of the period, though it too is not a historical narrative.

The end of the nineteenth and the beginning of the twentieth centuries saw renewed interest in the history of the Revolution. Of the many works produced, the following are the most important: Alphonse Aulard, *Histoire politique de la Révolution. Origines et développement de la démocratie et de la République* (Paris, 1901; English translation, London, 1910); Jean Jaurès, *Histoire socialiste de la Révolution française* (Paris, 1901–04; new edition edited by Albert Soboul, Paris, 1968–72); P. Sagnac, *La Révolution, 1789–1792* and G. Pariset, *La Révolution, 1792–1799* (Paris, 1920, vols. I and II of *L'Histoire de la France contemporaine*, edited by Ernest Lavisse); and Albert Mathiez, *La Révolution Française* (Paris, 1922–27; English translation, London, 1928) which stopped at 9 Thermidor and was continued by Georges Lefebvre, *Les Thermidoriens* (Paris, 1937; English translation, London, 1965) and *Le Directoire* (Paris, 1946; English translation, London, 1965).

The most outstanding modern history remains Georges Lefebvre, *La Révolution Française* (Paris, 1951; new edition with a bibliography by Albert Soboul, Paris, 1963; English translation, 2 vols, 1962–64). Albert Soboul, *La Révolution Française* (Paris, 1965; in the 'Que sais-je?' series), provides a concise summary. Other recent general works are M. Vovelle, *La chute de la monarchie, 1789–1792* (Paris, 1972), M. Bonboiseau, *La République jacobine – 10 août 1792 – 9 Thermidor an II* (Paris, 1972), and D. Woronoff, *La République bourgeoise de Thermidor à Brumaire, 1794–1799* (Paris, 1972).

Among histories of the French Revolution written in English, the best are: Crane Brinton, *A Decade of Revolution, 1789–1799* (New York, 1934); Alfred Cobban, *A History of Modern France*, vol. I, *Old Regime and Revolution, 1715–1799* (London, 1957); Leo Gershoy, *The Era of the French Revolution, 1789–1799* (New York, 1957); Norman Hampson, *A Social History of the French Revolution* (London and Toronto, 1964); George Rudé, *Revolutionary Europe, 1783–1815* (London, 1964); M. J. Sydenham, *The French Revolution* (London, 1965); and A. Goodwin, *The French Revolution* (London, 1966).

For the debate on the interpretation of the Revolution, see Alfred Cobban, *The Social Interpretation of the French Revolution* (Cambridge, 1964) and *Aspects of the French Revolution* (London, 1971); *New Perspectives on the French Revolution*, edited by Jeffry Kaplow (New York and London, 1965); and *The French Revolution: Conflicting Interpretations*, selected and edited by F. A. Kafker and J. M. Laux (New York, 1968). For the historiography of the Revolution, see H. Ben Israel, *English Historians of the French Revolution* (Cambridge, 1968).

For 1789 the essential works are Georges Lefebvre, *Quatre-vingt-neuf* (Paris, 1939; English translation, *The Coming of the French Revolution*, Princeton, 1947) and the same author's *La Grande Peur de 1789* (Paris, 1932; English translation, London, 1973). Also Albert Soboul, *1789, l'an I de la Liberté* (second enlarged edition, Paris, 1973), and, on 14 July 1789, Jacques Godechot, *La prise de la Bastille* (Paris, 1965; English translation, London, 1970).

For the insurrection of 10 August 1792 and the overthrow of the monarchy, the important works are F. Braesch, *La Commune du 10 août 1792* (Paris, 1911), M. Reinhard, *La Chute de la royauté* (Paris, 1969), and Albert Soboul, *Le procès de Louis XVI* (Paris, 1966). For the *journées* of September 1792, see P. Caron, *Les massacres de septembre* (Paris, 1935).

For the popular movement, the Revolutionary Government, and the Terror, see particularly George Rudé, *The Crowd in the French Revolution* (Oxford, 1959), and the works of Richard Cobb: *Les armées révolutionnaires. Instrument de la Terreur dans les départements, Avril 1793–Floréal an II* (Paris and The Hague, 1961), *Terreur et subsistances, 1793–1795* (Paris, 1965), *The Police and the People, French Popular Protest, 1789–1820* (Oxford, 1970), and *Reactions to the French Revolution* (London, 1972). See also Albert Soboul, *Les sans culottes parisiens en l'an II. Mouvement populaire et gouvernement révolutionnaire, v juin 1793 – 9 Thermidor an II* (Paris, 1958; abridged English translation, *The Parisian Sans-culottes and the French Revolution, 1793–4*, Oxford, 1964), the same author's *Paysans, Sans-Culottes et Jacobins* (Paris, 1966), and K. D. Tønneson, *La défaite des sans-culottes. Mouvement populaire et réaction bourgeoise en l'an III* (Oslo and Paris, 1959).

On the peasantry, nothing has surpassed the outstanding work of Georges Lefebvre, still the undisputed *maître* of the study of the Revolution. The main works here are *Les paysans du Nord pendant la Révolution française* (Lille, 1924), *Questions agraires au temps de la Terreur* (Paris, 1932; second enlarged edition, 1954), *Etudes sur la Révolution française* (Paris, 1954; second edition, with an introduction by Albert Soboul, 1963), and *Etudes orléanaises*, vol. I, *Contribution à l'étude des structures sociales à la fin du XVIIIᵉ siècle*, and vol. II, *Subsistances et maximum, 1789 – an IV* (Paris, 1963).

For bibliographies of the Revolution see P. Caron, *Manuel pratique pour l'étude de la Révolution française* (Paris, 1912; new updated edition, 1947), G. Walter, *Répertoire de l'histoire de la Révolution française. Travaux publiés de 1800 à 1940*, vol. I, *Personnes*; vol. II, *Lieux* (Paris, 1941–45), L. Villat, *La Révolution et l'empire, 1789–1815*, vol. I, *Les Assemblées révolutionnaires, 1789–1799* (Paris, 1936), and Jacques Godechot, *Les Révolutions, 1770–1799* (Paris, 1963; English translation, London, 1965).

Index

This index does not include minor characters mentioned in the book

Girondins, 8, 24, 262, 426; and aristocracy, 285, 308, 311; and bourgeoisie, 48, 276–7; and counter-
revolution, 255, 308, 311, 317, 319;
and Danton, 299; and economic
liberty, 244, 276–7; fall of, 309–11,
314; and monarchy, 118, 245, 246–8,
250, 283–4; and Montagne, 260,
267, 268, 272–82, 285, 292, 295,
305, 306–11; in National Convention, 271–311; origin of, 231; and
Paris Commune, 260–2, 276, 278,
308–10; and Robespierre, 273–5,
278–9, 306–7, 310, 409; and September massacres, 264, 385; trial
and execution of, 341; war policy
of, 234–8, 240–1, 243, 271–2, 279,
290–1
Gobel, Jean-Baptiste, 347, 361
Godoy, Manuel de, 291
Goethe, Johann Wolfgang von, 269,
589
Gohier, Louis-Antoine, 306, 535, 545
Gorsas, Antoine-Joseph, 154, 166
Gossec, François-Joseph, 399, 574,
594
Government: under Ancien Régime,
administration, 28, 34, 77–8, 80,
82–96; administrative divisions,
84–5, 101; agents of, 85–7; centralization of, 12, 82, 86, 96, 111, 143;
after 1791, administration of, 194–
195, 381, 583–5; administrative
divisions of, 184–5, 193–4; centralization, 319, 355–7, 378, 381, 384,
406–7, 419, 421, 470, 578–80, 584;
decentralization, 193–5, 470, 578,
584; under Directory, 469–71,
513–16, 518–22, 551, 580, 584;
Revolutionary, 257, 281, 303, 313,
339, 366, 379–84, 418, 578–9, 584;
stability and instability of, 419,
513, 542, 543, 551, 586; Thermidorian, 418–20
Great Fear, the, 58, 144–7
Grégoire, Henri, abbé, 150, 276, 287,
289; and education, 603; and lower
clergy, 128, 131–2; and monarchy,

272–3; on property franchise, 181;
reform of Church by, 431, 458
Grétry, André-Modest, 574
Greuze, Jean-Baptiste, 574
Guadet, Marguerite-Élie, 231, 236,
247, 260, 307, 309
guilds, 47, 53, 56, 111, 124, 125, 127;
abolition of, 189–91, 208, 556
Guillotin, Joseph, 46, 133
Guizot, François, 21, 181
Gustav IV, king of Sweden, 530
Guzmán, Andrés Maria de, 361, 377

Hague, Treaty of the, 464
Hanriot, François, 57, 310–11, 410
Hardenberg, Karl August, prince
von, 463
Hébert, Jacques-René, 187, 323–4,
327; arrest of, 309; attack on clergy,
347; attack on Robespierre, 374–5;
and conscription, 328–30; and Cordeliers, 368–9; terrorist campaign
of, 331, 333, 341, 360, 370; trial and
execution of, 256, 376, 391
hébertisme, 331, 407, 421–3, *see also*
neo-Hébertists
Helvetian Republic, 525–6, *see also*
Switzerland
Helvétius, Claude-Adrien, 68, 398,
412
Hérault de Séchelles, Marie-Jean, 121,
311, 323, 377
hoarding and speculation, 137, 244,
322, 334, 343, 378, 386, 520, 562–3;
law on, 324–5, 330, 389, 392
Hoche, Louis-Lazare, 352, 400, 500,
594; and defence of Dunkirk, 354;
and Irish expedition, 504; in the
Vendée, 432, 482; as War Minister,
507
Holland, 4, 10, 464, 580; Anglo-
Russian landing in, 539–40; war
with, 290, 298, 461
Hondschoote, battle of, 339, 352, 354
Hostages, Law of, 537, 545
Houchard, Jean-Nicolas, 339, 352,
354, 401
Houdon, Jean-Antoine, 574